# THE STRUCTURE OF CRIMINAL PROCEDURE

**Recent Titles in
Contributions in Criminology and Penology**

# THE STRUCTURE OF CRIMINAL PROCEDURE

## Laws and Practice of France, the Soviet Union, China, and the United States

**BARTON L. INGRAHAM**

Foreword by **JACQUES VERIN**

Contributions in Criminology and Penology,
Number 16

Greenwood Press
New York • Westport, Connecticut • London

**Library of Congress Cataloging-in-Publication Data**

Ingraham, Barton L.
  The structure of criminal procedure.

  (Contributions in criminology and penology,
ISSN 0732-4464 ; no. 16)
  Bibliography: p.
  Includes index.
  1. Criminal procedure.  I. Title.  II. Series.
K5401.I54  1987      345.73'05      86-27139
                     347.3055
ISBN 0-313-25431-1 (lib. bdg. : alk. paper)

Library of Congress Catalog Card Number: 86-27139
ISBN: 0-313-25431-1
ISSN: 0732-4464

First published in 1987

Greenwood Press, Inc.
88 Post Road West, Westport, Connecticut 06881

Printed in the United States of America

The paper used in this book complies with the
Permanent Paper Standard issued by the National
Information Standards Organization (Z39.48-1984).

10  9  8  7  6  5  4  3  2  1

To my parents, Lee and Margie Ingraham

# CONTENTS

# FOREWORD

Criminal procedure, faithful handmaiden of criminal law, is often dreaded by students who regard it solely as a collection of forbidding provisions. The complexity and minutiae of its rules discourage comparative research by specialists, who often remain on the level of the purely technical, which in no way facilitates an in-depth understanding of the subject matter. How often writers take delight in ridiculing its quibbles and its quibblers!

However, "the code of honest people," as some have called the code of criminal procedure, in contrast to the penal code made for criminals, deserves a more just appreciation. It is one of Professor Ingraham's achievements to have elevated criminal procedure by providing it with a conceptual framework which makes it possible to take a view of the whole of this domain and to restore to its study the scientific temper which people tend to misunderstand.

Having posed as his hypothesis that there is a fundamental underlying structure to every procedural system and having created an analytical grid which takes account of the different tasks of criminal procedure, the author undertakes to test this model by comparing the criminal procedures of four nations which are notably different from one another and are representatives of major legal systems. What better test could one imagine?

I would like to mention here the essential points of the author's thought and to bring out not only the uses he proposes for us to make of his analytical model but also the encouragement he provides for us to engage in new comparative studies or studies of individual systems in order to bring to light the interactions, the transfers of powers, buried beneath the surface.

But before going further, I must say how much I appreciate, with regard to French criminal procedure—others being more qualified than I to speak for other countries—the scrupulous precision, the profound knowledge, not only of the texts but of practice which the author evidences throughout his work. Were it only a comparative study of the procedural systems of the four nations concerned, perfectly up-to-date at the moment of its publication, this book would already be a valuable aid to knowledge. But it is much more than that, and I come now to that which constitutes its main interest and reflects its title aptly: the uncovering of the *structure* of criminal procedure. Professor Ingraham asks himself questions concerning the functions which criminal procedure is called upon to fulfill. Obviously, it is charged with giving full effect to the penal law itself and, consequently, to the investigation, prosecution, and conviction of the perpetrators of misdemeanors or crimes, whatever the objectives may be that we assign to the punishments pronounced—whether they be retribution, deterrence, rehabilitation, or, in addition, reconciliation of the criminal and society. But one would be mistaken, he believes, to limit the tasks pursued by the entire modern system of criminal procedure to the prevention and punishment of crime: it is also charged, and this is essential, with being awake to the fact that the task of protecting society and of restoring social harmony must be accomplished without doing injury to the fundamental values of our civilization. It must thus insure against the risks of judicial error, against the violation of human rights and more particularly the rights of defense, against the risk of the dehumanization of a bureaucratic process, the neglect of the interests of victims, the bypassing of the public interest, and so forth. The author arrives thus at establishing an explicit morphology for criminal procedure, comparable to that of vertebrates, which is common to all systems no matter how different they may appear to be. He thus places in relief in his comparative study the similarities of procedural systems much more than their differences. That is what makes for the originality of his work. Getting back to the analogy with zoology, he describes the skeleton common to all modern procedural systems, while at the same time noting that one can find significant differences in their muscles, viscera, and organs.

The traditional contrast between accusatorial procedure—a model inspired by conflicts in the private realm and by arbitration—and inquisitorial procedure—active investigations and prosecutions of the guilt of criminals by public authorities—is blurred, not only because a pure system does not exist (the French example is there to show the variations possible from one model to another in passing through various mixed models), but also because there are identical functions to be performed and common problems to be resolved whichever procedural system is adopted.

These functions, according to the author, are six in number. One reads the author's analysis of these with the greatest interest, proceeding in chronological order from intake through appeal; passing from the examination and screening of cases to the beginning of the prosecution and the guarantees of sound justice (the sector where the differences are most marked according to political system and culture), the judgment as to guilt, and finally to the sentence and its execution.

Perhaps one could quarrel with the author in regard to the singling out of these different functions. If it is completely justified to group into one single task the sentence and its execution, which, despite the considerable practical importance that it has acquired, is only an extension of the judicial phase and deserves only that we recognize its judicial character, is it also satisfactory to unite the "charging and protecting" functions which answer to two different objectives? By the same token, shouldn't one place appeal in the same general function as protection from error and excess on the part of lower-court judges?

But this critical remark is, on the whole, a minor matter. The important thing is that the author's analysis does not leave in the shadows any essential function of procedure and that it furnishes a particularly useful model (even though it is susceptible to further refinement).

Chapter 9 discusses some of the possible uses of the analytical model. It should significantly facilitate the comparison of different rules and practices which seek to fulfill the same function, permit one to distinguish national differences in procedure which are functional from those which are explained solely by history and culture, free the reformer from the limitations of ethnocentricity and resistance to ideas coming from abroad, aid the historian in better appreciating the nature of changes introduced in the course of time, and facilitate the understanding of dysfunctions in the system.

But I think that it is not only the comparativists, the reformers, or the historians who can draw profit from Professor Ingraham's analytical model. Criminologists, notably those with a sociological background, cannot fail to be stimulated in their research by this conception of criminal procedure *as a system*. There exists, as for a living organism, a strict interdependence between the organs charged with fulfilling different tasks. If one is failing, another comes to the rescue and adjusts itself to perform the task in its place. The researcher is thus encouraged to closely study the model in action, to bring to the full light of day phenomena disguised behind appearances which intervene so that the system can function: diversions, reinforcements, substitutions, etc.

I will give two illustrations of the usefulness of Professor Ingraham's analytical model drawn from French procedure. Following the liberation of France from Nazi occupation at the end of World War II, the legislator established a remarkable and very daring system of justice for juvenile offenders which departed considerably from the traditional, time-honored principles of criminal justice. In principle, educational measures replaced sanctions and punishments were supposed to be exceptional. The principle of the separation of investigation and of adjudication was abandoned since the juvenile judge could investigate a case, then decide on guilt, and impose an educational measure or certain sanctions.

Measures taken in regard to the juvenile ceased to be irrevocable, but, on the contrary, became always susceptible to revision depending on the progress of the delinquent. The public nature of court sessions was restricted. The juvenile judge, a professional magistrate and jurist like all of his colleagues, received, in addition, an initiation into the behavioral sciences and was provided with a team of social workers and psychologists as assistants, permitting him to take measures appropriate to the personality of the juvenile and to follow his development from the beginning to the end of the judicial intervention. Lay assessors later came to support him in forming the Juvenile Court, which was authorized to take the most serious measures.

This system, of which France was justly proud, has since the 1970s experienced a veritable crisis. The basic reason for this is that juvenile justice is resented as a foreign body within a penal system which remains classical. The spirit which animates it has not, as one might have hoped, impregnated criminal justice entirely. Quite the contrary, the separation of juvenile justice from the larger system was accentuated with the rejection of all coercive measures and the elimination of all the institutions of confinement. It is evident that society was no longer sufficiently protected against juvenile delinquents committing the most serious crimes. The function of "sanctioning" was no longer carried out seriously in their regard and it became necessary for other procedural mechanisms to come to the rescue of the failing organ. Thus, the prosecutor has progressively bypassed the juvenile judge in favor of an investigation judge and that incarceration for juveniles, an exception for a while, has now become very common.

Moreover, one observes in this corrective mechanism another change, which we are going to find more common for adults, and this will be my second example: detention before trial, decided by the investigation judge according to the needs of the inquest, has become in practice a virtual punishment, to the considerable embarrassment of the jurists.

In effect, at the very moment of playing its adjudicative role, the court finds itself, to a considerable degree, confronted with a fait accompli. In the case of petty and middle-grade offenses the court is limited to confirming the sanction which has already been carried out in prison, and in any event, is forced to choose that type of punishment rather than the substitutes for incarceration which the legislator has wracked his brain to place at his disposal. This procedural deformity is less scandalous than it may seem if one interprets it in the light of Professor Ingraham's analytical model; there again one can note a weakness: adjudication and imposition of the sanction are so slow that society would not be protected unless other mechanisms come to the aid of the failing organs. The prosecutor and investigating magistrate have now come to fill, tacitly, these indispensable tasks, thanks to temporary detention. One can thus uncover and scientifically examine the underlying system alongside the formal judicial organization and evaluate the merits, faults, and consequences, both foreseen and unforeseen, of the replacement mechanisms.

These two examples will give the reader an idea, I believe, of the dynamic aspect of Professor Ingraham's work, which, by its way of welding tightly together criminal law and criminal procedure into one coherent and well-analyzed system, can only advance both the concept and the study of criminal policy.

—Jacques Verin
Magistrate and Secretary General of the
International Society of Criminology and
of the Center for Research on Social Policy

# ACKNOWLEDGMENTS

I do not know about the experience of other authors, nor can I speak for them, but for me getting a book published has always been a long, arduous trek, with many hazards and traps, disappointments and defeats, relieved by sudden miraculous turns of good fortune. That is why a helping hand and good advice are appreciated so much when they are offered.

I would like to take this opportunity to express in print my deeply felt appreciation to the following individuals who, in one way or another, contributed to the preparation, writing, rewriting, editing, and final preparation of this book: Peter P. Lejins, Professor emeritus, Sociology and Criminology, University of Maryland, College Park; Jacques Verin, Judge, Tribunal de Grande Instance de Versailles, France; José María Rico, Professor, School of Criminology, Montreal, Canada; Louise Shelley, Professor, School of Justice, The American University, Washington, D.C.; Konstantin Simis, formerly Senior Research Assistant, Institute of Soviet Legislation, Moscow, USSR, now living in the United States; Fridrikh Neznansky, former procurator, Moscow District, RSFSR, USSR, now living in West Germany; Jerome A. Cohen, esq., formerly Associate Dean and Director of East Asian Legal Studies, Harvard University, Cambridge; Chun-tu Hsueh, Professor, Department of Government and Politics, University of Maryland, College Park; Lore Rutz, graduate student, Institute of Criminal Justice and Criminology, University of Maryland, College Park; and Rosemarie Culmone, secretary, Institute of Criminal Justice and Criminology, University of Maryland, College Park.

# ABBREVIATIONS

PC, RSFSR    Penal Code of the RSFSR [Russian Soviet Federated Socialist Republic] in Harold J. Berman, *Soviet Criminal Law and Procedure: The RSFSR Codes*. 2d ed. Translated by Harold J. Berman and James W. Spindler. Cambridge, Mass.: Harvard University Press, 1972.

CCP, RSFSR    Code of Criminal Procedure of the RSFSR. Berman, *Soviet Criminal Law and Procedure*.

CL, PRC    The Criminal Law of the People's Republic of China, adopted July 1, 1979. Translated into English by Jerome A. Cohen, Timothy A. Gelatt, and Florence M. Li, in *Journal of Criminal Law and Criminology* 73 (Spring, 1982): 138–70.

*CPD*    *Code Pénal, Dalloz ed.* (Paris: Dalloz, 1983–1984).

CPL, PRC    The Criminal Procedure Law of the People's Republic of China, adopted July 1, 1979. Translated into English by Cohen, Gelatt, and Li, *Journal of Criminal Law and Criminology* 73 (Spring, 1982): 171–203.

*CPPD*    *Code de Procédure Pénale, Dalloz ed.* (Paris: Dalloz, 1983–1984).

FBIS    Foreign Broadcast Information Service.

# I

# INTRODUCTION

# I _____

# OPENING REMARKS

Comparison is the only method for understanding the range of variation in phenomena of a particular type, as well as noting what is common to all of them.[1] It is the first step in theory building.[2] Ideally, in order to achieve this knowledge of the full range of exhibited variation, one should study and compare all known members of a species;[3] but, frequently, that is impractical and one is constrained merely to examine selected members who are known in advance to reveal very different characteristics.

In this search for an underlying structure in modern criminal procedure, I have chosen four modern societies which differ substantially from one another in their cultures and in their political and legal perspectives. Two are "Western" democracies—France and the United States—but, while sharing certain general cultural and legal traditions, they differ from one another in the manner in which cases are processed through the courts, the former using "inquisitorial" methods while the latter uses adversarial methods.[4] The other two—the Soviet Union and the People's Republic of China—share a common political philosophy (Marxist socialism) but have very different cultural traditions and perspectives toward law. Although there has been some borrowing and diffusion, the cultures of all four nations are significantly different although perhaps not as different from one another as they might be from some developing nations of the Third World.[5]

Nevertheless, they are all powerful and influential states in the late twentieth century, and in an advanced condition of technological and legal development. This makes their responses to problems of criminal law and enforcement interesting to study and compare, since their solutions are likely to be imitated by other nations falling within their zones of influence.

In these opening remarks I intend to lay the groundwork for the analysis of criminal procedures in four different legal systems, with different "legal cultures,"[6] by discussing their different approaches to criminal law and beliefs as to what their procedures and punishments should be designed to accomplish. The main theme of this opening chapter is that the system we are best acquainted with, the American adversary system, sees crimes in terms of two-party conflict (State versus offender, or victim versus offender) and procedure in terms of conflict resolution.[7] From that perspective, the interests of "outsiders"—principally the public-at-large—are frequently ignored since they are regarded as non-interested parties. The procedures of other systems, not founded on adversarial assumptions, however, either regard victims and the public as vitally interested parties or they tend, as in Communist countries, not to view criminal events as conflicts at all but as excuses for therapeutic intervention.

## THE POLITICAL AND LEGAL CULTURE OF THE SOVIET UNION AND CHINA

In the two giants of the Communist world, the U.S.S.R. and the People's Republic of China (P.R.C.), laws are seen as having explicitly political and moral objectives and as having didactic as well as regulatory functions.[8] Both societies are governed by elites, who are entrusted (theoretically by popular acclamation) with the task of ruling in order to accomplish a mission. This mission changes from time to time. It is not self-evident that it remains today what it was at the time each society was founded in its present form (the USSR in 1917 and the PRC in 1949). Today the mission of the ruling elites in both nations may be no more than the realization of internal order and economic prosperity at home, the creation of friendly and subservient states on the borders, hegemony within an appropriate sphere of influence beyond those borders, and security from incursions of hostile foreign states into these zones of influence.[9] Both societies are hierarchically organized with power flowing mostly from the top downward; the elite defends the state morality, and the primary obligation of the citizen is obedience and support of this state morality.[10]

The penal law in these two nations is not only regulatory but, in most cases, attempts to reconcile the citizen who violates the law to the proper observance of his civic duties.[11] Thus, a great emphasis is placed on rehabilitation, which is conceived of as expiation through labor and reindoctrination of the errant individual to believe in the invalidity of his past modes of thinking and behavior and to seek to conform them with socialist morality, thereby restoring himself to his former position in the community. It has been pointed out by many observers that this view of the relationship between citizen and state is extremely paternalistic and has deep roots in Russian and Chinese history.[12]

Criminal procedures in such societies, as will be seen in later chapters of this book, not only attempt to achieve the usual goals of criminal procedure—apprehension and temporary immobilization of the suspected offender, the investigation and determination of his guilt or innocence in a manner which has external validity and rationality, and the preservation of at least some human rights—but also attempt to accomplish the basic substantive objective outlined in the preceding paragraph. Communist countries, like the Soviet Union and China, seem to recognize the importance of process as an educative tool in commencing the reindoctrination of the offender; the sanctioning phase is supplementary and not the sole instrument of this purpose.

Courts in Communist societies have a very different status and role to play from that of their counterparts in Western societies, especially in the United States. First, they are not seen as having the power to make law or establish penal policy; these powers are entrusted solely to the legislative and executive arms of government.[13] Their function is to apply in individual cases the law given to them by these organs of government. In doing this, they are not bound by the decisions of other courts, even higher courts, in individual cases (although they are subject to the administrative regulations and judicial standards promulgated by higher courts for processing and adjudicating cases). They look to the written (but not always published) laws and decrees of legislative and executive organs for the guidelines to follow rather than to judicial precedent. Thus, the way they handle cases is flexible, according to the needs of the state at any given time, and does not strive for doctrinal consistency.[14]

Second, courts in the Soviet Union and China are agencies of an administrative apparatus controlled by the central governments and do actually not enjoy the independence which has been the hallmark of Western judiciaries in modern times. Although the importance of some degree of judicial independence is recognized in both societies,[15] it is not a matter of such overriding importance that much is done to strengthen or guarantee it. Courts as a sanctuary of opposition to the ruling elites of both societies would constitute a basic contradiction in the social order—a counterrevolutionary state organ.

Third, courts and lawyers are not seen primarily as guardians and defenders of individual rights but as performing public functions. Courts are regarded as defenders of socialism and *public* interests (which, of course, *can* include the interest of seeing that justice is done in individual cases and that the rights of the accused under law are not abused), and lawyers are viewed as assisting the court in this task. The duty of defense counsel in these societies is not to use his skills to defeat these objectives in order to preserve the freedom of his client, but simply to see that the law is observed in the processing of his client through the system. Much greater emphasis is placed on substantive justice than on procedural justice. Thus, if it becomes clear at any point in the proceedings that the defendant is guilty of the offense of which he is charged, there is little more the defender can do ethically than argue consideration for his client; he cannot subvert the process in order to produce an unwarranted exculpation.[16] This is not to say that in both countries there are not defenders who attempt to do more for their clients. They do so, however, at the risk of losing their right to function as authorized defenders.

It is sometimes argued by Western legal scholars that neither of the two Communist nations recognizes the presumption of innocence as a governing principle in the administration of criminal justice. If by "presumption of innocence" all that is meant is the allocation of the burden of proving guilt to the prosecutor or permitting conviction only after the presentation in court of evidence meeting the necessary standard of convincingness, this criticism may not be justified.[17] However, if one takes a broader view of the meaning of the phrase and includes within it many of the understandings of the adversary system—for example, that the accused has no burdens at all, no duty to cooperate with the state in the revelation of the truth if he is innocent, or that he may utilize procedures designed for his protection to obscure or obfuscate the truth or impede the prosecution if he is guilty—it is clear that the "presumption of innocence" in this sense finds little support, if any, in Communist societies.

## FRANCE AND THE UNITED STATES

Many of the aspects of criminal procedure in the Soviet Union and China just mentioned are attributable to the fact that both procedural systems are inquisitorial. Inquisitorial systems had their origin in the late Roman Empire, disappeared from Western Europe during the early Middle Ages, and were re-established there in the thirteenth century by the Roman Church.[18] Influenced by the liberal doctrines of the eighteenth century Enlightenment philosophers, inquisitorial procedure took its modern form (now mixed with accusatorial elements) in France after the Revolution of 1789. Since France was the *fons et origo* of modern inquisitorial procedure, it is not surprising that some of the aspects of law in the Soviet Union and China can be found in French law. For example, French law is also codified and primarily the product of legislative and executive bodies rather than of courts; it is also true in France that courts look to the substantive and procedural codes rather than to the decisions of other courts for rules to govern their decisions.[19] However, in France the courts and lawyers enjoy far more independence from state control than in either the Soviet Union or China. This independence can be traced to a Western European legal tradition which regards law and legal systems not as a subservient instrument of state policy but as a limiting force external to the state bureaucracy and controlling it.[20]

French law also stresses the rehabilitative functions of criminal sanctions but not to the extent it is done in Communist countries. Its conception of rehabilitation is to suppress the disposition of convicted criminals to engage in illegal conduct, but otherwise to leave them free to think and act as they choose. It thus rejects the idea that men and women should be indoctrinated in a particular political philosophy or ideology. Any attempt to do so would be resisted as opposed to the basic tenets of the liberal state which views the citizen as mentally and morally autonomous.

The American legal system has its roots in a cultural tradition, the English common law tradition, which is different from all of the societies discussed previously. It is different in two major respects: first, in possessing a system of procedure (both civil and criminal) which is described as being an "adversary system"—what that means and how long it has been a part of the "common law tradition" I leave for later discussion; and, second, in having a source of law *in addition to* usual sources of legislative statute and the administrative orders and decrees of executive or judicial agencies—namely, past decisions of other courts in similar cases and the guiding legal principles these past decisions establish. This source of law competes with other sources for preeminence. The principles and rules established in judicial decisions only have to give way to the command of the legislature when it is clear that the legislature intends to replace them with its own rules and when its doing so is constitutional. Secondly, when the legislature does act to replace common law with statutory law, courts, even then, have the power, and often exercise it, of limiting the scope of the legislature's innovation by construing words used in the statute in ways which are consistent with meanings they have acquired in past rulings of the courts. Third, common law decisional rules have a high degree of uncertainty, since it is never clear to what extent they can be generalized beyond the facts of the case or cases which gave birth to them. They are also highly particularized, and it is often pointed out by American lawyers that there is a decision or precedent for every argument.[21] Thus, common law rules can be manipulated by players to accomplish whatever objectives they have in mind, whether the player be judge, prosecutor, or defense counsel. It is generally acknowledged nowadays that American courts can and do make law. They do establish social policies of their own which may be at odds with state policies, and, as stated previously, they have it within their power to set at naught state policies in favor of their own, provided they find a constitutional justification for doing so. Thus, one of the most remarkable differences to be noted in the "American way of doing things" where legal matters are concerned is the enormous political power American judges have secured for themselves through their adaptation of the "common law tradition."[22]

In the light of this, one would suppose that American lawyers would be particularly sensitive to and aware of the political aspects not only of their judicial system and the way it works but also of the criminal law in general. But American lawyers, in general, resist the political implications of the power they have given to judges and lawyers because to do so would run counter to the sustaining myths of the "common law tradition".[23] These myths can be summarized in a series of propositions, which would probably command the assent of most of America's lawyers.

1. The American adversary system is grounded in English legal traditions which go back almost eight hundred years to the Magna Carta (1215 A.D.).[24]

2. This legal tradition establishes the independence of courts from the executive and (to a lesser degree) from the legislative power and thus constitutes the courts as the citizen's main defense against overreaching by the "political" organs of government.[25]

3. Courts operate according to politically neutral rules of substantive and procedural law and thus can act as arbitrators between the citizen and his government.[26]

4. When any conflict arises between the citizen and his government—and that conflict can arise in the context of a criminal prosecution—the courts should view the conflict in the same way they do a dispute between two private parties in a civil case: as one to be resolved by the application of these politically neutral rules of substantive and procedural law.[27]

5. The court should act as a referee in this conflict, having no particular stake in the outcome and leaving to the litigants the ability and right, within limits of course, to control the process by which evidence and law are adduced to support their respective positions.[28]

6. Somehow, the truth and public policy will be served by this adversary process, although its main objective is fairness, that is, the affording to

each disputant the maximum freedom to shape the case in the mode deemed most advantageous to presenting party.[29]

What this mythology overlooks, as far as criminal procedure is concerned, is (1) that there are certain important discontinuities between the "English common law tradition"—which is greatly misunderstood —and modern American practice: English and early American criminal procedure were considerably less adversarial than is generally believed;[30] and (2) that criminal law (public law) performs different functions from civil law (insofar as it is private law) and requires a different procedure. Public interests are involved in criminal law which are not necessarily involved in civil disputes between private litigants (for example, the safety interests of actual and potential criminal victims who are not "parties" to a criminal prosecution); and public interests are not always well served by the interests of those who are parties to the litigation or their legal representatives. In fact, so much time, thought, and effort not only of the court but also of the prosecutor and the defense attorney go into such purely administrative concerns as system maintenance that broader social policies and objectives often get lost in the process.[31]

In the United States lawyers play a role which is probably not matched in any other legal system in the world. They run the show. Their ethics and their concept of justice tend to be purely procedural and override larger public interests.[32] Insofar as the procedural rules reflect an attempt to advance larger public goals, the lawyers convert and manipulate them to achieve the private interests of their clients, the organizations they represent, or themselves. Being absolutely indispensable for the operation of the adversary system, they are virtually beyond the control of non-lawyers wishing to make their behavior conform to public policy goals which transcend private interests.

## AMERICAN THEORIES OF CRIMINAL PROCEDURE AND HOW THEY REFLECT THE PECULIARLY AMERICAN WAY OF LOOKING AT CRIMINAL JUSTICE

It could be argued, and probably will, that this critical description of the American adversary system is misguided because it assumes that there is an inherent conflict between private and public interests. It could be that private and public interests are more concordant than critics of the adversary system are willing to admit. Taking an extreme position, one could argue that the virtue of the American adversary system is that it starts with the presumption that protecting the private interest is promoting the public interest, since, in a nation as ethnically and politically diverse as the United States, there are few interests which could command such universal agreement as to be rightfully designated "public interests," as opposed, let us say, to the interests of specific interest groups. Under this view the proper role of the courts is to provide a forum and a procedure which allow litigants the maximum opportunity to advance and debate the interests they espouse to "neutral and detached" decision makers and let them decide what best accords with the "public interest." Of course, this assumes that the legal standards which apply to the case are vague and subject to more than one interpretation because, to the extent they are not, the decision maker is forced to conform to a policy decision made by someone external to the little group of adversaries and the third-party decision makers immediately involved in the litigation. Fortunately, common law, as we have seen above, provides the necessary legal ambiguity and freedom of action.

This perspective contains within itself several serious flaws, but before discussing these I want to clarify, and be specific about, what I mean by "public" and "private" interests in criminal matters.

"Public interests" are viewed here as interests which should enjoy the support of most, if not all, members of the usually law-abiding public. They include:

1. the interest in being protected by the legal system from criminal victimization committed by other members of the public;
2. the interest in being protected by the legal system from victimization by government and agents of government, including police, prosecutors, and judges; "victimization," as used here, includes both malicious acts (corruption, intimidation, and fraud) as well as non-malicious acts, committed in an over-zealous pursuit of the first interest, which trample on the rights of all persons, innocent and guilty alike; and
3. the interest in having simple, inexpensive justice which efficiently and expeditiously separates the guilty from the innocent and deals with the former in an appropriate manner within the limits established by law.

"Private interests" include:

1. defendant's interest in evading a criminal conviction or in reducing the penal consequences resulting from his or her conviction as much as possible;
2. the interest of agents of the criminal justice system, including judges and prosecutors in lightening their workloads below what they should be, in deriving private advantage for themselves or for the agencies they work for, and in engaging in compromises ("deals") with the opposing party (not to mention other, more nefarious, practices) in order to accomplish these objectives; and

3. the interest of the defense lawyer in feathering his own nest at the expense of his client—for example, giving him short shrift so that he can turn his attention to the cases of better-paying clients and/or increase the volume of the cases he accepts for handling—and his interest in "winning at all costs" in order to advance his reputation as a successful attorney.

The task of the legislator designing a criminal procedure which will work to protect "public interests" as defined above is to so design it that the private interests of all the involved actors except the defendant (defense counsel, judges, and prosecutors, etc.) will be controlled and made subject to the independent, overriding action of non-interested persons or agencies. There are various ways of doing this, but the most effective ways are by reducing the incentives of actors to pursue private interests in derogation of public interests and by introducing at various crucial points in the criminal process decision makers who have no private or professional interests which might conflict with public interests.[33]

The major flaw of the adversary system of criminal justice is not only that it largely ignores the conflict between public and private interests, but that it gives almost free rein to private interests to run rampant, without control or supervision exercised by disinterested public bodies such as grand and petit juries.

Recently, American social scientists from different disciplines—Easterbrook,[34] a lawyer-economist, and Thibault and Walker,[35] social psychologists—have advanced "theories" which purport to explain not only behavior of actors within the criminal justice system, but also the procedural rules which are meant to govern their behavior. According to both—even though they have very different explanations—the rules of procedure are geared to carry out policies which have not been made explicit, at least not until they came along and made them so.

Frank H. Easterbrook's main thesis is that "criminal process is a method of allocating scarce resources" and that it may best be understood as designed to "get the maximum deterrent punch [on a cost-efficient basis] out of whatever resources are committed to crime control."[36] He argues that procedural rules which apply to the highly discretionary (almost lawless) activities of American prosecutorial offense charging, plea bargaining, and judicial sentencing "seem reasonably designed to squeeze the maximum deterrence out of funds available to courts and prosecutors."[37] The astonishing aspect of Easterbrook's discussion is its almost total lack of concern with the accurate determination of whether an accused is guilty or innocent, or whether according to some objective standard, he receives the punishment that he, individually, ought to receive.[38] The argument seems to be that if the parties in a criminal prosecution deal with one another as private bargaining agents within an essentially free, but not completely unregulated, market system, then the state will realize (in most cases) the optimal benefit, the most deterrence at the least cost, and the defendant will achieve the maximum he can achieve, given the strength of his bargaining position. Such a stance is grossly insensitive to the kinds of concerns which have motivated jurisprudes and legislators in designing criminal procedures, concerns which I have adumbrated above in the listing of "public interests."

Easterbrook's economic explanation of the odd assortment of procedural rules he selects governing prosecutorial charging, plea bargaining, and sentencing "explains" virtually none of these rules, if by "explain" one means why they were formulated or what purpose they were meant to serve. Even if his economic theory could *predict* the behavior of individual actors (prosecutors, defense lawyers, and judges) in any one of these situations, it would still not "explain" the rules; the behavior in question may be in defiance of the rule, or a rule established for one purpose may be misused to serve a different purpose.

Even though the author, a sometime lawyer and presently a criminologist, has at least one leg in the camp of the social sciences, he still finds it odd that American social scientists attempt to explain *normative* systems in terms of the behavior of those who operate within these systems.[39] How the meanings, purpose, and significance attributed to those behaviors by others (which it is necessary to understand in order to understand a normative system) can be derived solely from observing people's behavior and regularities in that behavior is not apparent. American social scientists prefer to *impose* meanings on the behaviors they study according to their own theory of motives, which contains two cardinal principles: (1) that people are not conscious, or only dimly conscious at best, of why they act the way they do, and (2) that their conscious and stated goals ("purposes") are virtually *never* to be taken as their "motivations" and have little or no correspondence with the behaviors which are thought to be guided by them. It is thus the task of the social scientist to discover what people's true "motivations" (that is, what "moves" them, not their purposes) really are. Since what moves them is usually something external to their conscious will, there is no way of determining by direct observation what it is; it must be inferred from its behavioral product. Thus a tautology is created: people behave in a way they are motivated to behave [behavior = motivation]. It is apparently not the task of the social scientists to explore how people fail to accomplish their stated objectives or why they do so, since it is a fallacy to give credence to a stated objective as a motivating force. "Rules," thus, never perform (or rarely perform) the function that their originators designed them to perform, but some other function which the social scientist "discovers" and which conforms more rationally and congruently with the actual behavior of the actors.

John Thibault and Laurens Walker have advanced a social psychological theory of procedure which they claim applies to criminal as well as civil cases (no distinction of any importance is noted between these kinds of cases) and to all nations of the world, not only to the United States.[40] They first propound a number of assumptions that underlie their theory: (1) that "the main business of the legal process ... is the apportionment of outcomes; hence the appropriate goal of legal procedure is the achievement of [distributive] justice";[41] (2) that "distributive justice is attained when the ultimate outcomes are distributed to contending parties in proportion to their respective contributions or inputs to the transaction underlying the dispute";[42] and, (3) "hence, we argue that the procedure most likely to produce justice is that procedure which facilitates the fullest possible report of inputs prior to determination of the distribution."[43] Procedures designed to facilitate "the fullest possible report of inputs" are contrasted with those which seek to produce the most accurate reflection of reality (that is, the ascertainment of truth), such as scientific dispute-resolution methods. Thus, Thibault and Walker make clear at the outset that "justice" in the substantive or retributive sense is not what they believe legal proceedings are meant to accomplish. In criminal *as well as in civil proceedings*, as long as the parties immediately involved (the prosecutor, the defendant and his counsel, and the judge) are happy with the outcome of the proceeding—and they will be happy, win or lose, provided they have contributed all the input they desire—"justice" has been done. These statements, Thibault and Walker admit, are not supported on moral or jurisprudential grounds but instead are claimed to be based on *empirical* studies in the field of social psychology which probe popular conceptions of equity in the exchange of rewards and losses.[44]

Thibault and Walker go on to say that "it is not necessary or even possible to choose the truth objective or the justice objective," because these "goals are dictated by the underlying character of the dispute and hence cannot be established independently." What they mean by the "underlying character of the dispute" is whether it involves mainly a dispute over facts or the relevance of the facts to an agreed-upon objective ("cognitive conflict") or whether it also involves disagreement over the ultimate outcome of the dispute ("conflict of interest"). If the dispute involves merely "cognitive conflict," without any "conflict of interest" between or among the disputants, the truth objective will be the preferred goal of legal procedure, since there is no problem of allocating outcomes among the parties; but where there are "conflicts of interest" the procedure must be designed so as to distribute the outcomes among the disputants in a manner they perceive to be most just, and in this process the correct determination of the truth plays a subordinate role.[45]

They then formulate a typology of five methods of dispute resolution in situations involving cognitive conflicts and/or conflicts of interest. In each situation there are at least two and often three parties—two disputants and a third-party advisor or decision maker—and different degrees of control over the decision (decision control) and over the conduct of the proceedings (process control) exercised by these parties:[46]

1. In the first situation, the two disputants have complete control over the selection of information that will inform the decision and over the mode of presenting that information to each other. They then bargain to arrive at a mutually satisfactory solution ("bilateral bargaining").

2. In the second, a third party is present but merely advises the disputants in resolving their dispute and sometimes recommends a basis for settlement or compromise ("mediation").

3. In the third situation, the third party is given the power of exercising a veto because in this situation *all* three of the participants must agree on a decision or outcome (the "moot"). Along with this shift of "decision control" to the third party goes a certain amount of process control, since the third party in the "moot" situation acquires the authority to ask questions and to control to some degree the nature of the evidence and the mode of its presentation.

4. In the fourth situation, the third party gains the authority to impose a decision on the disputants, after listening to whatever evidence they submit for his consideration ("arbitration").

5. In the fifth situation, the third party acquires not only decisional control, as in the previous situation, but also the right to control the development and presentation of the evidence necessary for making a decision ("autocratic decision-making").

After presenting this framework for analysis of dispute resolutions proceedings, Thibault and Walker proceed to state their hypotheses:

1. In disputes which involve disagreements over facts or the relevancy of facts in the determination of the truth of the matter, the interests of the disputants in a particular solution being congruent (cognitive conflict only), the optimal procedure is "autocratic decision making," at least where the disputants agree on a standard for judging the validity of the proof. Thibault and Walker assert that giving the decision maker complete process control in this instance permits the creation of a single "selection strategy" which generates information appropriate to resolving the disagreement. It also

increases the likelihood that the decision maker will obtain relevant information, reduces the strain of assimilating information, and minimizes the risk of failing to reach the correct solution within a limited number of attempts. In addition, giving the decision maker authority to make a dispositive decision does not conflict with the interests of the parties in disagreement since their interests are supposedly congruent as to the outcome once the proper determination of the "truth" revealed by the facts has been made.[47]

2. In disputes where distributive justice is the objective of the disputants (*all* legal proceedings, according to Thibault and Walker, criminal as well as civil) the optimal procedure for achieving this objective is the Type 4 "arbitration" proceeding, in which almost complete process control is assigned to the disputants or their legal representatives rather than to a third-party arbitrator such as a court. The reasons given for this preference are: (a) that parties litigating a dispute will prefer to present their positions and evidence in the way *they* view them rather than allowing a third party to develop the case according to his biases and preconceived expectations regarding the nature of the case or the nature of the disputants; and (b) that they will tend to express greater satisfaction in whatever decision is finally rendered by the third-party decision maker if they have been given the opportunity of controlling or contributing to the evidence he considers; it is more likely that they will consider his decision to be impartial, disinterested, and based exclusively on what they consider to be the relevant evidence.[48]

It will be noted that the type 4 "arbitration" procedure closely approximates the model of American adversarial procedure. In fact, Thibault and Walker in all their writings have clearly identified their preferred procedure as "adversarial" and "autocratic decision-making" as "inquisitorial." Their theory, being psychological, would imply that human preferences for different types of procedure in resolving disputes would be transnational and cross-cultural, and they claim that cross-national studies they have conducted in inquisitorial countries (France and Germany) suggest that, when variants of type 4 and type 5 methods of procedure are presented to inhabitants of these countries (university students) in an abstract form without identifying labels, these foreign nationals express the same clear preference for adversarial proceedings as their American counterparts.[49]

The theories of criminal procedure of Easterbrook and Thibault and Walker are empirical theories whose basic principles are grounded in social science, very unlike the analyses of procedure offered by American legal scholars.[50] Nevertheless, both of these theories of procedure share one thing in common with the jurisprudential theories: they are typically American in regarding criminal proceedings essentially as *private* disputes between criminal defendants and agents of the state who are interested in seeing to it that criminal behavior is curtailed at minimum costs to themselves, their agencies, and the public treasury. Both sides to the dispute have interests which are usually diametrically opposed and criminal procedure is essentially the means by which those conflicting interests are adjusted so that the end results are "optimal" from the perspective of both sides to the dispute. In this view, plea bargaining is far from being an aberration in criminal procedure which must be tolerated even though it frustrates or debases many of the goals of criminal laws; on the contrary, it is criminal procedure—or, perhaps, simply procedure—at its best, since it is far more efficient than adjudication in "adjusting" conflicts of interest and in facilitating resolution of "disputes."

Almost completely neglected in this general view of criminal procedure are the larger political and moral objectives of criminal law which transcend the private interests of the "parties" to the litigation. Criminal law has *both* instrumental and symbolic functions to perform.[51] The public takes an interest in the outcome of these proceedings that it fails to exhibit in the outcomes of private disputes, except insofar as private disputes also embody public interests.[52] Criminal proceedings are exemplary and are (or should be) designed to educate the public in the policies and moral values of those who are in governing positions. Those who rule must take care that criminal proceedings reinforce and support governing norms and that public interests are not publicly compromised by the manipulations of the litigating parties, including their own agents. Otherwise, there will be a general public dissatisfaction with the administration of criminal justice such as exists in the United States today and which existed at other times in our history when the legal profession became insensitive to public interests greater than those of their individual clients.[53]

This is not to say that American legal scholars are completely blind to public interests, but, to the extent they concern themselves with them, their attention seems fixated on the problems of providing ever-greater protection of criminal defendants from the abuses of governmental agents and increasing the speed and efficiency with which cases are processed. Seldom does one ever encounter any evidence of a general philosophical reorientation toward the goals of the system or how criminal procedure can play its part in a unified and consistent way in the implementation of those goals.[54]

In approaching such a general philosophical reorientation, such as that achieved by Jeremy Bentham and Anselm Feuerbach and their followers at the beginning of the nineteenth century, or Leon Petrajitsky at the beginning of the twentieth, comparative studies of criminal procedures in different societies will help in freeing the mind to appreciate the true similarities and differences between them, their philosophical and ideological underpinnings, and how well each works out in practice in fulfilling the *stated purposes* of their designers.

The basic theme of this book is that there is an underlying structure common to all the procedural systems examined herein. Nations may differ from one another in the manner of collecting evidence, the way they sift it, refine it, and evaluate it prior to trial, and the way they present it at trial, but they all have procedures to do these things. They may also differ in their views as to the appropriate relation between the citizen and the state and this may substantially affect the rights they are willing to grant the accused and, beyond him, members of the public in general; but all nations recognize that some human rights exist and must be respected. I will attempt to identify these in the course of this book.

Once the basic structure is outlined, it is possible to compare apples with apples and oranges with oranges—that is, different ways similar tasks are performed in different societies. These tasks, set forth in chapter 2, are not always performed well in any society. No nation's procedural system will be held up as a model for others to imitate. It is hoped that, better understood, the strangeness of certain foreign procedures will begin to dissipate for the American reader and that their advantages in certain areas over the way things are done in the United States will be seriously considered. I will attempt to show that there is no necessary connection between a procedural device and the kind of political system in which it is employed. Adversary procedure is not always found in free and open liberal societies (it can also be found in the Union of South Africa), nor are inquisitorial procedures always found in "totalitarian" states (it is found and has existed for a long time in democratic France, West Germany, Italy, and many other liberal states). I will ask the reader to shed the parochial bias which rejects everthing with a foreign label and which clings to what is familiar simply because it is familiar. The best procedural system to meet our present needs in this country will undoubtedly combine elements of both inquisitorial and adversarial procedures, each contributing its particular advantages to problem areas where it seems to work best.

With these opening remarks concluded, I now turn to a description of the basic framework which seems to underlie all the procedural systems discussed in this book—those of France, the Soviet Union, the People's Republic of China, and the United States.

# 2

# THE ANALYTICAL MODEL: THE MORPHOLOGY OF CRIMINAL PROCEDURE

In this chapter I intend to present an analytical model of modern criminal procedure which will aid in the explanation and comparison of the procedures in criminal cases in all parts of the world, regardless of culture or political orientation. I believe the time has come to begin pointing out the similarities and commonalities of these procedures rather than their differences. In subsequent chapters I plan to apply this analytical model to the criminal procedures of four nations— France, the Soviet Union, the People's Republic of China, and the United States of America—in order to see how much they resemble one another in the functions they perform and in the manner they are carried out in actual practice.

After describing the structural functional model, I offer a historical explanation of how the modern structure of criminal procedure developed and of two opposing methods of seeking justice and of controlling private and public harms which have guided the uneven course of this development not only in the West but also in great Eastern civilizations, such as China.

Although comparisons of criminal procedures in different nations have been done before, these comparisons have usually been of specific procedures, such as the law of arrest and detention, searches and seizures, discovery, exclusionary rules, and so forth, and moreover they have emphasized differences rather than similarities.[1] It is always good to be sensitive to differences where they exist and not to be misled by false similarities or parallels. On the other hand, the analyst who wishes to make valid generalizations about criminal procedure must look for similarities, whether they are facial or subdermal. That is the bias which affects this work, and my earnest prayer is that this bias does not lead me to make too many false comparisons.

There have been a few comparative studies done of entire procedural systems in criminal law.[2] These systemic studies, such as those comparing the inquisitorial and common law adversarial systems, have unfortunately been somewhat limited by the cultural boundaries implicit not only in the nations compared (Western European nations and their overseas ex-colonies) but also in the method of analysis itself. There still remains to be developed an analytical framework, or "grid," which can be superimposed on any modern procedural system extant in the world today in order to determine whether any parts are missing in that particular system of criminal procedure or what parts are elaborated in a unique way.

To construct such an analytical "grid" or model, the analyst must start with the assumption—a "working hypothesis"—that, whatever the purposes of the substantive criminal law may be, the tasks of criminal procedure are basically the same. However, by saying this, I do not mean to imply that these purposes are limited to the detection, apprehension, prosecution, guilt-determination, and punishment of offenders. John Griffiths, in his criticism of Herbert Packer,[3] correctly observes that the positivist conception of criminal law and procedure unduly narrows the conception of the social functions both perform. His point is that Packer's view of procedure is too adversarial in not incorporating within its range of possibilities a procedure designed to restore harmony between the offender and his society through reconciliation. I do not wish to be misunderstood as making the same mistake. The "tasks" which I ascribe to all modern systems of criminal procedure are not limited to the functions of the prevention and punishment of crime after a process of detection, apprehension, prosecution, and guilt-determination, even though no modern state fails to attend to these very important functions. I intend also to include within each task I assign to criminal procedure a symbolic component: to do what is to be done (but not everything that is to be done) publicly, ceremonially, and in a way likely to reinforce rather than undermine the legitimacy of the laws of the ruling power. There is also a conciliatory, peace-restoring component, as Griffiths points out. There is no modern state on the face of the globe which neglects these very important symbolic and conciliatory functions of criminal procedure, although obviously some states, engaged in re-educating their peoples in non-traditional values and in attempting to harmonize their interests, are going to emphasize them more than others.

Major changes in the social purposes which substantive criminal law is supposed to accomplish (such as occur during and after revolutions) will produce procedural changes in the way criminal law's basic functions are performed. In some cases a profound social change may reduce the performance of some procedural functions to a vestigial remnant of what was done before. However, the position taken here is that all these things may occur without modifying the basic skeletal structure of the criminal procedural system in its most abstract form. Here, as in the morphology of vertebrates, there is a structure common to all non-primitive procedural systems, no matter how facially dissimilar, by which they can not only be recognized but also compared.

As stated before, in this book I shall be comparing the criminal procedural systems of France, the Soviet Union, the People's Republic of China (PRC), and the United States according to the analytical model presented in this chapter. The selection of nations is deliberate. I wanted to compare not only inquisitorial (France, Soviet Union, China) and adversarial (USA) systems, but also a capitalist-Western-inquisitorial with a socialist-Western-inquisitorial system (France and the Soviet Union) as well as a socialist-Western-inquisitorial with a socialist-Eastern-inquisitorial system (the Soviet Union and China). The procedural system of each of these nations will be examined at each stage of the criminal process from both the perspective of the "ideal" and the "actual": the "ideal" being according to its written law, and the "actual" being according to the way the law is used or manipulated to carry out the functions the analytical model proposes must be performed by every legal procedural system. In demonstrating the adequacy or usefulness of the analytical model, I shall be stressing similarities in the structure of procedural systems and the common problems they must address. This approach does not necessitate the view, however, that the muscle, viscera, and organs that hang from the similar skeletons be similar; thus, I will be pointing out, especially at the end of this book, interesting and fundamental differences in the way eastern and western, capitalist and socialist, inquisitorial and adversarial, procedural systems attempt to address and solve the common procedural problems of enforcing criminal justice.

## ANALYTICAL MODEL

Whatever one believes the main purpose of substantive criminal law and its sanctions to be, whether it is the public condemnation of very serious acts of wrongdoing or the prevention of those acts through deterrence, incapacitation or reform, the procedural task of processing persons accused of crime from arrest to disposition is basically the same. Analytically, this process can be broken down into six tasks which modern criminal procedure must perform to be complete.

First, some method must be devised whereby reports of criminal activity are brought to the attention of officials and the offender taken into custody for investigation or prosecution. If government adopts a purely reactive attitude toward crime suppression, it will simply provide officials with whom complaints may be registered and will invest them with authority to issue summonses and make arrests. If government also takes a proactive stance, it may authorize its officials to ferret out criminal activity through investigations, informer networks, and traps set for willing but unwary offenders. Intake procedures are essential to all formal systems that have progressed beyond the stage of legalized self-help and private retaliation. They involve the making and filing of complaints with appropriate authorities, the making of arrests and searches with or without warrants, and the detention of suspects or accused persons during investigation or pending trial. In proactive intake systems, because of the difficulty of learning about crimes committed in the context of exchange transactions (for example, victimless crimes, or business crimes committed by or within an organization) where there is not likely to be a complainant or voluntary informant, there is a growing realization that procedures must exist to control and regulate police activities which (1) lay traps for unsuspecting criminals ("sting" operations), (2) infiltrate organizations with spies (paid informers and undercover police agents), and (3) purchase information and evidence from members of the public and the criminal underworld, by offering informer fees and rewards to the first group and withdrawals of prosecution to the second group.[4] Unattractive as these police methods may be for a person accustomed to reactive intake procedures, they can be fairly conducted within proper limits and are absolutely essential if a certain type of criminal wrongdoing (fraud, corruption, and subversion) is to be dealt with at all by the criminal law.

Second, it is necessary to sift and screen these complaints and reports of crime to determine their factual validity, to decide what laws have been violated and whether sufficient evidence exists to support criminal charges, to separate the prosecutable from the unprosecutable complaints, and finally to divert to other social control agencies the unprosecutable cases or cases which do not involve sufficiently public interests. It is generally believed that this task should be performed as early as possible, before formal charges are made, so that official energies are not wasted in litigating groundless or trivial accusations and accused persons detained or otherwise inconvenienced because of them. This sifting or screening may take place at various stages of the process before trial, but, ideally, should be completed before the prosecutor files his formal complaint. In the American system of criminal procedure, the process of screening cases prior to formal accusation is carried on by three different official bodies: (1) the police, when deciding whether to arrest, (2) prosecutors, when deciding which of those cases received from the police should be prosecuted, and (3) magistrates or grand juries, when deciding whether the prosecutor has adduced sufficient evidence to warrant a prosecution. In inquisitorial systems, in addition to screening by police and prosecutors, an investigation judge or other official may perform the same screening function that is performed by the grand jury or preliminary hearing in American criminal procedure.

The third task is to formally charge the defendant and to provide him some procedural protections for his defense, such as protection from: (1) prolonged detention pending trial without sufficient cause, (2) illegal searches and seizures of his person and property, (3) ignorance of the nature of the charges and evidence against him, (4) ignorance of the procedural law and lack of means to defend himself properly, (5) coerced self-incrimination, (6) secret proceedings, (7) redundant proceedings, and (8) arbitrary and unjust proceedings. Included here would be procedures limiting the time and the grounds for an accused person's pretrial detention; procedures limiting the government's right to invade the suspect's privacy or seize his property as evidence; procedures prescribing the form and content of the government's accusation, the method of giving defendant notice of the charges and of the evidence against him, and some method of responding to the charges; procedures indicating when and whether defendant shall be allowed the assistance of legal counsel; procedures limiting the government's right to interrogate the accused and compel him to give evidence against himself; procedures requiring a public trial and public participation in the adjudication process; procedures limiting the government's right to prosecute and punish the defendant more than once for the same offense; procedures permitting the defendant to challenge improper or illegal acts committed by his processors and to have these acts reviewed by other disinterested officials with the power to correct and remedy them; and so on. It is here, in the performance of these tasks, that procedural systems throughout the world differ most radically, since different nations take different positions with respect to an accused person's standing before the bar of justice. Some countries, regarded by Americans as despotic, seem to feel that it would be better if the citizen were to conduct himself like Caesar's wife—that is, above suspicion of wrongdoing—failing which he owes a duty to authorities to cooperate in the confirmation or removal of the suspicion. In such countries protective procedural devices which Americans deem essential are either not provided, or if provided, are ignored in the actual operation of the process.

The fourth task is to provide a method or procedure whereby the actual guilt or innocence of the accused may be determined. Procedures may differ as to who is to make this determination, how facts are to be presented to the decision maker, and the amount and kind of proof necessary for conviction. However, most "trials" (since I am talking here of the trial stage) are usually a review of facts collected by someone else (for example, by police, prosecutors, investigators, investigation judges or other officials, and defense lawyers) and presented to the decision maker in open court or through a written record. It is rare in modern criminal proceedings in any country for facts to be discovered for the first time at the trial stage. Thus, the significance of the trial is that it is a final, authoritative resolution of disputed facts and law by decision makers who are other officials than those who have collected the facts and who are presumed to be impartial and to represent the judgment of the community. Procedures at the trial stage usually include: (1) rules governing the reception of evidence, the order and burden of proof, competency of witnesses to testify, and so forth (rules of evidence); (2) rules governing the selection and duties of participants in the process (judges; jurors; attorneys; witnesses; and judicial assistants, such as clerks, bailiffs, and others); and (3) rules governing the way the official decision of conviction or acquittal is made and registered.

The fifth task of a system of criminal procedure is to prescribe how criminal sanctions are to be imposed and administered. For example, in the American system there are rules governing sentencing of convicted criminals, the administration of prisons and jails, judicial or administrative supervision of correctional administration, early release from confinement (parole, pardon, commutation of sentence), and civil disqualification.

The sixth and last task is to provide means by which decisions as to guilt or innocence and any other pretrial or postconviction official decision regarding the accused may be reviewed by higher authorities to make certain that justice has been done and the laws complied with. Review may be direct or collateral, interlocutory or postconviction, judicial or administrative.

Summarizing, we may classify these six tasks or functions of criminal procedure as: (1) intake, (2) screening, (3) charging and protecting, (4) adjudication, (5) sanctioning, and (6) appeal. As I shall demonstrate in the following chapters, the four modern systems of criminal procedure examined herein contain procedural rules in each of the six areas, although different systems emphasize different tasks or functions according to what they consider to be the most important overall function of the criminal process.

For example, "inquisitorial" systems emphasize abstract truth and substantive justice, believing that justice is impossible without truth. "Adversarial" procedural systems, on the other hand, stress the autonomy and dignity of the litigant (even if he is morally in the wrong) and insist on a "fair fight" under procedural rules that are so designed that there is a fair distribution of wins and losses, regardless of merit. Adversarial systems are open to compromise outcomes, which reflect a fair accommodation between the parties in dispute (in criminal as well as civil cases) considering the strengths and weaknesses of their respective legal positions. These two traits or tendencies control the internal logic of many procedural rules and practices (for example, plea bargaining in the United States or the leniency in sentencing shown to those who confess in China) and account for most of the differences which are found. However, as we shall see, because there are no longer "pure" inquisitorial or adversarial systems in the world, these traits are no longer as dominant as they were during earlier historical epochs when each system prevailed in a more undiluted form.

## THE HISTORICAL ROOTS OF MODERN CRIMINAL PROCEDURE

### Third-Party Arbitration-Adjudication of Private Disputes

Individuals and groups have always committed wrongs against other individuals and groups and these have given rise to sufficient conflict between them to disturb the public peace and to alarm others who are not immediately involved in the dispute. Anthropological as well as historical evidence indicates that in primitive societies, which ordinarily lack disinterested third parties who are sufficiently powerful to force a reconciliation, unilateral or bilateral methods of dispute resolution predominate, such as socially sanctioned self-help, retaliation, or negotiation. Laws and customs may assist in the process of dispute resolution by prescribing legitimate methods of self-help (for example, forcible recapture of stolen property) and retaliation. Third parties may occasionally become involved in advising, mediating, or subtly coercing the disputants to reach a satisfactory resolution of the dispute.[5]

Eventually, a level of political organization is reached—usually under a tribal chief, or early "king," supported by powerful clan headmen—where arbitration and adjudication of interpersonal or interfamilial disputes are possible.[6] The disputing parties and their supporters may wish to submit their disputes to tribal courts or popular assemblies or to the "king" himself for an authoritative resolution, or one of the disputants may compel the appearance of his adversary by invoking the jurisdiction of the tribal court in a way that the adversary cannot ignore.[7]

Proceedings in these early courts are likely to have the following characteristics:

1. The distinction between private and public wrong—except where wrongs against the king and his family or some sacral offenses are committed—is vague and imprecise. Most acts which today are regarded as criminal (homicide, theft, rape, and robbery) are at this stage usually private wrongs. There are rarely different procedures for arbitrating or adjudicating criminal and civil wrongs.[8] The main concern of the court is to reconcile the parties by forcing compensation of the injured party and thereby avoiding future hostilities, rather than to punish sin or regulate behavior through the terror of law.[9]

2. Criminal proceedings in these primitive courts are almost always accusatorial, in the sense that there is no action without an accuser (normally the injured party), who takes the initiative in commencing the lawsuit and prosecuting it before the courts.[10]

3. The arbitrating or adjudicating third-party, court, council, or popular assembly is, or is expected to be, neutral between the opposing sides and mainly referees a contest of proofs rather than actively seeking out evidence of guilt or innocence. Proofs at this stage, we shall later note, consist not of evidence but instead of the outcome of ordeals, divinations, and oath-takings, all carried out with formality, ceremony, and punctiliousness.[11]

4. The emphasis is on procedure rather than on substance, perhaps reflecting the fact that the third-party adjudicator/arbitrator does not wish to appear to take sides, leaving the determination to the outcome of the tests and ordeals prescribed by law which reveal the truth without anyone's determination of it. The parties are given an approximately equal opportunity to manipulate the procedure to their advantage, thereby better assuring distributive justice.[12] Procedure is extremely formal; so much so that procedural error can have a substantive effect. Thus, litigation often takes on the appearance of a complicated game whose outcome is unpredictable but nevertheless accepted because it is viewed as either divinely ordained or fairly arranged so that outcomes are not disproportionately in favor of one of the parties.[13]

5. The method of proof is one using indirect indicators of guilt or innocence. By "indirect indicators" I mean methods of proof other than eye-witness testimony and confessions, such as divine signs, tests and ordeals, eloquence or skill in advocacy, procedural mistakes or omissions, contumacy and default—in other words, evidence or events which do not involve investigation or necessitate the weighing of evidence according to its credibility but which are believed to have reliability because of their "magical" efficacy in revealing the truth or else are considered, in the absence of better proof,

sufficient to dispose of the case. Inasmuch as the trial is viewed as a *contest*, rather than as a human quest for the truth, it is more important that these methods of disposing of the case be accepted as dispositive by both litigants than that they actually reveal the truth.[14]

6. In adjudication proceedings at this primitive level there is rarely anything that might be described as screening of complaints or as appeals from adverse judgments to higher levels of authority.[15] Screening is not needed or desired: authority and revenue often accrue to him who can attract litigants to his court and the need to forestall vendetta is overarching. Moreover, the test or proof of right resides in the outcome of oaths, tests, and ordeals; it is not subject beforehand to human evaluation. Appeals are also unnecessary, not only because there are rarely higher authorities before whom there could be a retrial but also because, considering the method of proof (considered intrinsically reliable), no increase in reliability could be expected from a repetition thereof.

7. Punishments tend to be retributive rather than preventive (that is, deterrent, incapacitative, or reformative). Private disputes are best resolved by compensation, and in primitive societies, compensation tends to be whatever restores the honor of the injured person or family in the eyes of the community. Therefore, compensations are usually measured not as much by the extent of the injury inflicted (the extent of the loss in material terms) but rather by the status of the person whose honor has been damaged by the wrong. For this reason many primitive compensations impress us today as essentially punitive.[16]

In Western Europe during most of the early Middle Ages legal proceedings for the reparation of wrongs such as homicide, mayhem, rape, abduction, robbery, burglary, and theft possessed all of the characteristics described above.

## Third-party Investigation and Determination of Public Wrongs

The history of Western Europe reveals that the method of dealing with acts which today are regarded as criminal changed radically over a period of several hundred years (1200 A.D. to 1500 A.D.) under the impact of an ideological revolution which was religious in nature.[17] The nature of crime itself altered, so that acts formerly regarded as private wrongs now were viewed as damaging to public interests as well. The intervention of third-party adjudicators was no longer the solicited arbitration of disruptive private disputes but became the suppression of morally wrongful behavior (sin) or of behavior deemed contemptuous of royal authority.[18] This change demanded an official inquiry to determine the existence of such behavior, official action to suppress it, and an accurate determination through investigation of what had happened. An assessment of the culprit had to be made to determine the extent of his sin (his culpability) and the degree of his dangerousness (the intentionality of his behavior). Thus, procedures and methods of proof had to be invented to distinguish between individuals who were guilty and dangerous in this ontological sense and those who were not.[19] The public interest was involved in a major way since crime as sin threatens divine retribution or at least the destruction of social and political order. The central authority—king or emperor, pope or bishop—now bears the primary responsibility for seeing to it that substantive justice is done and that God is satisfied. This can no longer be left to the disputants themselves who are too concerned with private satisfaction to concern themselves with these more general and distant interests.

It is clear that a similar transformation of criminal procedure can be found in the history of nations in other parts of the world. We know that a parallel, if somewhat delayed, transformation took place in Russia between the fourteenth and sixteenth centuries.[20] It may have taken place in China between the fifth and first centuries before Christ.[21] It undoubtedly occurred in the last two centuries of the Western Roman Empire, especially under the Christian emperors after Constantine.[22] It may have occurred early in the dynastic history of the Egyptian pharaohs.[23]

Once this transformation takes place, criminal proceedings are likely to develop the following characteristics, as they did in Western Europe during the thirteenth to sixteenth centuries:

1. Public officials begin to supplant private complainants as prosecutors of wrongs previously viewed as private but now regarded as public. Thus, proceedings tend to become one-sided in the sense that investigating and adjudicating officials are looking into the deeds alleged to have been committed by the suspect/accused in order to determine whether there is evidence to support the charges. Theoretically, no personally affected complainant is required, provided sufficient facts warranting an investigation are brought or come to the attention of these officials, who may institute charges ex officio.[24]

2. Proceedings are no longer merely reactions to complaints voluntarily initiated by private persons who have suffered an injury. Efforts are made to seek out and discover incidents of wrongdoing, although police forces are still very far in the future. Investigating officials or bodies are established to investigate and inform royal or ecclesiastical officials of such incidents or to act as reception points for private complaints. These official persons or organs are instructed to assemble evidence which will lay the foundation for the later adjudication of guilt.[25]

3. Since proceedings are likely to pass through the hands of several officials in their progression toward judgment (we see the beginnings of a court

bureaucracy here), written records are kept of the testimony of witnesses, which may be used later in the process without the need for repeated appearances or oral testimony by those witnesses. The investigation, as well as the trial, may be conducted in secret, behind closed doors.[26]

4. Defendants are recognized as having rights for their protection, but these rights tend to be viewed in a teleological way—that is, as instrumental in preserving the integrity of the truth-seeking process and preventing false accusations from becoming erroneous convictions.[27] Defendants' rights are not regarded—as there is a tendency to regard them in the earlier system —as an entitlement which the defendant can use or not use at his discretion (since it is *his* status-right, after all) or as a counterweight offsetting the accuser's natural advantage and balancing opposing forces, but rather as functional in insuring that the truth is not bypassed or distorted in an excessively zealous quest for justice.[28]

5. The emphasis is clearly on substance rather than procedure. This feature is marked not in the lack of procedural rules, because they tend to proliferate in any rationalized system of justice, but rather in the increasing amount of freedom judges and other officials have to digress from procedural rules whenever necessary to achieve a substantively correct result.[29] Unfortunately, in the search for substance, officials tend to proceed *ex hypothesi* with predetermined suspicions and assumptions, and these subtly influence all subsequent investigations and evaluations of the evidence.[30] Procedures must be built in to counteract this tendency, and one of the first chosen is independent appellate review by officials at a higher level in the bureaucracy. Next, legal counsel may be provided in a representative, advisory, and/or advocate capacity.[31] Ultimately, the worth of the procedure is judged by its ability to extract the truth, not by its ability, in the words of some contemporary apologists for the adversary system, to "satisfy litigants and onlookers" or to be perceived by them as "fair" whether they win or lose.[32]

6. The method of proof is very different than what it replaced: it is one which depends on evidence (testimony, documents, and the thing itself brought into court) to demonstrate the fact of guilt, not one which depends on signs from the Almighty or procedural error and default. There is a preference for those kinds of evidence which most strongly establish factual guilt— direct proof, consisting primarily of eyewitness testimony and confessions. If necessary, judicial torture is utilized to extract the needed confession, when other types of proof are deemed inadequate.[33] It has been argued that in Western Europe the medieval canon law of proof, which regarded the testimony of two eyewitnesses to the crime or the accused's confession (combined with other lesser proofs) as essential for conviction whenever a serious crime was charged, was compelled by a public skeptical of circumstantial evidence.[34] Yet, such skepticism seems oddly lacking in England, which never adopted the canon-law system of mathematical proofs even though it was equally well acquainted with it and under the same pressure to adopt something in place of the earlier method of proof.[35] Either "inscrutable English jury verdicts" had the same attributes of divine revelation formerly possessed by ordeals, wager of law, and trial by battle, or else some other

explanation must be found for the unique English willingness to convict on the basis of what must have been considered at the time an extremely low grade of evidence as proof. Proof of the type we are speaking of here required investigation, and in these early European inquisitorial proceedings the emphasis is placed on ensuring the reliability of the investigative process.[36]

7. Two essentially new elements are added to criminal process by the inquisitorial method: screening of complaints during investigation to eliminate weak, false, and malicious accusations, and a system of appeals by which errors committed at lower levels of the judicial hierarchy can be corrected.[37] Because lower strata invariably commit errors, both procedural and substantive, and because (the process being lopsided in favor of the prosecution and defendant not having legal counsel) these lower strata are not likely to be aware of and correct errors at the time they are made, appeal becomes essential in the pursuit of substantive justice. In the previous system, human error on a question of substance could hardly be committed, inasmuch as the results were the product of God's judgment (*judicium Dei*), and procedural error was either corrected contemporaneously or not at all.

8. Punishments in an inquisitorial system can have many goals, but the significant difference from "punishments," if they are properly so labeled, in the earlier era is that they begin to serve some broader, public purposes— purposes which transcend the narrow objective of satisfying the litigants (particularly the plaintiff) and restoring the peace; purposes such as deterrence, the prevention of recidivism through incapacitation and branding, or the saving of souls through rehabilitation.[38]

## The Amalgamation of the Two Systems

With this transformation of criminal procedure into the bureaucratic inquisitorial mode in most of Western Europe (except England) in the first half of the second millennium A.D., the basic structure of criminal procedure with its six component parts was formed. But, before diffusion of this basic model throughout the world occurred during the second half of that millennium (the period of European exploration and colonization), one further important historical development occurred which accounts for the present configuration of modern criminal procedure and its remarkable comparability across nations.

English criminal procedure had retained many characteristics of the ancient accusatory (private-dispute) method of administering criminal justice. Although English-Norman kings developed a system of royal courts early, they never erected an elaborate bureaucracy to prosecute, try, review, and punish crimes; they left most of the administration of criminal justice in the hands of local magistrates and popular institutions of the vicinage, such as grand and petit juries.[39] In theory, complaints were initiated by private complainants, although the ancient methods of proof were abandoned and transformed into others which approximated in some respects inquisitorial procedures found on the Continent.[40] The trial, however, rather than the pretrial judicial investigation, remains the focus of the English procedure; the proceedings are still open and public and proofs still consist of the oral testimony of witnesses in court during the trial, instead of their written depositions.[41] Although during most of this period (1500 A.D. to 1800 A.D.) defendants were severely limited in the way they could present their evidence (although not as limited as on the Continent), procedural loopholes for evading conviction or full punishment prescribed by law were many, even though few procedural mechanisms existed for correcting errors committed at the trial level.[42] Moreover, the English were the first to feel the effects of the political and philosophical movement toward anti-monarchical republicanism and the "rights of man." Thus, the English were the first to make liberalizing changes restoring the rights of criminal defendants to introduce proof of innocence through witnesses and to permit the accused assistance of counsel in an advisory, if not a representative, capacity.[43]

For those on the Continent who were dissatisfied with inquisitorial procedure as it developed between 1200 A.D. and 1700 A.D.—especially with regard to its less pleasant aspects: judicial torture in extracting confessions, secret trials and denunciations, requiring the accused to answer questions while under oath, and denying them means to prepare and conduct their own defenses—English procedure offered an attractive contrast, as did a better understanding of what Roman accusatory procedures were like under the Roman Republic.[44] Much ink was spilled on this subject by the French philosophes of the seventeenth and eighteenth centuries. The force of "enlightened public opinion" became so powerful during the eighteenth century that several important reforms, such as the elimination of judicial torture, were achieved even before the French Revolution of 1789. Thereafter, in France and later throughout Europe, many reforms were made in judicial proceedings in criminal cases. The direction of these reforms was to introduce into inquisitorial procedure many accusatorial elements, outlined below, thereby creating a "mixed" system, combining (supposedly) the best of both systems.[45]

A. Esmein summarizes these developments in France as follows:

1. Accusations must now be made by the public prosecutor acting in the name of the state; judges can no longer take cognizance themselves of criminal denunciations by secret informers.

2. The judgment is rendered by magistrates and/or lay jurors.

3. The proceeding is divided into two stages: the first, the preliminary investigation, is entrusted to an investigating magistrate and results in an official evidentiary record (dossier) which becomes the basis of the prosecutor's

accusation; the second, the public trial, in which the evidence is presented orally or in documentary form and the defendant is given the opportunity to confront his accusers and to submit evidence of innocence as well as evidence of justification.

4. The canon-law system of mathematical proofs is abolished and replaced with a system of free evaluation of the evidence by the triers-of-fact, subject to the standard of their being "thoroughly convinced by it" before finding guilt. However, the judge or jury is no longer required to state the evidentiary basis of his or their judgment. Something approaching the "inscrutable" general verdict of the English jury is imported into Continental criminal procedure.[46]

While modern European nations following the Civil Law tradition have become increasingly more adversarial in their criminal procedures in the twentieth century,[47] England and nations once its colonies, including the United States, which retained its common law tradition, have adopted some inquisitorial institutions, procedures, and practices. Among these are:

1. a public prosecutor who can file criminal charges on his own information without the intervention of a grand jury;[48]

2. extensive preliminary investigation and screening of criminal complaints and reports by police and prosecutors acting together;[49]

3. new means of judicially assisted discovery through which evidence in the possession of one's adversary may be obtained, though these discovery devices are still limited in criminal cases;[50]

4. greater control exercised by the court over evidence that the jury will be permitted to consider, thus reducing the control of the parties over the introduction of evidence (less process control by the litigants);[51]

5. judicial supervision of negotiated pleas to ensure that substantive justice and the public interest are not totally compromised;[52] and

6. the hypertrophy (at least in the American criminal justice system) of appellate and collateral review of final judgments to correct both procedural and substantive error.[53]

Adversarial and inquisitorial systems of administering justice no longer stand in sharp contrast to one another. They are now both mixed systems, in the sense that they contain elements of both in different proportions.[54] Nevertheless, they use similar personnel to carry out the same six tasks that we have assigned to modern criminal procedure. In short, the present configuration of modern criminal procedural systems is the historical result of the merging of the two systems which had developed at an earlier stage in European history and which were then transmitted to other parts of the world during the era of European exploration and colonization through the process of cultural diffusion.

## KEEPING AN OPEN MIND

It has long been a failing of American parochialism to believe that foreign criminal procedures are lawless, leave too much to the discretion of officials, and omit necessary elements for the fair and accurate determination of guilt and innocence. This belief confirms our preference for our own systems and our resistance to ideas imported from abroad, notwithstanding our recognition of the deficiencies of American criminal procedure.[55]

First, we tend to harbor certain illusions about the role of law in "totalitarian" societies,[56] believing that law is simply window-dressing masking a reality of official lawlessness. All rules of law—and rules of procedure are no exception—both confer authority and limit authority. Laws which invest officials with authority to exercise their powers with respect to a certain subject matter necessarily restrict that authority as to other subject matters, and, insofar as laws prescribe the method of their operation, limit officials' discretion to perform in other ways. Even though a totalitarian regime might be reluctant to have explicit rules of criminal procedure narrowly circumscribing the authority of its officials in using their powers to benefit the regime and its policies, it still might desire to have its rules made explicit and definite for reasons of administration.[57] If a large volume of criminal suspects and accused persons are going to be processed by the system, it is in the interest of even a totalitarian state to have the power of dealing with such persons delegated to trusted officials whose jobs and powers are clearly demarcated and separated in order to prevent conflicts among them and jurisdictional disputes. In reviewing the actions of these officials, totalitarian regimes are also likely to want cases administered in a regular and prescribed manner so that reviewers will face a limited number of review problems routinely involving a few and, for the most part, *substantive* issues, rather than procedural or technical issues.[58] Finally, in the administration of criminal justice in non-political cases, it is no more in the interest of totalitarian governments than of any others to have innocent people convicted of crimes they did not commit or guilty offenders escape justice. No government could long endure which did not deal with the problem of ordinary crime and which did not at least give the appearance of attempting to do justice. All fictional accounts of governments so tyrannical that the issue of guilt or innocence becomes subordinate to the higher goals of demonstrating the regime's absolute power and of eliciting abject submission to that power (for example, Orwell's *1984*) are just that, fictions.

Therefore, the possession of great power over a subject people does not necessarily mean that legal procedures for the processing of criminal cases will be neglected or left to the unregulated discretion of government agents and officials. Whether governments are democratic or undemocratic, we should expect them to have rules of criminal procedure in most, if not all, of the six areas described above. I shall now attempt to demonstrate this point by comparing American criminal procedures with those of three inquisitorial systems: France, the Soviet Union, and Communist China. Two of these states, the USSR and China, are considered in the West to have undemocratic "totalitarian" regimes. Thus, comparisons can be made not only between an adversarial system of criminal procedure and inquisitorial systems but also between non-Communist "democratic" procedural systems (France and the United States) and Communist "totalitarian" systems (the Soviet Union and Communist China). The respects in which all systems are similar and in which they differ will be reviewed at the end of the book.

# II

# USE OF THE MODEL IN THE COMPARISON OF FOUR MODERN PROCEDURAL SYSTEMS

# 3

# INTAKE

Considering the many reasons people have for not reporting crime—
fear of retaliation by the offender or his supporters, reconciliation between the offender and his victim, unwillingness of the victim to involve himself in official proceedings, lack of faith in the ability of
officials to render effective aid, feelings of guilt or uncertainty about
one's own role in the commission of the offense, and so forth—it is not
surprising that in every nation crime occurs that is never brought to
the attention of authorities. This cannot be a matter of indifference to
authorities whose duty is to preserve public order and protect people
from victimization, since the detriment to public welfare does not depend on whether victims *feel* themselves to have been injured or
whether they are ready to complain about what they have suffered.
Indeed, victims may be unaware that they have been victimized or
their failure to complain may be based on some selfish motive indif-
ferent to the public objective of preventing the continuation of similar
activities. Civil remedies are usually available for those who feel injured enough to resort to the law on their own initiative. Criminal law,
on the other hand, is not designed for the purpose of settling, amicably
or otherwise, interpersonal or interorganizational disputes; it has the
purpose of rectifying wrongs to public interests whether or not there
is a private complainant. Moreover, it cannot be assumed that the
greater the injury to the public interest, the greater the likelihood that

the crime will be reported. Crimes, known in the United States as "white collar crimes" (business crimes such as employee theft, consumer fraud, regulatory violations), "victimless crimes" (transactions in prohibited drugs, prostitution, corruption of youth), and "political crimes" (espionage, subversive activities) are rarely reported to authorities and yet may cause great injury to public interests. Victimization studies conducted in the United States by the Census Bureau reveal that even some crimes of violence (for example, rape and robbery) are not reported with the frequency one might expect considering the gravity of the wrong and the fact that the victims, at least, are always aware of their occurrence.[1]

For the reasons just stated, no nation can safely ignore unreported crime and must do what it can to stimulate reporting by members of the public and to search out and discover crime likely to be hidden from public view. It goes without saying that not everything presently labeled as a crime either can be or should be processed by criminal justice agencies. Any existing criminal justice apparatus would be incapable of managing the resulting monstrous overload. Much of what at present passes for crime could be handled informally by civil administration, social control, or mediation of disputes between the parties immediately involved. But, even if crime were greatly narrowed in definitional scope, the problem of encouraging its revelation so that criminal justice agencies can deal with it would still remain.

## INTAKE PROCEDURES IN FRANCE

In France the police must report all crimes which come to their attention to the public prosecutor (*procureur*), who is vested with the ultimate authority of deciding whether they will be prosecuted.[2] The police are given the authority to arrest and conduct searches without warrants in cases of crimes committed in flagrante delicto,[3] and to detain persons suspected of criminal activity for limited periods of time while conducting a preliminary investigation regardless of how the crime was committed.[4] Although crimes may also be brought to the attention of the prosecutor directly by the victim, they seldom are; thus the police are the principal entry point for the processing of criminal complaints in France.[5] Later on in the process, before the decision is made by the prosecutor to proceed with a formal prosecution, the investigation may be turned over to an independent magistrate, an "investigation judge" (*juge d'instruction*). However, this is only required in the case of serious crimes or felonies (*crimes*), is discretionary in cases of serious misdemeanors (*délits*), and not required at all for petty misdemeanors (*contraventions*).[6] Even in the case of serious crimes, much of the investigative work of the investigation judge may be delegated by him to the police, so that in actual practice the entire investigation of criminal complaints is performed by the police in the great majority of cases.[7]

The police in France do not merely respond to complaints and reports of crime made by citizens. As with all police, they have extensive networks of informers, both inside and outside the ranks of the criminal underworld, who advise them of criminal incidents or ongoing activities; and even without the help of these informers, much crime comes to their notice during the performance of their normal policing activities.[8] Occasionally—as in the enforcement of drug laws, for example —they engage in what we would describe as entrapment tactics in order to catch elusive offenders in the commission of crimes, although probably not to the degree of their American counterparts.

## INTAKE PROCEDURES IN THE SOVIET UNION

In the Soviet Union the office of the state prosecutor (the Procuracy) controls every aspect of the administration of criminal justice from arrest through punishment, with the exception of the defense function and the judicial function of determining guilt or innocence.[9] As far as the initial phases of a criminal proceeding—the complaint reception, detention, and investigation—are concerned, the work is done by the procurator's investigator, the police (*militsiia*) or the agencies of state security (KGB), subject to the procurator's supervision. Reports are received by police and other "agencies of inquiry" from various sources. Some indication of what they are is given in Article 108 of the 1960 Code of Criminal Procedure of the Russian Soviet Federated Socialist Republic (RSFSR):

*Reasons and Grounds for Initiating Criminal Case*

The following shall constitute reasons for initiating a criminal case:
1. Declarations and letters of citizens;
2. Communications of trade union and Communist Youth League organizations, people's guards for the protection of public order, comrades' courts and other social organizations;
3. Communications of institutions, enterprises, organizations, and officials;
4. Articles, notices, and letters published in the press;
5. Giving oneself up;
6. Direct discovery of a crime by an agency of inquiry, investigator, procurator or court.

A case may be initiated only in instances where there exist sufficient data indicating the indicia of a crime.[10]

Of the various ways listed in Article 108 criminal complaints may come to the attention of authorities, the first and last ways are the most common; the least common way, as might be expected, is offenders "giving themselves up."

Officials are required to act promptly after receipt of such reports by deciding whether to "initiate a criminal case," refuse to initiate it, or transfer the complaint to another investigative or judicial jurisdiction.[11] When the recipient of the complaint or crime report is an "agency of inquiry," one of the three agents or agencies mentioned above, it is required to take steps to investigate the crime and to take whatever additional measures are necessary to prevent or suppress it.[12] If the case is one where a preliminary investigation conducted by an investigator assigned by the procurator is obligatory, the police are expected to transfer it to the investigator as soon as possible after conducting whatever urgent investigations, detentions, interrogations and acts to preserve the evidence are immediately required.[13] Where a preliminary investigation is not obligatory,[14] they have up to a month to complete their investigation and decide whether to criminally charge, terminate, or suspend the case, although this period may be extended by the procurator.[15] Persons may be detained for periods of up to seventy-two hours for purposes of interrogation and preliminary investigation, but longer periods may be authorized in special cases.[16]

Serious criminal cases are usually investigated by an "investigator" (*sledovatel'*) assigned by the procurator.[17] The investigator conducts a "preliminary investigation" (*predvaritel'noe sledstvie*) rather than an "inquiry" (*doznanie*), which is conducted by agencies of inquiry, such as the police, in less serious cases. The preliminary investigation is the Russian equivalent of the supposedly thorough work-up of the case which the investigating magistrate performs in France. It will constitute the basis for the procurator's decision to indict.[18] Theoretically independent of the procurator to the extent of being permitted to disagree with the procurator's decision to indict or not to indict and to appeal his decisions to a higher level of the Procuracy,[19] the investigator's independence is severely limited by other provisions of the Code which permit the procurator to reverse his decisions and even to remove him from the case completely.[20] Even where the preliminary investigation is conducted by an investigator of the Procuracy, the Code provides, like its French counterpart, for enlisting the aid of other "agencies of inquiry" in the investigation through rogatory commissions or assignment of investigative tasks.[21]

Therefore, as in France, in the Soviet Union the police and procuratorial investigators are the principal organs for the receipt of criminal complaints and the discovery and investigation of crimes. Unlike France, however, the Soviet Union goes much further in attempting to involve the citizen in the war against crime. Citizens are encouraged to participate in the administration of criminal justice and are given many opportunities to do so. They are indoctrinated in the civic morality of informing, and, as we note from Article 108 of the Code of Criminal Procedure quoted above, there are many civic organizations (trade unions, collectives, youth groups, and people's guards) who consider themselves auxiliaries of the police in detecting and reporting crime.

## INTAKE PROCEDURES IN CHINA

Criminal procedure in the People's Republic of China is now governed by the Law on Criminal Procedure adopted at the second plenary session of the Fifth National People's Congress on July 1, 1979,[22] supplemented by additional regulations, such as the Regulations Governing the Arrest and Detention of Persons Accused of Crimes adopted by the Standing Committee of the Fifth People's Congress (PRC) on February 23, 1979.[23] The promulgation and publication of these written laws and regulations represent a major departure from past practice and procedure in Communist China. Until July 1, 1979 the People's Republic never had a formal penal code, in which all acts deemed criminal by the government were set down in writing and defined.[24] Its criminal procedures were an admixture of procedures copied from the Soviet Union during the Stalinist era, procedures of long-standing but of indigenous character which had been adopted by revolutionary committees in provinces and districts under their control before their successful overthrow of the Kuomintang government in 1949, and a series of procedural innovations and experiments introduced by secret regulation during the period 1949 to 1979. Only a few of these—such as the Arrest and Detention Act of December 20, 1954, for example,— were ever published. In fact, in the period before 1979, if laws were "published" at all, it was for internal administrative use rather than for popular consumption or enlightenment of foreigners. Most of our information about them, therefore, is based upon accounts given by expatriate refugees who fled mainland China and the scant written material, including newspaper articles, published in China and disseminated abroad.[25] In the past eight years these sources of information have been supplemented by foreign visitors who have been invited to China to observe its legal institutions in action.[26]

Because of the radical changes in both internal and external policies in the PRC since the death of Mao Zedong and the fall of the "Gang of Four," there have been equally significant changes introduced in the administration of criminal justice in the last few years, best illustrated by the publication of the penal and procedural codes mentioned above.[27] Thus, much of what has been written about Chinese criminal procedure in the past is already, to a certain extent, outdated and inaccurate. Nevertheless, there is reason to believe that many former practices and procedures are so well entrenched that it will take time for the provisions and ideology of the 1979 code to be implemented. China is a large country, with a huge population (slightly over one billion), comprising a large number of ethnic subnationalities, and divided into many governmental subdivisions. There always has been, and will continue to be, resistance by some local cadres (army, police, and Communist Party officials) to the implementation of national laws with whose purpose or underlying philosophy they disagree.[28] Secondly, although the People's Procuracy was given supervisory powers over the administration of justice in the 1978 and 1982 Constitutions, as well as in the 1979 Procedure Code, to ensure that the policies of the new laws are carried out, it lacks the power and authority of its Soviet counterpart.[29] Finally, China still lacks a trained cadre of lawyers to administer and utilize its judicial system; and lawyers are probably the best guarantee that legal procedures will be followed. It has been estimated that there are probably no more than ten thousand trained lawyers in all of mainland China. The government is engaged in a strenuous effort to train more,[30] but it is doubtful that for a generation, at least, there will be a sufficient number to change the system from one operated by legal amateurs concerned primarily with substantive justice to one run primarily by professionals equally concerned with procedural justice.

In discussing criminal procedure in China, whether at the intake stage or later in the process, it will be necessary to adhere to the description of the process presented in the criminal law and procedural codes themselves, because of the unavailability of information concerning the actual operation of the system in practice. Occasionally, I will supplement the discussion of the Chinese law-as-it-is-supposed-to-operate, with some comments as to procedures which antedated the 1979 reforms in order to provide a context in which to view these reforms.

In the period before the promulgation of the substantive and procedural criminal codes in mid 1979, it was not always a simple thing to determine when a crime was committed.[31] The same act might be responded to in a variety of ways: it might be subject to mediation by the offender's residency committee or by his work group; it might be subjected to the application of administrative sanctions by the local public security bureaus (police); or it might be the basis of a criminal prosecution, all at the discretion of the police acting in coordination with other local officials, including party officials.[32] Under the new codes this situation has changed considerably, in that it is now much clearer which acts violate the criminal law and which acts are appropriate for mediation, for administrative sanction ("rehabilitation through labor"), and for criminal prosecution, even though a residual vagueness remains in the area of lesser offenses against public order, which could probably be handled in any of the three previously mentioned ways.[33]

But before these largely discretionary decisions are made as to how to handle a complaint, how are criminal complaints brought to the attention of public authorities and how are they supposed to respond to these complaints, assuming they suspect a criminal violation has occurred?

There are essentially two different methods prescribed by Chinese procedural law, depending on whether the making of a complaint by a citizen or organization with the police, procurator, or local people's court *precedes* or *follows* the detention or arrest of the offender. The first procedure, covered by Articles 59 through 61 of the Procedure Law,[34] stipulates that, upon discovery, governmental organs, citizens, or non-governmental organizations have the right and duty to make complaints to the police, procuracies, or courts, which shall have the duty of accepting and registering these complaints for possible investigation, unless the matter falls outside their jurisdiction, in which case the receiving agency shall transfer it to the organ which has jurisdiction to investigate it.[35] Complaints of this nature may be made orally or in writing, but oral complaints must be reduced to writing and attested to by the complainant who is warned beforehand as to the legal penalties for making false accusations. The complainant has the right of requesting anonymity, at least as long as the investigation lasts.[36] Upon receipt of these complaints, the receiving agency (police, procuracy, courts), if the matter lies within its jurisdicition, is enjoined to promptly review the facts of the accusation—or confession, if there has been a voluntary surrender and the first report of the crime comes from the offender himself—and to determine whether to "file a case" (initiate an investigation which may lead to formal charges). On the other hand, the receiving agency may decide that the accusation or confession is factually baseless or that the facts are so minor in importance as not to warrant a criminal investigation, in which case it is authorized to reject the case. If the latter is done, the agency is supposed to inform the complainant of the reason for its action, and the complainant then has the right of applying for reconsideration if he disagrees with the decision.[37] Under this procedure, investigative detention or arrest,[38] both of which will be discussed in greater detail hereafter,[39] usually follow the decision to commence an official investigation.

The second typical method of bringing offenders before the appropriate authorities for criminal investigation and possible prosecution is the procedure provided for by Articles 41 and 42 of the Procedure

Law, which allow for the immediate apprehension and taking into custody of a criminal suspect by a public security officer (policeman) or citizen in any of the following circumstances:

1. the suspect is caught in the process of preparing to commit a crime, during its commission, or immediately after committing it;[40]
2. the suspect is identified as having committed a crime by the victim or an eyewitness;
3. the suspect is discovered to have criminal evidence on his person or in his residence;
4. the suspect attempts to commit suicide, escape, or is a fugitive after committing a crime;
5. an emergency exists because the offender may destroy or fabricate evidence or collude with others in devising a consistent exonerating story or alibi;
6. the offender's identity is unclear and there is a strong basis for suspecting that he will flee and commit other crimes unless detained;
7. the offender is carrying on "beating, smashing, and looting" and is gravely undermining work, production or social order;[41]
8. the offender is wanted for arrest, is being pursued for arrest, or has escaped from prison.[42]

Under this procedure, whenever a citizen is authorized to seize and detain an offender in flagrante delicto or a wanted person, prison escapee, or fugitive, he is required to turn him over to the police, local procurator, or people's court for handling.

In a variety of ways the new Procedure Law encourages and facilitates the reporting of crime. First, Articles 59 and 60 provide an extremely simple method for uneducated people to file oral and written complaints with several complaint-reception agencies; Article 60 (para. 3) guarantees the complainant's anonymity, if he desires it, during the investigation phase. Second, although the Chinese penal code does not, like its Soviet counterpart, make non-revelation or concealment of a crime a criminal offense,[43] and although it does provide criminal penalties for making false accusations,[44] there are no penalties, civil or criminal, for making improvident but non-malicious accusations based on ignorance or good-faith mistake. Third, Chinese law *does*, as do most inquisitorial systems, provide for the joinder with criminal prosecutions of "supplementary civil actions," whereby a victim suffering material loss as the result of defendant's behavior can recover compensation in the same proceeding in which criminal guilt is determined by way of court-ordered restitution or damages.[45] Thus, it is often to the victim's advantage, and seldom to his disadvantage, to report crime to the authorities.

## INTAKE PROCEDURES IN THE UNITED STATES

In the United States most of the crime which comes to the attention of authorities comes to the police by way of citizen reporting. Little is done to encourage such reporting, however, with scattered exceptions here and there of local citizen groups voluntarily engaged in crime prevention efforts.[46] Officially established citizens groups, such as grand juries, determine the prosecutability of complaints which are brought before them by prosecutors for possible indictment; they no longer perform, to any significant extent, their ancient function of "presenting" criminal charges on the basis of information in their possession.

Private prosecutions are not allowed, as they are in England, nor may citizens intervene in criminal proceedings in order to recover civil damages or to ensure that their interests are not neglected by the state, as in France and the Soviet Union. The United States continues to maintain a sharp distinction between criminal and civil jurisidiction, whereby victims have no official standing in criminal proceedings and are not permitted to participate in them, except when called to testify as witnesses. Victims are relegated to separate, and often prohibitively expensive, civil proceedings against the same defendant for the same wrong that constitutes the subject matter of the criminal proceedings if they wish to obtain relief of a kind which has personal value to themselves. With the exception of restitution, sometimes imposed as a condition of probation or voluntary diversion programs officially or unofficially sanctioned as a part of adult and juvenile delinquency proceedings, criminal law in the United States has no punishments which are of tangible benefit to victims, and this further discourages their reporting crime to authorities.

The United States utterly neglects to instill in its citizenry moral beliefs of mutual dependence and civic obligation, including the duty to inform regarding known or suspected criminal activities, whether or not personal advantage can be derived from such reporting. Indeed, the mutual suspicions of ethnic groups in our society and their suspicions of the police are fostered, and "minding one's own business" is elevated to the level of a positive virtue. Few, if any, efforts are made by government to organize the population into self-regulating local units which could exercise informal, but legally sanctioned, measures of social control in cases of minor crimes and delinquencies, thus saving official agencies the burden of regulating and controlling them.

Intake procedures in the United States usually commence with the arrest of a criminal suspect by the police on the basis of information supplied by victims and witnesses or on the basis of the policeman's own observations. This information must be sufficient to furnish the arresting officer with "probable cause" to believe that a crime has been committed and that the arrested person committed it.[47] The arrested person is then taken into custody and held until such time as he furnishes bail security which the magistrate has imposed as a condition for his release or until the magistrate releases him "on his own recognizance" without bail.[48]

One of the major differences between the inquisitorial intake procedures previously described and intake procedures in the United States is that in the United States there is no provision for more than a momentary detaining of a criminal suspect by police for an investigation into the facts prior to making an official arrest.[49] However, provided that the original facts which come to the attention of the arresting officer at the time of arrest do meet the standard of "probable cause," the arrested person can remain in police custody without further investigation or corroboration until such time as the prosecutor is required to present to someone—a magistrate at a preliminary hearing or a grand jury—adequate evidentiary support for a prosecution. This may not occur for weeks or even months after the arrest. In inquisitorial systems, on the other hand, the "arrest" of the defendant is likely to come long after his initial investigative detention and usually represents a decision by the police, prosecutor, or investigating magistrate that evidence exists to warrant criminal prosecution. This results in fewer cases being dropped for lack of evidence after the formal "arrest" has been made in inquisitorial systems.

In summary, the procedures of France, the Soviet Union, and China seem better designed than those of the United States to encourage the reporting of crime by citizens to authorities and allow officials, particularly police, more freedom in investigating crime and ferreting it out.

# 4

# SCREENING

Screening out cases which do not merit criminal prosecution goes on from the moment a crime first comes to the attention of a government official (usually the police) to the time someone (usually the prosecutor) makes a decision to file a formal accusation in a court of appropriate jurisdiction. In the United States, for example, the police may decide not to arrest a suspect, even when they have sufficient evidence to do so.[1] Prosecutors, in their almost boundless discretion, may decide not to prosecute, or to withhold prosecution while the accused submits voluntarily to a diversion treatment program or informal probation. Magistrates (usually judges of lower criminal courts of limited jurisdiction) may decide at preliminary hearings or grand jurors at a grand jury hearing that the prosecutor has not adduced sufficient credible evidence to justify prosecution.[2] The definition of screening should also be extended to include decisions other than those not to arrest or prosecute, such as decisions to settle the case by trading possible criminal charges or penalty recommendations for the accused's agreement not to contest the prosecution or to enter a plea of guilty. Even though such agreements do not avoid the formalities of accusation and prosecution, they do eliminate or abbreviate later stages of the proceeding, such as trial and appeal, and, like other screening procedures, reduce the administrative burdens on the system.

Screening practices may or may not be regulated by legal rules of procedure. Where they are not, they may still be regulated by supervisory officials of the agency which has screening powers; otherwise, they are left to the unreviewable discretion of the official who exercises the power. The danger always exists that decisions not to arrest or prosecute will be made for improper reasons, reasons which are extraneous to the accomplishment of the system's major goals. Criminal procedural systems differ in the extent to which they seem cognizant of this danger and attempt to cover it in their rules of criminal procedure. In the United States, for example, until very recently, discretionary decisions of police not to arrest and prosecutors not to prosecute were left completely unregulated, either externally by the courts or internally by the agencies or offices themselves. The movement of the United States during the last two decades to reduce official discretion in these two areas has produced two major sets of guidelines (recommended rather than prescribed standards) for the exercise of these powers, but neither has had much impact on the way police and prosecutors actually screen cases.[3] In the remainder of this chapter I will compare the procedures and practices followed in France, the Soviet Union, China, and the United States to screen out unworthy cases from the mass of complaints they receive and the devices they have to ensure that worthy cases are not also screened out for improper reasons.

## SCREENING PROCEDURES IN FRANCE

In French inquisitorial procedure the state official who should have the greatest control over the investigative and screening phase of criminal procedure is the investigation judge (*juge d'instruction*). In theory, screening is supposed to work as described in the following passage:

> The police must report all offenses to the prosecutor who must then open a file—a dossier—and refer the matter to a judge for "examination." Police are placed at the disposal of the examining judge, who must decide whether there is enough evidence to justify prosecution. To that end, he is given the power to order arrests and searches, take testimony under oath, and interrogate the accused—all the while recording the results of the investigation in the dossier. The critical investigative and charging decisions are to be made by the judge, or authorized and reviewed by him. And non-judicial officials have no authority to terminate a case reaching a certain level of evidentiary sufficiency, or even to determine the seriousness or number of the charges on which a defendant is ultimately tried.[4]

In France today, however, it is actually the police and the prosecutor (*procureur*), not the investigation judge, who make most of the important screening decisions. And, contrary to what is suggested in the preceding quotation, the prosecutor is not required to open a file and refer the matter to an investigation judge. The investigation judge does not even participate in the proceedings unless the prosecutor assigns the case to him and that is only required in the case of serious crimes (*crimes*).[5] A recent study reveals that in 1974, serious crimes (*crimes*) and misdemeanors (*délits*) were sent to the *juge d'instruction* for judicial investigation in less than 15 percent of the cases.[6] Under Article 79 of the Code of Criminal Procedure the French prosecutor enjoys the discretionary power not to assign a misdemeanor case to a magistrate for examination. He can also avoid doing so as to serious crimes by ignoring their aggravating circumstances and treating them as lesser-included *délits*. This practice is known as "correctionalizing" a serious crime,[7] and has the same semilegal status in France that plea bargaining had in the United States before the United States Supreme Court gave the practice its constitutional blessing in the early 1970s. Nevertheless, "correctionalizing" is a major device available to the French prosecutor for simplifying cases procedurally so that they may receive an expeditious disposition.[8]

The French prosecutor also enjoys by law a broad discretionary power not to prosecute no matter how serious the offense, unlike his counterpart in other inquisitorial countries, such as Italy and West Germany.[9] He may dismiss the case for policy or evidentiary reasons and need not explain his decision to the court.[10] This power must be exercised before the case is placed in the hands of the investigation judge, but we have already seen how the prosecutor can prevent that from occurring. The only instance in French criminal procedure where the prosecutor's discretion to nolle pros (*classer sans suite*) a criminal case is limited is when a victim intervenes in the case and becomes a civil party (*partie civile*). When the *partie civile* files a felony or misdemeanor complaint directly with the investigation judge (Articles 85 through 87, *CPPD*), or in the case of misdemeanors directly with the *tribunal correctionnel* (Art. 392), the prosecution must usually proceed regardless of the prosecutor's judgment as to its merits.[11] However, this occurs with relative infrequency.[12] A. V. Sheehan states that statistics for the Paris prefecture for 1970 show that approximately 80 percent of all criminal complaints made known to the *procureur* were marked "*classer sans suite*" (no further proceedings), although the greatest number of these complaints were for insufficient funds where restitution was probably made.[13]

A significant amount of screening of criminal complaints in France is probably done by the police themselves. Theoretically, according to law, police have no discretion in reporting crimes to the prosecutor, whether or not they have a suspect, or in conducting a preliminary inquest (*l'enquête flagrante*) into the facts reported to them.[14] In actuality, the police enter many reported crimes and complaints in a register known as the "*main-courante*" without transmitting formal "*procès-verbaux*" to the prosecutor.[15] During the year 1970 in Paris where a strict reporting requirement prevails, only 13.9 percent of all *crimes* and *délits* reported by the police to the prosecutor were prosecuted.[16] Of the original 477,870 incidents reported, about 28 percent (134,000) were cases where the offender was not identified.[17] Therefore, we may assume that roughly one-third of all felony and misdemeanor-grade offenses in France are probably screened out by the police and over 85 percent by both police and prosecutors at a very early stage of the investigation.

Screening is done by investigation judges in those cases which are assigned to them at the completion of their investigation. They have the authority to order no further proceedings (*ordonnance de non-lieu*), to remit the case to the appropriate court for trial (*ordonnance de renvoi*), or to arrange for the case (if it involves a serious crime) to be placed before the indicting chamber (*chambre d'accusation*) of the appeals court, so that it may review the magistrate's decision to charge prior to remitting the case to the assize court which has jurisdiction over serious crimes.[18] The magistrate's decision that there be no further proceedings in the case can be appealed to the indicting chamber of the appeals court by the *procureur* and the *partie civile*, but such appeals are seldom made and seldom successful.[19] Also, decisions by the indicting chamber to reverse or alter the decision of the investigation judge to proceed are likewise rare.[20]

The question of whether French prosecutors screen cases by engaging in practices comparable to American plea bargaining has recently been addressed by two American legal scholars who traveled to France to study criminal law in practice in the context of its procedural code.[21] Abraham S. Goldstein and Martin Marcus found no evidence of "explicit" charge bargaining (that is, reduction of charges in return for an agreement not to oppose conviction of these lesser charges) or sentence bargaining (that is, the prosecutor's recommendation of a lenient sentence in return for a similar agreement on defendant's part). However, they did find some evidence of "implicit" bargaining.[22]

First, it must be understood that the guilty plea, as we Americans know it, does not exist in inquisitorial procedure. If the defendant confesses his guilt of the crime or crimes of which he is charged, whether before trial or during the trial, the confession is never treated, as the guilty plea is, as defendant's acquiescence in the immediate entry of a judgment of conviction. Instead, it is treated as evidence which must be evaluated with all the other evidence pointing to the defendant's guilt. Thus, trials cannot be avoided by extrajudicial or judicial confessions in inquisitorial procedure. Nevertheless, *uncontested* trials—trials which consist of the president of the court reading selected items from the accused's dossier and receiving his confirmation as to their validity and little more, trials which consume less than fifteen minutes of the court's time—are still possible. Indeed, according to Goldstein and Marcus, they are a common feature of the inquisitorial judicial scene.[23] They report that prosecutors, judges, and defense counsel in France, Italy, and West Germany steadfastly deny that they engage in bargaining in order to produce a smooth flow of uncontested criminal cases through the courts, and from all the evidence it would appear that these officials are sincere in their opposition to, and abstinence from, explicit plea bargaining. However, as Goldstein and Marcus also observe, this does not rule out the possibility of prosecutors exercising their discretionary powers in such a way as to encourage non-resistance on the part of defendants.[24] In all procedural systems, accusatorial as well as inquisitorial, they argue, defendants who cooperate with their accusers by acquiescing in their decisions, by saving authorities time and expense and by accepting some punishment for the crimes they have allegedly committed, receive better and more lenient treatment than those who obstinately resist and bog down the system. This being the case, implicit "understandings" tend to arise between officials, accused persons, and their counsel that non-resistance and acquiescence will be rewarded with either reduction of charges (in France, *correctionalisation*) or with recommendations by prosecutors and sentences by courts involving more leniency than they could expect after full proceedings. These "understandings" may never be arrived at by consultations or negotiations carried on between prosecutors and defense counsel, and expectations based on them may be betrayed by the atypical behavior of a participant, such as a prosecutor or a judge; but, insofar as they are given substance and legitimacy by the routine conduct of all participants in the system, Goldstein and Marcus argue that cases are being expedited in inquisitorial systems by a form of "implicit" plea bargaining.[25]

Thomas Weigend, however, argues, somewhat more convincingly, that it is doubtful that even implicit plea bargaining underlies the French prosecutor's practice of reducing felonies to misdemeanors through *correctionalisation*. He gives three reasons: (1) most defendants do not have counsel to represent them at the stage of proceedings where *correctionalisation* decisions are made and thus no one to bargain for them; (2) by the time the prosecutor makes his charging decision, he has a complete dossier containing all the evidence available to the police, and if it were lacking in anything he would be more likely to forward the matter to the investigation judge for further investigation than to reopen the preliminary inquiry and negotiate with the defendant; and (3) unlike American law regarding guilty pleas, a French defendant can always repudiate and withdraw his confession prior to conviction, and therefore a French prosecutor who traded a *correction-alisation* for a confession would never be certain that the defendant would not present a full-scale defense before the *tribunal correctionnel.*[26]

Thus, although the French screen a large portion of all criminal complaints referred to them by the police and even though they do attempt to expedite and simplify the adjudication of cases by switching them away from the cumbersome assize court to the faster-paced *tribunal correctionnel* through the device of *correctionalisation,* they do not seem, in the better analysis, to engage in the American practice of plea bargaining, either explicit or implicit, in order to coerce the cooperation of the accused in screening cases away from trial. They do not, not only because the idea of bargaining with a wrongdoer over his guilt and punishment is repulsive to them, but also because there is no need to do so.[27] The system is flexible enough to permit prosecutors to achieve most of what they want without soliciting the cooperation or collusion of the accused.

## SCREENING PROCEDURES IN THE SOVIET UNION

There is little information available as to informal screening procedures in the Soviet Union. We do not know the extent to which the police, procuratorial investigators, and security agencies sift out of the mass of crimes brought to their attention those they consider too unimportant to report to the procurator's office or those which they consider better handled administratively.[28] Nor do we know the extent to which the procurator himself consigns cases reported to him to oblivion or refers them to another agency.

Information received by the author from *emigré* Soviet officials formerly employed in the criminal justice apparatus suggests that the greatest number of citizen complaints—the actual percentage varying by region and republic—are screened out of the system by police officials who make the decision not to register them. If complaints are not registered, they do not get into the pipeline and there is no need to justify to the procurator the decision to discontinue investigation and terminate or divert the case in accordance with the provisions of the procedural code. This practice of "hiding cases" (that is, screening but not reporting) is quite prevalent in the Soviet Union and is done routinely by all agencies of inquiry, with the possible exception of the KGB, for a variety of reasons, many unrelated to the systemic need of alleviating the burden of an excessive number of cases. For example, Soviet procuratorial and police investigators often manipulate the crime statistics collected by their offices by not reporting criminal complaints, often for the same reason American police do: to make themselves look good in terms of goal accomplishment.

Notwithstanding these informal methods of screening cases, the RSFSR procedural code provides a number of formal mechanisms to the procurator and investigator for screening and diverting criminal cases out of the system.

Article 3 of the General Provisions of the 1960 Code of Criminal Procedure of the RSFSR states:

A court, prosecutor, investigator, and agency of inquiry shall be obliged, within the limits of their competence, to initiate a criminal case in every instance in which indicia of a crime are disclosed and take all measures provided by law for ascertaining the occurrence of the crime and the persons guilty of committing it, and for punishing them.[29]

This provision would seem to exclude the discretion on the part of Soviet police and prosecutors in managing the intake of reported and discovered crimes, but it is clear from subsequent provisions that such an interpretation would be incorrect. Article 5 states the usual legal grounds for non-initiation of a criminal case or its early termination once initiated: non-occurrence of the crime, absence of an element of the crime, expiration of a period of limitation for the commencement of prosecutions, amnesty or pardon, the offender's incapacity due to infancy, and so forth. Article 6 provides that a court, procurator, or investigator or agency of inquiry with the consent of the procurator has the right to terminate a criminal case if any one of them decides on the basis of its investigation that "the act committed by the guilty person has lost its socially dangerous character or the person has ceased to be socially dangerous."[30] Article 7 permits the same officials to terminate criminal proceedings for certain petty offenses and to transfer the case for consideration by a comrades' court.[31] Article 8 permits the same officials to terminate criminal cases involving minors under the age of eighteen and "not representing a great social danger" and to transfer them to a "commission for cases of minors," which has the power to administer non-criminal sanctions. Article 9 allows a similar termination and release of the offender on sureties to a petitioning social organization or collective of working people for re-education and correction. Article 10 permits diversion, *even before initiation of criminal cases*, to comrades' courts, commissions for cases of minors, and social organizations mentioned in Article 9 where "a person commits a crime that is insignificant or does not represent a great social danger, and when the fact of the crime is obvious and the person who has committed it may be corrected by measures of social pressure."[32] The RSFSR Penal Code contains a number of vague provisions incorporating a broad span of petty crime and anti-social conduct (for instance, "hooliganism" defined in Article 206, which includes deliberate evasion of methods of control by persons previously administratively determined to be living a "parasitic existence"). It also contains an elaborate system for subjecting criminals and other anti-socials to social control measures such as "social censure" and "corrective labor."[33] It is thus quite probable that these provisions are designed to give officials the discretion needed to divert from the investigative and court processes the bulk of minor offenses which, if not diverted, would hopelessly congest and overburden the criminal justice apparatus.

Article 113 also grants the procurator, investigator, agency of inquiry, or judge the right to refuse to initiate a criminal case.[34] However, it also provides that the reasons for such refusal should be justified in writing to the person, institution, enterprise, or social organization which has notified authorities of the violation, and that the refusal may be appealed by such persons or organizations "to the proper procurator or higher courts, as appropriate."[35] Article 29 of the procedural code allows intervention in the criminal proceeding by persons suffering material loss as a result of the offender's behavior, but a civil suit in a criminal case may only be brought *after* initiation of the criminal case by official agencies.[36] Only Article 27 provides, in a very limited number of cases, for the initiation of a criminal case solely on the complaint of the victim. Therefore, there would appear to be very little recourse, except political, for anyone who might object to the non-prosecution of criminal cases by police and procurators or to the diversion of cases to other agencies for handling.

Screening in Soviet criminal procedure also takes place later in pretrial proceedings. The investigator who conducts the preliminary investigation may terminate the case at the conclusion of his investigation with the approval of the procurator if the participation of the accused in the commission of a crime has not been proved or if any of the bases for termination provided in Articles 5 through 9 of the Code exist.[37] This decision by the investigator is subject to appeal to the procurator,[38] and may be reversed by the procurator,[39] but this provision is seldom effective since the procurator has previously authorized the termination of the investigation. The procurator also enjoys broad powers to terminate a criminal case prior to trial and transfer it to another agency for handling.[40] Indeed, these powers of the procurator in the pretrial phase of criminal proceedings are so great as to suggest that he may use it to "deal" with defendants for their cooperation. One can only speculate as to whether bargains are struck between procurators and defendants in the Soviet Union, but it seems unlikely that they are. Except to furnish information and testimony regarding crimes in which they participated as accessories, there is little the average defendant has to offer the Soviet procurator in return for his consideration. Soviet courts are usually not overburdened with criminal cases and the procurator's burden of proof, if he has one,[41] is not heavy or difficult to discharge. Thus, there is no pressure on the procurator to relieve that burden by bargaining for the defendant's cooperation.

## SCREENING PROCEDURES IN CHINA

In China screening of complaints is done mainly by the police rather than by procurators. Even though the office of the procuracy has been restored in the most recent constitutions,[42] the procuracy is still in its infancy at this time, there being few officials with sufficient legal training to perform the task of supervising the administration of criminal justice. In the new Procedure Law (1979) the police were given a certain amount of discretion in deciding whether to initiate a preliminary investigation into complaints they receive,[43] and whether to recommend the arrest of a criminal suspect to the procuracy for their approval.[44] It is they, the police or "public security bureaus," rather than procuratorial investigators as in the Soviet Union, who conduct most of the preliminary investigation of criminal complaints.[45]

The procuratorates (prosecutors' offices at various levels) also screen cases insofar as they have limited authority to decide whether a certain category of criminal complaint will be investigated,[46] but mainly in their overall authority to decide whether "arrests" shall be made and prosecutions initiated.[47] Article 96 of the 1979 Procedure Law provides that, in reviewing cases, procurators must ascertain, among other things, whether the facts and circumstances of an alleged crime are clear and supported by reliable and complete evidence, whether criminal conduct has been omitted from the charges, whether there are other persons connected with the crime whose involvement and responsibility should be investigated, and whether the investigation activities of the police were lawful. Article 100 provides that if the procurator deems the facts of the complaint as elucidated by the investigation to be "reliable and complete,"[48] he should initiate a prosecution in the appropriate people's court. Article 101, on the other hand, states that the procurator has the authority to exempt a case from prosecution "in cases where, according to the provisions of the Criminal Law, it is not necessary to impose a sentence of criminal punishment or an exemption from criminal punishment may be granted . . . ."[49] If he does exempt a case from prosecution, his action is reviewable by his superiors in the procuracy. Also the public security bureau which investigated the case initially and transmitted it to the procuracy for prosecution has a right to be informed of the decision and to request reconsideration. If that fails, the public security bureau may protest the decision by seeking review by the next higher level of the procuracy. The crime victim likewise has the right of being advised of a decision not to prosecute and to request that the local office of the procurator review its own decision.[50] Finally, the procurator can, if he wishes, conduct a supplementary investigation of his own into the facts of the case, or he can return the case to the public security bureau for further investigation.[51] Thus, the Chinese procurator has considerable latitude—although not unreviewable latitude, to be sure—to screen out of the process complaints which he and his coworkers believe lack merit or are not sufficiently serious to warrant criminal prosecution.[52] In the recent Procedure Law, as in the past, the people's courts also have the power to screen cases before they reach the trial stage. Under Article 108 the people's court which receives a case after the decision to prosecute has been made, must conduct a threshold ex parte review of it to determine whether it is ready for public trial. If, in the judges' opinion, the facts are not clear nor the evidence complete, they may remand the case to the procuracy for supplementary investigation, and, where there is "no need for a criminal sentence," they may demand that the procuracy withdraw the prosecution entirely.[53] Thus, it would appear that, before a criminal case is finally litigated in the People's Republic of China, not only the factual, but also the legal, sufficiency of criminal accusations is sifted by officials of at least three organs of government—police, prosecutors, and court officials—all of whom have the right, albeit not the final and unreviewable right, of withdrawing the case from the criminal process.

## SCREENING PROCEDURES IN THE UNITED STATES

In the United States the two formal screening mechanisms in criminal procedure are the grand jury and the preliminary hearing; three informal screening processes are the arrest policies of the police, the policies of the prosecutor's office which determine which complaints will be prosecuted, and, finally, the plea bargaining process, which serves a screening function in addition to the many other functions it performs for those involved in it.

The grand jury today is a notoriously ineffective device for screening out a weak or oppressive prosecution, and in that sense it is an anachronism.[54] Grand juries usually consist of a body of from twelve to twenty-three citizens convened to hear evidence brought before them by a prosecutor bearing on the probable commission of crimes by certain individuals or groups. They hear only the prosecutor's evidence and decide, on the basis of the prosecutor's explanation of the law in relation to this evidence, whether there is probable cause to believe that a certain individual or group committed an indictable offense.[55] As one might have predicted—given the fact that laymen are involved, that they have no legal or other special knowledge that would enable them to evaluate the evidence critically, that in the ordinary non-political case they see no reason to distrust the prosecutor's evaluation and judgment of the case, and, lastly, that the grand jury hearing is closed and nonadversarial—grand juries tend to do what prosecutors want them to do: they affirm a screening decision already made by the prosecutor's office to push the case to prosecution.[56] Thus, although grand juries *may* act as a great bulwark against tyranny in the extremely rare "political case," they are an empty formality when ordinary crimes are submitted to them for screening.[57]

The preliminary hearing, introduced as an alternative to the grand jury in many states of the United States during the nineteenth century, is not much better than the grand jury as a screening device.[58] In theory, it should be. The sufficiency-of-the-evidence-to-prosecute decision is not made by a body of lay persons untutored in the law but by a legally trained judge or magistrate. It is made in an open, adversary setting in which the defense attorney can hear the prosecutor's prima facie case and can cross-examine his witnesses.[59] The defendant may, if he wishes, introduce whatever exculpatory evidence he has through witnesses, documents, and physical exhibits in order to weaken or destroy the effect of the state's evidence. The sad truth is, however, that this potential for critically screening the state's evidence has not been realized. The major reason for this is undoubtedly the easily satisfied burden of proof resting on the prosecutor and a tendency of magistrates, like grand jurors, to rubber-stamp the prosecutor's decision to prosecute. The willingness of the magistrate to ratify the prosecutor's decision to proceed may be an acknowledgment of his trust in the prosecutor—an assumption that the prosecutor has already done a careful job of screening. It may also reflect a feeling that the prosecutor should not be put prematurely to his proof and that, even if his case is weak at the time of the hearing, he should be given additional time prior to trial to develop it further. If either of these hypotheses is true, the preliminary hearing cannot operate as an effective screening mechanism. Defense attorneys soon learn the futility of an early effort to have the prosecutor's case dismissed at the preliminary hearing stage, and either waive the hearing altogether or use it to obtain some foreknowledge of the prosecutor's evidence.[60]

Most of the screening of criminal complaints in the United States, as elsewhere in the world, is probably done informally by the police.[61] There is nothing inherently wrong with this fact, since many complaints of "criminal" conduct turn out not to be criminal after all or not provable. On the other hand, there is very little knowledge of the way this screening activity is performed by police or how to control it.[62]

After the police, public prosecutors undoubtedly account for most of the remaining screening of criminal complaints.[63] This screening takes place in two stages: the first being prior to the filing of criminal charges and the second stage coming after. Pre-charge screening, if it occurs at all, consists mainly of prosecutors sifting the mass of cases dropped in their laps by police to decide whether sufficient evidence exists to support a criminal charge, and, if so, in what court the charges should be brought.[64] Post-charge screening is more complicated and involves decisions influenced by pressures emanating from many sources: defense counsel, the court, the police and correctional officials, politicians, the media, and others.[65] It may involve nolle pros (voluntary dismissal) decisions of less important cases in order to alleviate the docket situation in certain courts or overcrowding in correctional facilities; or it may involve trading charges for testimony on the part of some of the defendants in a multi-defendant criminal case; or it may involve plea negotiations with defense attorneys, in which charges are dropped in a certain court and trials avoided in return for guilty pleas. This, too, is a method of screening criminal cases from the criminal justice system before major resources are committed.

Plea bargaining is the most common form of post-charge screening.[66] The bargains that are struck take several forms. Sometimes the negotiated guilty plea is "on the nose"—that is, to the original charge— and a deal has been worked out as to the sentence the prosecutor will recommend to the judge. The prosecutor may agree to forego an enhancement of the penalty under an habitual offender statute in return for a guilty plea to the original charge. At other times lesser charges made at the same time as the greater charge may be dropped, or, to the much greater benefit of the defendant, the greater charge may be abandoned in favor of the lesser. Finally, the complaint, indictment, or information may be re-drawn to allege different charges, carrying lesser penalties than the original charges.[67] The possibilities for bargaining are almost always present to some degree in every case. Convictions are rarely certainties, and the prudent management of the prosecutor's time frequently necessitates such bargaining. However, even if the time and docket pressures did not exist, the unreasonableness of many legislatively mandated penalties for crimes, the variability of aggravating and mitigating circumstances surrounding the commission of every crime, and the relative "unimportance" of many criminal incidents in the eyes of prosecutors, would still dictate the extensive use of plea negotiations in the United States in order to bring the final result in each case within the limits of what is reasonable in the eyes of both prosecutors and defense attorneys.[68] This is not to say that plea bargaining as a method of screening is inevitable in the United States. It does suggest, however, that if plea bargaining is abolished, it must be replaced by something which performs at least as well the numerous functions, among them screening, that plea bargaining performs.

In summary, it can be seen that the screening of criminal complaints in all the nations, except for a small percentage (usually the most serious cases), is done in a very haphazard, unregulated way by police and prosecutors at the earliest stages of the process. Although great efforts are being expended in some nations, such as the United States, to understand the motivations of the actors involved in this process, the enormous variety of screening methods and motivations will probably defeat any efforts to deal with the problem in a comprehensive way for a long time to come.

# 5

# CHARGING AND PROTECTING

The third task of a criminal procedural system is formally to charge a defendant so that he may respond to the state's accusation and to give him some means of protecting himself from abuse of the process by his accusers. Without intending to cover all those procedures regarded by Americans as necessary for fairness ("due process"), I have listed eight protections which are regarded by many as fundamental. These are:

1. protections against prolonged and unnecessary pretrial detention;

2. protections from illegal searches and seizures;

3. notice given to defendant of the charges and evidence against him;

4. right of counsel and other measures to afford defendant the means of defending himself properly;

5. protections against coerced self-incrimination;

6. protections from secret (non-public) adjudication proceedings carried on by officials without public participation;

7. protections against repeated prosecutions and punishments for the same offense; and

8. measures to enable defendant to appeal and obtain review of arbitrary and unjust decisions to higher, and presumably more impartial, authorities.

Most of the above procedural rights have achieved world-wide recognition in the Universal Declaration of Human Rights of the United Nations (December 10, 1948). Most of them can also be found in the American Bill of Rights (1791), in the European Convention for the Protection of Human Rights and Fundamental Freedoms (November 4, 1950), in the Inter-American Convention on Human Rights (November 22, 1969), as well as in the constitutions of many nations, states, and republics throughout the world. Two of these rights—protections against self-incrimination and the right of appeal—are less frequently mentioned than others; still, it will be argued that, kept within reasonable limits, they are necessary for procedural fairness and legality and should be included within a list of fundamental rights without which the whole process can become a farce. Thus, a sound argument can be made that they are all "fundamental" in the sense that Supreme Court Justice Benjamin Cardozo once used the term in a leading case in American constitutional law,[1] and would be so regarded by any member of the international legal community regardless of nationality.

In the following pages, I intend to review the procedures of France, the Soviet Union, China, and the United States in regard to each of the eight protections with the exception of the right to a public trial and the right of appeal, which will be left for discussion in chapters 6 and 8, respectively.

## PROTECTIONS AGAINST PROLONGED AND UNNECESSARY PRETRIAL DETENTION

### France

France has several provisions in its code of criminal procedure which limit the duration an accused may be detained prior to trial. In the case of "flagrant" felonies and misdemeanors the police may detain a suspect without warrant for twenty-four hours in order to conduct an investigation; if there are grave and concordant indications of guilt (*indices graves et concordants*), the prosecutor may extend this period of detention an additional twenty-four hours.[2] Afterwards, the police must release the defendant unless the prosecutor has turned the investigation over to an investigation judge and that judge has authorized temporary detention (*détention provisoire*).[3] Temporary detention is strictly limited when the accused is charged with a misdemeanor. It cannot be used where the punishment authorized is less than two years imprisonment and judicial supervision (*contrôle judiciaire*) is adequate and when there are not grounds to believe the accused may flee, exert pressure on witnesses, engage in fraudulent collusion with his accomplices, destroy evidence, commit new offenses, or disturb public order. Moreover, in cases of felonies and misdemeanors carrying certain penalties, the period of detention is limited to four months, with additional four-month extensions if the investigation judge deems it necessary.[4] France does not utilize the bail system much[5] and does not have the writ of habeas corpus, but it does have provisions whereby the defendant may obtain his liberty with or without judicial supervision from the investigation judge after the latter has consulted with the prosecutor and the civil party.[6] "Judicial supervision" (*contrôle judiciaire*) is a conditional release on such terms as the magistrate may wish to impose, such as not leaving the area, not visiting specific places, presenting oneself to persons specified in the release order at stated intervals, and so forth.[7]

## Soviet Union

The Soviet Union follows somewhat similar procedures, with two major differences: (1) the periods of authorized detention are longer, and (2) there is no judicial control or supervision of pretrial confinement. As to detention of suspects prior to accusation (*zaderzhanie*), the 1960 RSFSR Code of Criminal Procedure provides in Article 122 that in certain cases (cases analogous to the French "flagrant offense") the police have the authority to confine a suspect for twenty-four hours before notifying the procurator, and an additional forty-eight hours while the procurator makes up his mind whether to order the supect's release or continued confinement under guard.[8] Article 90 of the RSFSR Code provides that "in exceptional circumstances, a measure of restraint may be applied against a person suspected of the commission of a crime even before the presentation to him of an accusation." There are no time limits set on the period of detention under this article as there are under Article 122, except for the further provision in Article 90 that the accusation must be presented within ten days of the time the measure of restraint is applied for and cancellation of the measure if this is not done. In practice, Article 90 is applied to a broad range of cases, not just to "exceptional instances" as the language of the article suggests. Apparently, persons confined during investigation under this article are held for months without the protections afforded by Article 122 (seventy-two–hour limitation).[9]

Confinement under guard (pretrial detention) during the preliminary investigation of *persons already accused* would seem to be governed by Articles 89 and 97. Article 89 provides that "if there exists sufficient grounds for supposing that an accused will hide from an inquiry, preliminary investigation, or court, or that he will hinder the establishment of the truth in a criminal case, or that he will engage in criminal activity ... the person conducting the inquiry, investigator, procurator, or court shall have the right to apply to the accused one of the following measures of restraint: signed promise not to depart, personal surety, surety of social organizations, confinement under guard."[10] The last measure of restraint mentioned, confinement under guard of persons during investigation (comparable to the French *détention provisoire*), is limited by Article 97 in ordinary cases to two months, in some cases to six months, and in exceptional cases can be extended to nine months with the permission of the Procurator General of the USSR.[11]

The office of the procuracy oversees the whole process of arrest and detention. Article 11 of the Code states that a procurator is obliged to release immediately anyone illegally deprived of his freedom and detained for a period longer than provided by law or judgment of a court. If one wishes to obtain one's release from detention before trial, one has to appeal the detention decision to the procurator.[12] If the decision to detain was made or approved by the local procurator, the appeal must be made to the procurator's superior in the procuracy.[13]

### China

In China, prior to the most recent legislation, there were very few procedural safeguards against prolonged and arbitrary detention before trial. Articles 7 and 11 of the 1954 Arrest and Detention Act limited to seventy-two hours emergency detention by police before arrest, but in the past these limitations were often ignored by the police.[14] Under the 1979 Procedure Law the public security bureaus may now detain a suspect for up to three days; under "special circumstances" this three-day period may be extended from one to four days; thereafter the prosecutor has three days to approve the arrest of the detained suspect if he wants to hold him for a longer period during the pretrial investigation.[15] Criminal suspects who are not "arrested" and formally charged within ten days of their detention must be released. However, if they are "arrested," they may be held for an additional two months, unless the case is complex and the investigation cannot be concluded within that time period. In this event, the pretrial detention may be extended for an additional month with the approval of the procuracy at the next-higher level of administration. Additional extensions may be granted only in "especially major or complex cases" and, then, only by the Standing Committee of the National People's Congress at the request of the Supreme People's Procuracy.[16] Article 38 of the Procedure Law states that a criminal suspect "summoned for detention" may obtain his release during pretrial investigation by securing a guarantor of his continued availability or by living at home, if this is permitted. If he is restricted to his home under surveillance, he is not free to leave the designated area—he is under "house arrest," in other words. It is not clear from the procedural code in exactly which cases these alternatives to pretrial confinement may or should be granted.[17] It is also not clear who—the people's court, the procuracy, or the public security bureaus—has the right to authorize these alternatives. A literal reading of Article 38 would suggest that it is whichever of these three agencies caused the arrest or detention in the first place. The conditions under which prolonged detention of accused persons before trial is permissible is now clearer than it was before 1979, but there is little empirical evidence that the situation has changed much for the average offender under the law.

## United States

In the United States police have extraordinarily limited powers to detain and search a person on the street who is merely suspected of crime without "probable cause" existing which would justify an arrest. Police may detain a suspect for a very limited time if there is grounded suspicion to believe he may be engaged in criminal activity in order to ask him some questions about his identity, activities in the area, and so forth, and may, for their own protection, frisk him if there is reason to believe he may be carrying weapons.[18] They may not, however, transport him to the station house for further questioning or investigation or engage in more extensive searches of his person, clothing, portables, or automobile without arresting him or without a warrant.[19]

Once a person is arrested, however, he is taken to the police station where he is "booked" and then is supposed to be promptly taken before a magistrate to be advised of his rights regarding bail and the appointment of counsel, should he be too poor to hire one of his own. Thereafter, he is either released on money or property bond (bail), on his own recognizance (without bail), or is returned to jail where he remains confined until trial. If the accused is not released on his own recognizance or does not make bail, he may be confined during the entire pretrial period which in the United States, depending on the locality, may be a lengthy period.[20] Other methods of obtaining pretrial release are: (1) on a writ of habeas corpus on proof that his detention is illegal (rarely granted); (2) dismissal of the case by the magistrate after the preliminary hearing (also very rare); (3) decision by the prosecutor not to prosecute; and (4) furnishing of the required bail after the amount of bail originally set has been lowered (the most common of these other methods of pretrial release).

Because the standard of proof necessary to make an arrest ("probable cause") is not arduous and because arrest is so infrequently challenged, many arrests are made and many persons are detained awaiting trial. Bail is often required and arrested persons frequently are too poor to raise the necessary security. Thus, although the procedural system in the United States provides many safeguards against arbitrary and prolonged detention of accused persons before trial, in practice it operates to deprive poor defendants of this protection in many cases. Also, by failing to provide for limited periods for investigative detention prior to arrest as inquisitorial systems do, it forces the police to initiate the proceeding by making an arrest, thus setting in motion the almost irreversible process of extended detention.

## PROTECTION FROM ILLEGAL SEARCHES AND SEIZURES

### France

In the case of flagrant felonies and misdemeanors French police possess broad powers of search and seizure of persons whether at the scene of the crime or at home.[21] When the offense is not "flagrant," however, the police must obtain the written consent from a person whose home they search.[22] Once the investigation is turned over to the investigation judge, he may conduct or authorize searches and seizures almost without limitations. The restrictions which are imposed on searches are that none may be conducted between 9:00 p.m. and 6:00 a.m. without the consent of the homeowner, they must be conducted in the presence of witnesses, and the property taken must be inventoried. The French do punish the conducting of illegal searches and seizures by the exclusion of the evidence obtained thereby, but in a narrower way than is done in the United States.[23]

### Soviet Union

In the Soviet Union protection against illegal arrests; illegal searches and seizure conducted in the home; and illegal searches of private correspondence, telephone conversations, and telegraphic communications is theoretically guaranteed by Articles 54 through 56 of the 1977 Constitution of the USSR. Article 12 of the RSFSR Code of Criminal Procedure guarantees the "inviolability" of the home and secrecy of correspondence and provides further that searches of a citizen's residence, the impounding of his correspondence, and its seizure at postal and telegraph offices may be conducted only according to legal procedures. The RSFSR procedural code sets a number of limitations *on the manner* in which the search is conducted. For instance, witnesses and occupants, when present, are required to be present during the search and seizure process; no nighttime searches are allowed except in instances not permitting delay; occupants of the premises are requested to surrender voluntarily the items desired before the search begins; the property seized must be inventoried; intimate facts about the residents or occupants must be preserved in confidence by those conducting the search if the facts are unrelated to the purpose of the search; and so on.[24] However, there are not an equivalent number of provisions protecting the citizen from extensive searches of his home based on mere suspicion. Article 168 states merely that "if an investigator has sufficient grounds to suppose that the instruments of a crime, or articles or valuables criminally acquired, or other articles or documents which may be of significance for the case, are on some premises or in any other place or are in someone's possession," he may conduct a search to find and remove them. What "sufficient grounds" consist of is never stated by the code. If there is sufficient time to obtain the sanction of a procurator, the search can be conducted with a warrant ("reasoned decree") prepared by the investigator himself and approved by the procurator; if there is not, the investigator can conduct the search on his own unreviewed warrant, provided the procurator is informed within one day of the search.[25] Thus, except for certain amenities in the way the search is conducted, there are few burdensome restrictions imposed on police and investigators as to when and where they will search. Also, the provisions of the procedural code relating to searches and seizures[26] are extremely flexible and permit numerous evasions based on emergency clauses; they also provide no substantive and realistic remedies for their violation by persons conducting the search.[27]

## China

The Chinese make, and have made ever since the 1954 Arrest and Detention Act,[28] a clear distinction between "detention" and "arrest." Detention is the emergency apprehension and confinement of a suspect without an arrest warrant for the purpose of investigating whether there is sufficient evidence to justify his arrest on formal charges.[29] I have already dealt with the conditions under which investigative detention is authorized,[30] and for how long detention is permitted before formal charges must be made and arrest authorized.[31] Arrest consists of the apprehension and confinement, or continuation of confinement, of an accused on the basis of an arrest warrant for the purpose of investigating whether there is sufficient evidence to justify prosecution.[32] In this section I will discuss the new arrest procedures and provisions regarding searches of premises for evidence of criminal activity.

Under Article 37(2) of the 1982 Constitution and Article 39 of the

1979 Procedure Law, all "arrests" made by police of criminal suspects must be approved or ordered by the procuracy or by a people's court.[33] Therefore, the first step for a public security organ wishing to place a person under arrest is to fill out and submit to the office of the procurator an application for approval of the arrest, together with the materials in the case file and the evidence. In major cases the police decision to do so may be preceded by consultation with the procuracy.[34] The people's procuracy then reviews the case file and evidence and may either approve or disapprove arrest or may order a further investigation.[35] If the decision is made not to arrest the accused, the police must immediately release the detained person, but they may also demand that the local procuratorate reconsider its decision. If their opinion regarding the arrest decision is not accepted after reconsideration, the police may request a review by the procuratorate at the next-higher level, which has the power of reversing the decision of the local procuratorate.[36] In making an arrest, the police must produce an arrest warrant, and the family of the arrested person or his residency unit must be notified within twenty-four hours of the fact of the arrest, the reasons for it, and the place where he is being confined, except in circumstances where notification would hinder the investigation or where it is impossible.[37] Interrogation of the accused must be conducted within twenty-four hours of his arrest, unless this has already been done; and, when it is discovered that the accused should not have been arrested, he must be released immediately and issued a certificate of release.[38] Article 52 provides that the procuracy, in reviewing a case file for arrest, may notify the police to correct any illegalities which they have committed during their investigation.

Search procedures are now covered by Articles 79 through 87 of the Procedure Law.[39] Article 79 provides that investigators may conduct searches of the person, articles, residences, and other relevant places of defendants and persons who might be concealing criminals or evidence of the crime. Article 80 places a duty on every residential unit and individual to cooperate with investigators in turning over to them material and documentary evidence relating to the crime. Article 81 states that a search warrant must be shown to the person being searched except when carrying out an arrest or detention in an emergency situation. The person searched or members of his family, neighbors, or other witnesses must be present during the search; females may be personally searched only by other females.[40] A written record is to be kept of all the circumstances of the arrest; the property seized, which can only be property of evidentiary value, must be inventoried in the presence of witnesses, who must sign and confirm the removal of the property seized, retaining a copy of the inventory for themselves.[41] These provisions, reminiscent of similar provisions in the Russian code,[42] are simplicity themselves: they preserve the basic amenities of search procedure; they attempt to prevent theft and misappropriation of private property by agents of the state; but they fail to indicate, and thus fail to limit, the grounds for conducting a search. There are no constitutional or statutory provisions in Chinese law requiring prior approval by the procuracy or the people's court of a search by police, as there is in the case of arrest. Thus, the warrant requirement provided by Article 81 is largely meaningless; the police can issue such a warrant to their own investigators on whatever gounds they view sufficient.

## United States

In the United States searches and seizures are governed first by the provisions of the Fourth Amendment,[43] next by any more restrictive provisions of the constitution of the state wherein the crime occurred, and finally by any more restrictive provisions of the state's criminal procedural code. Search and seizure law in the United States is a thicket of complexity and detail so great as to prohibit any extensive discussion here.

In general, the following statements regarding the law of search and seizure in the United States are valid as of the date of present writing (June, 1986):

1. A criminal suspect may be arrested in his home only if the police have first obtained a valid warrant except in exigent circumstances.[44]

2. Arrests outside the home may be made without warrants if, at the time of the arrest, police have probable cause to believe that the person has committed or is committing an arrestable offense.[45]

3. Police may detain persons for short periods of time where they stop them in order to ask questions and may conduct limited frisk searches of their persons to locate weapons whenever there is "reasonable suspicion" (a lower standard than "probable cause") to believe they may be engaged in crime, and, in the case of the frisk search, that they may be armed and dangerous and need to be disarmed before the interview can proceed with safety.[46]

4. Searches conducted by the police of the suspect's home for evidence, or of the home of another for evidence or for a person whose arrest has been ordered can only be made by police with search warrants, unless an emergency exists requiring immediate entry without a warrant.[47]

5. Both arrest warrants and search warrants must be obtained from magistrates or other authorized officials not connected with the police or prosecution upon a showing by police of probable cause that a crime has been committed, that the person to be arrested has committed it, or that the place to be searched contains seizable property and evidence (which must

be described with particularity in the application for the warrant and in the warrant itself.)[48]

6. Police may seize evidence, fruits and instrumentalities of a crime, or contraband, not described in the warrant, or even without any warrant, if such seizable property is discovered "in plain view" while they are conducting a valid arrest or search and are lawfully where they are at the time that the seizable evidence or property comes into plain view.[49]

7. The need for a search warrant when searches are conducted for evidence in various places depends on whether the person whose Fourth Amendment rights are claimed to have been violated has a legitimate right to expect privacy (that is, freedom from unlawful governmental intrusion) in the place where the police search; thus, no Fourth Amendment rights of the suspect are violated if some other person's rights of privacy are violated by police action, if the place searched is not one where anyone has a "legitimate" right to expect privacy, or if the search is not conducted by the police or by someone else acting on their instructions.[50]

8. Police, except in exceptional cases, must knock and announce their identity and purpose before entering a house without the owner's consent, but neither the owner's consent nor the presence of witnesses to the search are required if the police have authority to search the premises pursuant to a duly issued search warrant. [51]

9. Police are not required to have search warrants to conduct searches in many situations outside the home where obtaining a warrant would run the risk that evidence would be lost, removed, or destroyed during the time necessary to get a warrant, or where security risks of not conducting immediate, routine, and unselective administrative searches without warrants would be too great or carry too great administrative burdens.[52]

All of the above rules—and the list is by no means exhaustive—are largely the product of case decisions of the United States Supreme Court, interpreting the Fourth Amendment of the United States Constitution. Thus, they are binding on all fifty states, as well as the District of Columbia, Puerto Rico, several U. S. territories, and jurisdictions in which federal law applies exclusively. Each of these jurisdictions has separate and additional rules of procedure which further limit and control the way arrests are made and searches are conducted, but they are too diverse to discuss here.

The Supreme Court of the United States does not have a record for consistency in the Fourth Amendment area.[53] Therefore, these rules are in a constant state of flux. For example, many of the foregoing rules (numbers 1, 3, 4, and 7) are of relatively recent origin, being less than twenty years old. They are all "enforced" by the American "exclusionary rule" which excludes evidence which, either directly *or indirectly*, is obtained as the result of a violation of one of these judicial or statutory rules of procedure by police or by agents acting on their instruction, *whether or not such violation was intentional, negligent, or committed entirely in good faith in a condition of excusable ignorance.*[54] The result of such a strict rule of exclusion is that an element of pure chance is introduced into the game of American criminal procedure. There are unexpected lucky breaks for guilty offenders against whom reliable evidence of guilt cannot be used because of the draconian operation of the exclusionary rule; while, on the other hand, there is the constant possibility, always attractive to police who are willing to gamble, that a search or arrest of dubious legality may be upheld after all by a court interpreting the many exceptions to the warrant requirement. Thus, it became an open question for debate whether American search and seizure law actually provided as much protection of the average citizen from illegal searches and seizures as it did in protecting guilty offenders from a conviction based on illegal police activity during the investigation stage of the process.[55] Perhaps, as a result of this, the Supreme Court has recently modified the exclusionary rule, first, in limiting the situations to which it applies, and most recently, in denying its application whenever the police do not intend to violate a suspect's rights and act under circumstances where their ignorance of legal requirements is excusable.[56] Even with these substantial limitations, the American exclusionary rule, unknown in most parts of the globe, goes much further in excluding illegally obtained evidence than any other English-speaking nation.[57] There is the possibility that, in future years, the exclusionary rule may be abolished entirely or that it may be reinstated in its previous form; however, both prospects seem unlikely at this time.

## NOTICE OF THE CHARGES AND EVIDENCE AGAINST THE ACCUSED

### France

In France an accused will be notified of the charges against him at his first appearance before the investigation judge, assuming he has not already been informed of them by the police or prosecutor during the period of his investigative detention.[58] However, as stated before, he will not as a rule be examined by a magistrate except when he faces serious felony or misdemeanor charges. In the case of misdemeanors an accused may learn of the charges from the *procureur* after his arrest, but if he is not arrested he may not learn of the charges against him until he receives a citation (*cédule*) by which he is commanded to appear before the *tribunal correctionnel*.[59] French criminal procedure not only assures that the defendant has early notice of the nature of the accusation, but it allows his counsel full access to the evidence compiled by the police and investigation judge during the course of the investigation.[60]

## Soviet Union

In Russian criminal procedure notice of the charges is given to the accused within forty-eight hours after the decision to prosecute has been made.[61] When the investigation has been completed, the defendant or his counsel will be presented with all the materials and proceedings of the investigation for inspection.[62] On the other hand, he will only see the evidence against him to the extent it has been summarized or included in the investigator's official report. He will not see the original statements of witnesses or documents collected by the investigator unless he makes a special request to the procurator for such inspection or petitions the court for such relief during the trial. He will also never see the evidence that was collected by the investigator but not included in his official report. Nevertheless, Soviet criminal procedure seems adequate with respect to protecting this aspect of due process. The remark of Robert H. Jackson in his book relating his experiences as a judge at the Nuremberg trial of Nazi war criminals is pertinent here:

It was something of a shock to me to hear the Russian delegation object to our Anglo-American practices as not fair to the defendant. The point of the observation was this: we indict merely by charging the crime in general terms and then we produce the evidence at the trial. Their method requires that the defendant be given, as part of the indictment, all evidence to be used against him—both documents and the statements of witnesses—[our] method, it is said, makes the criminal trial something of a game. This criticism is certainly not irrational.[63]

## China

In China the accused is not informed of the charges until after the decision to initiate a prosecution has been made, and, in any event, not later than seven days before his trial. At this time he is served with a bill of prosecution which outlines the charges and is informed that he may appoint a defender or have one designated for him.[64] It is only *after* the accused is informed of the charges against him and has had a lawyer appointed for him that the *lawyer* acquires the right to inspect the prosecution's evidence against the accused; other nonprofessional defenders may obtain access to this evidence before trial only with the permission of the court.[65] Thus it would seem that the defendant may be kept in the dark about the charges he faces during the pretrial investigation and even during his interrogation. Commentaries on the 1979 Procedure Law state that the police interrogator has the duty of informing the defendant of the reasons for his arrest or for being subpoenaed for interrogation and also refer to his right to request the calling of witnesses and obtaining of evidence for his defense.[66] However, there is little in the law itself which supports such an interpretation.[67] Articles 62 through 66 of the Procedure Law deal with the interrogation of an accused during an investigation; there is no mention in these articles of any such rights. Article 64 states:

> When interrogating a defendant, investigation personnel shall first ask the defendant whether or not he has engaged in a criminal act and let him state the circumstances of his guilt or explain his innocence, and then put questions to him. The defendant shall answer the questions put by the investigation personnel according to the facts. However, he has a right to refuse to answer questions which have no relation to the case.[68]

It is possible to interpret this provision as implying a duty on the part of the interrogators to inform the defendant of at least some of the charges he faces, since it is difficult to understand how, in exercising the right to refuse to answer *irrelevant* questions given to him by the last sentence of Article 64, the defendant could determine the *relevancy* of the questions without knowing the nature and point of the investigation. On the other hand, the first sentence of the article merely requires the interrogators to begin the interrogation with a general request for information about whether or not the defendant has engaged in "a criminal act," not whether or not he has engaged in a specific criminal act. In the past, police interrogators in China typically began an interrogation with questions such as, "Why are you here? What crimes have you committed? Are you going to resist or be honest?" leaving interrogees in ignorance of the specific charges against them so that their confessions would not be limited to what police already knew.[69] Except for the duty implied in the last sentence to inform the accused of the reasons for his arrest or detention and his interrogation, there is nothing in the Procedure Law itself which indicates this past police interrogation practice is now illegal. Therefore, of all the procedural systems reviewed in this comparative study, the Chinese is the most restrictive in affording accused persons early notice of the specifics of criminal charges facing them.

## United States

In the United States adequate provisions are made in the procedural laws of the fifty states and federal government for giving defendant notice of the criminal charges a sufficient time in advance of trial to permit the preparation of a defense. In fact, notice of the nature of the accusation is a right protected by the Sixth Amendment of the United States Constitution, and could not be curtailed by any criminal jurisdiction in the United States even if a legislature were disposed to do so. Nevertheless, discovery of the evidence in the government's possession is another matter, as the quotation from Justice Jackson above indicates. Except for information which is clearly exculpatory, the American prosecutor has no obligation to disclose witnesses' statements and other evidence in his file to the defense, and discovery of this information by court order obtained by motion (petition) is severely restricted in many jurisdictions.[70] Such disclosure is often granted to defendant's lawyer informally as a matter of professional courtesy, but can be denied by the prosecutor when he believes it would hinder the prosecution of the case. Therefore, many plea bargains are made between prosecutors and defense attorneys when the defense attorney knows little more about the case than what his client has told him, and trials may commence with the defendant and his attorney still in the dark as to the strength of the state's case.[71]

## RIGHT OF COUNSEL

### France

In France the assistance of counsel, retained or appointed, is guaranteed defendants in most criminal cases. In minor criminal proceedings in the *tribunal de police*, which can impose minor fines and jail sentences of up to two months, there is no statutory authority for the appointment of counsel for those too poor to retain their own, but retained counsel may appear for the defendant.[72] Similarly, there is a limited right to appointed counsel in appellate proceedings, such right being discretionary with the appellate court.[73] In felony and misdemeanor cases, the accused is informed of his right to counsel at his first appearance before the investigation judge, at which time he is informed of the charges against him,[74] and if detained is allowed to consult with him immediately thereafter.[75] Defense counsel has the right to be present at all interrogations of the defendant and confrontations staged between him and adverse witnesses by the investigation judge, although this right can be waived. He also has a right to examine the dossier twenty-four hours in advance of such interrogations and confrontations.[76] Generally speaking, there is no right under French law to have counsel present during earlier phases of the proceeding, such as the forty-eight–hour period of investigative detention (*garde à vue*) when the accused is being questioned by the police or the pros-

ecutor.[77] Of course, the defendant enjoys the right of counsel, summoning witnesses in his favor, and so forth, when he goes to trial.
Lawyers from adversarial systems often criticize French and other
Continental defense lawyers for passivity during the conduct of the
judical examination of witnesses, for their failure to vigorously cross-
examine the state's witnesses,[78] and for reserving their efforts for the
final summation to the court, which is often more a plea in mitigation
than in exculpation.[79] The criticism is valid but not entirely fair. Guilty
pleas are not allowed in inquisitorial systems, notwithstanding the
frequency of confessions. Thus, all cases which are not dismissed must
be processed through trial, and, as a result, very many are in effect
uncontested—the exact result which would transpire if guilty pleas
were abolished in adversarial countries and all cases forced to adjudication. Therefore, the appearance of passivity may result, in part,
from the fact that guilt is well established prior to trial in most cases
adjudicated in France and that the only issue truly in doubt or in
contest is the sentence the defendant will receive.[80]

### Soviet Union

In the Soviet Union the right of assistance of defense counsel is
provided in general terms by Articles 158 and 161 of the 1977 Constitution and in the Russian Soviet Federated Socialist Republic by
Article 19 of the RSFSR Code of Criminal Procedure. This right accrues
"from the moment the accused is informed of the completion of the
preliminary investigation and is presented with all the proceedings in
the case," except when the procurator by special decree permits defense
counsel to participate earlier in the investigation from the moment.
when the accusation is presented (that is, immediately before interrogation of the accused by the investigator).[81] In cases where a preliminary investigation is not conducted, defense counsel is permitted to
participate in the proceedings from the moment the accused is brought
to trial.[82] This is somewhat later than counsel is allowed to participate
in most Western European inquisitorial systems and is less favorable
to the accused than the situation which prevails in the United States.

Once appointed, the Soviet defense lawyer has the right to consult
with his client alone and may examine the investigator's dossier. He
may also challenge the investigator and other officials in the case,
petition for supplementary investigations, and contest the investigator's conclusion to indict. However, his objections regarding the investigation must be made first to the office of the procuracy, not to the
court, except as to the procurator's conclusion to indict which may be
protested to the single judge or administrative session of the court that
reviews the conclusion to indict forwarded to them for adjudication. If

the procurator refuses to conduct the necessary supplemental investigation requested by defense counsel, the latter may request the court to order him to conduct such investigations.[83]

Soviet law provides for lay counsel, and the defendant may choose to represent himself.[84] Usually, however, defense lawyers are selected from the college of advocates (*advokatura*), which constitutes an officially sanctioned bar association of lawyers outside the official structure of the criminal justice agencies of the Soviet republics, territories, regions, and municipalities.[85] Although their independence of the state, which manages their profession and the amount of their fees, is dubious, they are not considered adjuncts of the procuracy or the courts, and are enjoined by law to "use all ways and means specified by law for the defense of rights and legal interests of citizens, enterprises, institutions, organizations and collective farms that turn to [them] for legal assistance."[86] Western observers of Soviet criminal proceedings have reported that defense counsel is not always the passive advocate whom skeptics would expect in a justice system as dominated by the state; at least, he is no more passive than lawyers in most other inquisitorial nations.[87] I am speaking here not of the criminal cases with political implications, but of advocacy in ordinary, run-of-the-mill criminal cases.

### China

In the 1982 Constitution of the People's Republic of China, Article 125 states that "the accused has the right of defense." Presumably, this means the right to have the assistance of a defender at one's public trial, since Article 125 deals exclusively with this stage of the proceedings.[88] As indicated already, this interpretation is borne out by the 1979 Procedure Law which indicates that defenders are not appointed for defendants until shortly before trial, at which time they may begin to consult the materials of the case and consult with their clients.[89] Unlike the procedure in the Soviet Union,[90] defense counsel in China do not participate in the pretrial investigation of the case, and thus their ability to attack the evidence and the witnesses in the case is limited to whatever they are allowed to do at the trial.[91] In general, the responsibility of a defender is to present evidence and opinions proving that the defendant is not guilty, or that his crime is a minor one, or that he should receive a mitigated punishment, or be exempted from criminal responsibility.[92] Although some attempts have been made recently to improve public understanding of the role of the criminal defender, particularly the lawyer defender, his position is at best an ambiguous one, since there is a long-standing tradition in Chinese culture among the lower classes, as well as officials, to view lawyers as obstructionists whose purpose is to defeat, rather than to assist, justice.[93] Observers have commented upon the extreme passivity of defenders during public trials and on their reluctance to do much more than argue for leniency at the end of the trial.[94]

Defendants have the right to defend themselves,[95] but in most cases in which a procurator appears for the state, the court will appoint a defender for the defendant. The court *must* appoint one where the defendant is deaf, mute, a minor, and is not represented by a defender of his own choice.[96] Defenders may be either lawyers, citizens recommended by a people's organization, by the defendant's residential unit, or those who are authorized to act in such a capacity by the people's court, or they may be close relatives or guardians of the defendant.[97] Due to the shortage of lawyers in China, it is not at all unusual to find lay counsel representing defendants in public trials, especially in not-so-serious criminal cases. Finally, the defendant is given the right to discharge his appointed defender during his trial and to entrust the defense to another defender.[98]

## United States

In the United States the right of assistance of counsel is protected by the Sixth Amendment of the United States Constitution, enforced on the states through the due process clause of the Fourteenth Amendment.[99] The Sixth Amendment assistance-of-counsel provision has been interpreted by the United States Supreme Court to require the appointment of counsel at state expense for indigent defendants who are sentenced even to one day of imprisonment.[100] As a result, legally trained counsel are now required in all criminal proceedings in the United States, even down to the petty misdemeanor level, as long as imprisonment of any duration is the assessed penalty. Defendants may waive this right in serious as well as minor cases, since the Supreme Court has also held that the Constitution protects the defendant's right to defend himself.[101] However, the waiver must be explicit, voluntary, and informed.[102] The presence of counsel, retained or appointed, is required at every "critical phase of the prosecution,"[103] which can be as early as police interrogation if formal charges have been filed; if they have not, counsel must also be present during the accused's interrogation in police custody if the accused, having been advised of this right, demands counsel's presence.[104] Presence of counsel is also required at other pretrial and posttrial hearings in addition to trial proceedings.[105] It is usually not required during an investigation which does not necessitate defendant's presence or cooperation, such as tests conducted on real evidence or viewing of photographs by identification witnesses.[106]

In the United States defense counsel is expected to conduct himself as an adversary and to challenge the state's "search for the truth" at every stage of the process, employing every device short of fraud or perjured testimony to obstruct the defendant's conviction or to minimize its consequences.[107] The United States has probably expanded this protection far beyond the bounds of reason or necessity, but there remains one major defect in the full implementation of this right: because of the limitations already mentioned on counsel's access to the prosecutor's file and information possessed by the police and because of the financial limitations which often restrict the defense lawyer's ability to conduct his own investigation, defense counsel must make important tactical decisions (for instance, whether to plea-bargain or go to trial) in the absence of information concerning the strength of the state's case. The result of this defect is often to discourage the defendant's lawyer from making a defense on the facts and to push him toward plea bargaining or making dilatory motions or technical objections in order to improve the consequences for his client.

## PROTECTION AGAINST SELF-INCRIMINATION

The protection against self-incrimination is an important one for any procedural system which attempts to reach a just result, and its importance is recognized in all inquisitorial as well as in accusatorial systems. The *core* of this protection in almost all systems is the desire to prevent investigation or adjudication procedures from coercing unreliable confessions from the mouths of accused persons. It is *not* the desire to prevent investigators from asking accused or suspected persons questions relating to the crime, nor the desire to keep the person from answering them (although defendants are usually given the option of doing so), nor the desire to keep people from drawing adverse inferences from an accused persons's refusal to answer questions. If there are procedural rules which seek to accomplish these ancillary objectives, they are intended to make it more certain that the core objective will be realized.[108] Therefore, in this brief review I will concentrate on procedural rules which relate immediately to the core objective of preventing coerced confessions.

### France

As Robert Vouin has stated, a fundamental rule in French criminal procedure is that nobody is bound to accuse himself or to give evidence against himself.[109] The accused is never required to answer questions put to him by the police, the prosecutor, or the investigating magistrate (except to identify himself); and he may even maintain his silence, if he wishes, at his trial without fear of being punished for doing so. Moreover, confessions obtained by police or others by violence, trickery, or some other strategem incompatible with defendant's right to a fair trial are considered too unreliable to serve as evidence for a conviction.[110]

The major problem with this protection in the inquisitorial system—and France is no exception to the general rule—is that certain disadvantages are likely to flow from an accused person's exercise of the privilege of silence, even though these disadvantages are not prescribed by law nor do they amount to coercion in the eyes of civil law jurists. For example, Manfred Pieck states that an accused who maintains his silence in face of questioning by the police or magistrate is more likely to be subjected to provisional detention pending trial than one who cooperates in the investigation.[111] Second, although the prosecution has the burden of proof and the accused is presumed innocent until proven guilty, under French law all evidence, including the demeanor and attitude of the accused, is subject to the free and unrestricted evaluation of the court.[112] Therefore, not only the investigators but also the adjudicators are likely to draw adverse conclusions as to guilt from a refusal to answer questions and are not prevented by law from doing so. There is also the problem of warning accused persons of their legal right not to respond to police questioning during a preliminary inquest. Article 114 of the Code of Criminal Procedure requires such a warning when an accused is first brought before the investigation judge, but as we have already seen this is done in less than 15 percent of the criminal proceedings.[113] Even when a warning is given, the accused may have already been questioned by the police, who are under no obligation to give such warnings. In a legal culture where a cooperative attitude by the accused is the norm rather than the exception, a warning of the right to remain silent may never be given, or, if given, may come too late to do the accused any good.[114]

French law has another rule of procedure which is related to the privilege against self-incrimination: the rule that persons against whom "grave and concordant indications of guilt" exist should not be questioned under oath.[115] The rationale for this rule is that probably guilty persons should not be questioned under conditions which subject them to the risk of liability for perjury, not that they should not be subject to questioning at all. Article 105 provides that neither the investigating magistrate nor police acting pursuant to a rogatory commission authorized by a magistrate may take the testimony of a suspect under oath "with the purpose of defeating the rights of the defendant."[116] The effect of violating this provision may be "nullification" of the testimony so taken (that is, striking it from the dossier). But the application of this provision is very limited: it may not apply to interrogations conducted by the police on their own behalf before the investigating magistrate enters the case; it requires intent on the part of the investigators to defeat defendant's rights; and the violation nullifies only the statements so obtained, without "tainting" derivative evidence.[117]

## Soviet Union

The Soviet Union also officially recognizes the defendant's privilege not to accuse himself and to refuse to answer questions.[118] If the accused does not speak, his silence alone may not convict him, although as in France it may be counted along with the other evidence as a factor to be considered.[119] Article 77 affords the accused the right to give testimony, if he so wishes, concerning the circumstances of the case, and then states: "An acknowledgment of guilt by the accused may become the basis for an accusation only if the acknowledgment is confirmed by the totality of evidence in the case."[120] A similar right is extended to "suspects."[121] The privilege against self-incrimination applies only to the accused; it does not extend to other parties and witnesses, who are required to divulge all they know about the case, even at the risk of incriminating themselves.[122] This includes family members, priests, and physicians, who do not enjoy a legal privilege not to testify; other than the accused, only the defendant's counsel and a mentally or physically disabled witness enjoys this privilege.[123]

I do not maintain here that criminal justice officials in the Soviet Union regard the privilege against self-incrimination in the same light as American civil libertarians. They take the position common to all lawyers reared in the civil law tradition that the accused should be encouraged to participate in the pretrial investigation of the case and to provide authorities with whatever exculpatory evidence is in his possession rather than concealing it until the judicial examination of the evidence (hence Articles 76 and 77). Moreover, it would be unrealistic not to assume that they share with the law enforcement brotherhood all over the world the desire to trench upon the privilege and to do whatever they can to get a statement from the accused, except when other evidence of guilt is overwhelming or pressures placed on the defendant to talk would jeopardize the prosecution. The point made here is simply that the Soviet Union officially recognizes the principle and has some procedures which allow it to be exercised.

## China

The Chinese have several provisions in their procedural law which seek to avoid coerced confessions, which strain against the tendency of police and prosecutors to rely too much on confession evidence, and which protect in the same minimal way as the Russians, a right to remain silent. To this extent they recognize a privilege against self-incrimination.[124] For example, Article 32 of the Procedure Law provides, inter alia, that "[t]he use of torture to coerce statements and the gathering of evidence by threat, enticement, deceit or other unlawful methods are strictly prohibited."[125] Article 35 states, in part: "In the decision of all cases, the emphasis should be placed on evidence and investigative research, and credence should not be readily given to oral statements. In cases where there is only the testimony of the defendant and there is no other evidence, the defendant cannot be found guilty and sentenced to criminal punishment . . . ."[126] As for the right to remain silent, the procedural code is somewhat ambiguous. Article 37 (para. 1) states, "[a]nyone with knowledge about the circumstances of the case has a duty to testify."[127] However, a commentary on this provision remarks that it has application only to witnesses and not to defendants, and, given the context in which the provision is found, this would appear to be a correct interpretation.[128] Article 64, which relates to the pretrial interrogation of the defendant, provides that "[t]he defendant *shall* answer the questions put by the investigation personnel according to the facts,"[129] but it also gives him a right to decline to answer irrelevant questions. More importantly, the same provision talks about the interrogators "allowing" the defendant to explain the circumstances of the crime, his guilt, or his defense, rather than demanding such an explanation. This, taken together with Article 32 above, could be read to suggest that a defendant may maintain his silence during interrogation without fear of *legal* punishment for doing so. It is the same at the defendant's trial: during the questioning of the defendant, which is usually the first order of business as far as the testimony phase of the trial is concerned,[130] the defendant is permitted to make whatever inculpatory or exculpatory statements he wishes. If he decides to make none and to maintain an adamant silence,[131] he is subject to no contempt penalty. However, it is clear that such a tactic would be and is viewed by adjudicators as a silent confession of guilt. It is doubtful that there is in Chinese procedural law anything approaching the presumption of innocence found in Western law.[132]

## United States

The privilege against self-incrimination is considered to be one of the most essential features of accusatorial procedure, inasmuch as it places the entire burden of proof through non-confession evidence on the shoulders of the state and reduces the defendant's participation in his own conviction to zero.[133] The rules of American criminal procedure guaranteeing this right and fortifying it are many and complex and cannot be covered here.[134] Suffice it to say that these rules go very far in ensuring that the defendant's lack of cooperation in the development of proof of his own guilt will not be held against him or prejudice his case. Failure to admit his guilt, to respond to questions, or to take the witness stand in his own defense cannot in American criminal procedure be legally considered by the fact-determiner as inferential evidence of guilt.[135] Penalties may not be increased vindictively for those who refuse to cooperate and insist on a trial or an appeal.[136]

The reality of the expression of this right in American criminal process is somewhat less spectacular than the promise held out by judicial decisions. Judicial confessions, otherwise known as guilty pleas, are the most common basis of criminal convictions in the United States. These are not produced by investigation employing third-degree tactics of interrogation but by a negotiation process carried on by prosecutors and defense attorneys, usually after police have completed their investigation and before or after formal charges have been filed. The forces impinging upon defendant's decision to "cop a plea" and obtain a reduction in the charges or a lighter sentence are not always free from coercion, but this coercion most often arises from uncertainty as to the charges which *might* be made, the sentence which *might* be passed after trial, and the testimony which *might* be adduced at the trial.[137] None of these uncertainties is regarded as the kind of official coercion which renders a confession of guilt nugatory.[138] Thus, confessions, in the guise of guilty pleas, are no less common in the United States than in foreign countries employing inquisitorial procedures, even though they may be purchased at a price rather than being coerced.

## PROCEDURES PROTECTING DEFENDANT FROM SECRET TRIALS

Under this heading I include procedural provisions guaranteeing public trials and public participation in the adjudication process. Since I will be discussing the adjudication phase of criminal procedure in the next chapter, I will defer for the present any comparison regarding procedural protections of this kind.

## PROTECTIONS FROM REPEATED PROSECUTIONS AND PUNISHMENTS FOR THE SAME CRIME

### France

In France repeated prosecutions for the same crime are prohibited, as are retroactive increases in punishment already imposed. A. V. Sheehan states:

Another plea which could successfully bar criminal court proceedings is "res judicata." If a criminal court has already decided on the same matter—i.e., the same accused, offense, etc.—subsequent criminal proceedings may not be based thereon. Thus, an accused acquitted of murder cannot be retried for the same offense under the "nomen juris" of culpable homicide. As a general rule only the verdict of a criminal court will act as "res judicata." The decision by the procureur not to prosecute is regarded as an administrative decision and not the verdict of a court. The decision of a juge d'instruction might in some cases act as "res judicata."[139]

## Soviet Union

In the Soviet Union a plea in bar to further criminal proceedings may be interposed whenever there is a judgment of a court relating to the same offense which has taken legal effect or a decree of a court, agency of inquiry, investigator, or procurator to terminate a case involving the same facts and charges.[140] There are limited circumstances (for example, procurator protests sentence as too lenient) in which a court of first instance may increase the punishment previously imposed or apply the law for a graver crime after an appeal has been taken and the original judgment vacated.[141] However, if the case is reviewed by higher courts by way of supervision, the punishment may not be increased but only mitigated, and applying the law for a graver crime than the one under which the accused was sentenced is also forbidden.[142]

## China

Prior to 1980 when the new procedural law went into effect, there did not appear to be any law or regulation in Chinese criminal procedure which specifically prohibited repeated prosecutions of the same defendant for the same offense. This situation remains unchanged under the new code. In the Chinese analogue (Article 11) of Article 5 of the Russian Code of Criminal Procedure, which in effect establishes the defenses of former conviction or acquittal as bars to prosecution, there is no mention of this defense among those listed as bases for immediate termination of a criminal investigation or prosecution, unless such a defense would be included within the last clause which mentions "other laws or decrees [providing] for exemption from investigation of criminal responsibility." It seems probable that there is a law prohibiting vexatious and repeated prosecutions for the same offense since I am unaware of any reported case where this particular evil was perpetrated by authorities. Somewhat clearer now under the new law is the answer to the question of whether a defendant's punishment may be augmented on retrial after he has successfully appealed his first conviction. The law prior to 1980 permitted this, and it discouraged many from appealing their convictions or sentences.[143] Article 137 of the 1979 Procedure Law now forbids this practice. However, the offender's punishment may be increased if it was the procurator, either public or private, who appealed ("protested") the judgment of the court of first instance or its sentence on the ground of excessive leniency.[144]

### United States

In the United States the double jeopardy provision of the Fifth Amendment of the United States Constitution protects defendants from repeated prosecutions for the same crime and from vindictive augmentations of penalties originally imposed after the defendant has taken a successful appeal and obtained a retrial of his case.[145] It is possible in rare instances in the United States for the state to appeal an inadequate sentence; except in these rare instances, there is no possibility of an increase in the penalty if defendant does not appeal his conviction or the sentence of the court.[146]

## RIGHT OF APPEAL

As stated earlier in this chapter, I will be discussing the appellate stage of criminal procedure in chapter 8. Discussion of defendants' right to appeal adverse decisions in the four countries compared will be deferred until that time.

# 6

# ADJUDICATION

The fourth task, adjudication, covers procedures regulating what is known as the "trial" phase in Anglo-American adversarial procedure. The word "trial" in English suggests an ordeal or a contest between competing champions. Both connotations of the word suggest what is unique about adversarial procedure: the degree to which the question of guilt or innocence is left to the game-playing skills of two adversary lawyers. I will not enter the debate here as to whether the real purpose of the adjudication phase of our criminal procedure is the pursuit of truth in an adversary setting, as opposed to some other objective—let us say, maximizing participation by the defendant in the final determination of his case. There are grounds for arguing that the revelation of truth about a criminal incident is not what Anglo-American criminal procedure is all about.[1] Nevertheless, it is clear that the search for the truth and the achievement of substantive (and not merely procedural) justice are the main objectives of inquisitorial procedural systems. In these systems the search for the truth begins with the investigation and receives its final testing at the trial where the evidence is reviewed by judges and/or jurors so that mistakes or oversights can be corrected and only the guilty convicted. In adversarial procedure, on the other hand, the search for the truth, if there is one, begins officially at the trial phase because all previous investigation by the police has no standing and is given no consideration until it is presented in court through witnesses and other evidence. There each side, the prosecution and the defense, presents its own private version of the truth and the adjudicators have to decide between them.

Criminal procedures relating to adjudication proceedings vary greatly from nation to nation. They differ as to the rules of evidence; the composition and functions of the adjudicators; the duties of attorneys, witnesses, judicial assistants, and others who participate in the trial; and the degree to which the public is involved in the proceedings, either as spectators or as participants. In comparing the adjudication procedures of France, the Soviet Union, China, and the United States, I shall concentrate on the last-mentioned aspect of adjudication: public participation.

There is reason for my choice of this aspect. Legal proceedings to determine guilt are fundamentally different from administrative methods of determining facts, which can be carried out secretly, but with accuracy and impartiality, by police or other investigators. Legal proceedings, however, must give the appearance of being fair and accurate, and the best way—perhaps the only way—to give that appearance is by allowing the community either to witness the process through which the decision is made or to participate in some way. This lends the proceeding legitimacy, avoids suspicion and rumor of official prejudice and arbitrariness, and gives the public a feeling of security. In the second place, public adjudication proceedings perform an important function in the administration of criminal justice which cannot be achieved by administrative fact-finding: they dramatize moral issues and inform the public of the sad consequences which attend violation of the law. Through their public ceremonies adjudication proceedings condemn, educate, and deter. The administrative determination of guilt carried on behind closed doors can perform none of these necessary functions.[2]

## TRIAL PROCEEDINGS IN FRANCE

In France adjudication proceedings in criminal cases are conducted in three courts: the assize court (*cour d'assises*) for felony complaints, the correctional court (*tribunal correctionnel*) for serious misdemeanors, and the police court (*tribunal de police*) for petty misdemeanors.[3] The lowest court, the *tribunal de police*, is presided over by a single full-time judge, who decides all matters coming before him without lay participation. However, its proceedings are conducted in public.[4] The *tribunal correctionnel* for serious misdemeanors (*délits*) consists of three full-time professional judges, of whom one acts as president of the court and the other two as associate judges.[5] They may decide by majority vote. There is no jury, but proceedings are held in public, except when closed by order of the court because publicity would be dangerous to public order and morals.[6] The trial court for felonies, the *cour d'assises*, is a court of special and limited criminal jurisdiction and is composed of three professional judges (one of whom acts as president of the court) and nine lay jurors. The jurors sit with the judges and retire with them to consider the verdict and the sentence after closing arguments of counsel. Verdicts unfavorable to the defendant (which are special verdicts responsive to specific questions rather than general verdicts) must have at least eight votes to be binding, thereby requiring at least a majority of lay jurors to concur with the three professional judges. Verdicts as to the sentence must be agreed upon by a simple majority vote (that is, seven votes). The defendant's presence during the adjudication proceedings is required except in unusual circumstances.[7]

In general, trial proceedings in France commence with the reading of the charges; the questioning of the defendant by the president of the court may follow, and often does, in the misdemeanor courts. At the conclusion of this examination by the court, the *procureur* may question the defendant; the lawyer for the civil party, if one has intervened, and defense counsel may suggest additional questions for the court. Vigorous cross-examination, if there is any, is likely to be conducted by the president of the court rather than by any of the lawyers present. The president may question witnesses in any order he thinks appropriate. The subpoenaing into court of witnesses who have already given written depositions or statements to the police or investigating magistrate is usually required only in the assize court where the "principle of orality" obtains, but not in the correctional court where judges may rely on evidence in the dossier.[8] At the conclusion of the evidence the lawyers present address the court regarding the evidence and the sentence. The lawyer for the civil party must address the court first, then the prosecutor, and then defense counsel, with the defendant himself given final leave to supplement the remarks of counsel if he so desires. At this point in the proceedings in the *tribunal correctionnel* the judges retire for deliberation, but in the *cour d'assises* the president will address the jury, outlining the specific questions they will be required to decide. The parties may dispense with such a public lecture. When the court (or court and jury) return after deliberation, the verdicts are read and the sentence is announced. If there is a civil complaint, proceedings are suspended and resumed before the court (sitting without lay jury members) to examine the question of civil damages. Civil damages are awarded either to the civil party or to the defendant if the victim has wrongfully and maliciously prosecuted him.[9]

## TRIAL PROCEEDINGS IN THE SOVIET UNION

During the Stalin era (1927-1953) secret criminal proceedings conducted by special boards of the state security agencies and military tribunals were not uncommon in the Soviet Union.[10] They were eliminated prior to the enactment of the 1960 RSFSR Code and similar codes in other republics of the Soviet Union. Also eliminated were provisions of earlier codes (for instance, Articles 381, 382, and 391 through 397 of the 1923 Code) which allowed provincial courts sitting as courts of first instance to exclude the prosecutor and defense counsel from the proceedings as well as witnesses who had testified in the preliminary investigation, to terminate the questioning of witnesses, to consider evidence not produced at trial, and to refuse to hear the oral arguments of the parties.[11] Today criminal trials in district people's courts are usually heard in public[12] by a professional judge and two people's assessors (that is, lay judges).[13] Each judge has an equal vote but unanimity in agreeing upon a verdict is not required; a majority of two may decide all questions and the dissenting judge may state his or her objections to the decisions in writing for the file.[14]

The trial begins with the presiding judge (the professional member of the three-judge court) reading the charges to the accused and asking him whether or not he admits guilt.[15] Although a different order of proof may be chosen,[16] the presentation of evidence usually begins with the presiding judge requesting the accused to testify concerning his version of the circumstances of the case, subject to questioning by members of the court if some facts need clarification. After the conclusion of questioning by the court, the prosecutor, the victim, the civil plaintiff, the civil defendant, or their counsel, and defense counsel may question the accused. If he is on trial with co-defendants, their counsel may likewise seek the opportunity to question him.[17] Other witnesses are then called and are questioned by the court, the parties, and/or their counsel after being warned of their civic duty to tell all they know about the case and of their criminal responsibility for refusal to testify and for false testimony. Sequestration of witnesses prior to their testimony is also followed.[18] Physical and demonstrative evidence may be presented, and the court may adjourn to the crime scene if that is felt to be necessary.[19] With the court's leave, the parties may add other evidence to what the court has already adduced, and with that finished, the presiding judge announces that the judicial investigation into the facts is concluded.

The trial then enters into its second phase—the judicial "debate"—where arguments of counsel are heard. All parties, their counsel, and the defendant himself, may be heard.[20] Supposedly, these arguments may not be interrupted or terminated by the court, although interruption is not uncommon, especially when the presiding judge feels that a party, accused, or counsel, has strayed into irrelevant matters.[21] Every party is permitted to make a reply argument.[22] The accused has the right to the last word.[23] The parties and their counsel then submit written proposals to the court concerning the disposition of the case.[24] The court then retires to consider its verdict and judgment, which, when decided upon, is announced in open court to those present.[25]

The adjudication procedure just outlined may not accurately describe many, or even most, criminal proceedings conducted in Soviet courts, which can be considerably abbreviated if the allegations of the indictment are not disputed. Moreover, it does not describe adjudication procedures in comrades' courts to which many minor criminal complaints are referred for informal sanctions ("measures of social pressure") and minor penalties.[26] An interesting feature of the procedure just described, however, is the provision it makes for the public participation and the strengthening of the trial's educational effect on these participants. Not only is there public participation in the decision making by two people's assessors, but Soviet criminal procedure allows for the intervention and active participation of "social accusers" and "social defenders," who are representatives of social organizations (for example, Communist party organizations, youth groups, trade unions, and "collectives" of various kinds) with an interest in the outcome of the case or in the defendant.[27] They are allowed to present evidence, question witnesses, present petitions and challenges, participate in the oral debate at the end of the trial, and express opinions on the law and the sentence.[28] This device for introducing public opinion into court proceedings in order to maximize their educational effect and to keep court functionaries in close touch with public sentiments about the administration of justice is characteristic of criminal justice in Communist nations, and we shall see an even more vivid illustration of it in Chinese public trials.

## TRIAL PROCEEDINGS IN CHINA

In China the adjudication phase of the criminal proceedings has gone through a series of historical stages of development. During the years 1949 to 1953 (the immediate postrevolutionary years) the criminal process was used as an instrument of terror to suppress sources of potential political opposition (bourgeois and rich-peasant "counterrevolutionaries") and anti-social elements, such as a horde of small thieves and opportunists who survived the fall of the Kuomintang regime. Although most of the work of identification, adjudication, and punishment was carried out administratively by the army and the police, who enjoyed unfettered powers to handle all phases of the process, occasionally demonstration "trials" were convened before thousands of hostile onlookers, who were allowed to vent their rage on the persons in the dock and suggest a punishment, usually death. The second historical stage, 1953 to 1957, saw the enactment of a Constitution (September 20, 1954) and the attempt to adopt Soviet legal procedures. Among these borrowed procedures was the public trial held in a courtroom, presided over by a judge and two people's assessors, and before which appeared a procurator, a defender, the defendant himself, the victim, and the witnesses.[29] This brief period of experimenting with Western procedures was brought to an abrupt end with the outbreak of the "anti-rightist" campaign in the latter half of 1957 launched by Party leaders hostile to the reforms. The third period, which lasted at least until the Cultural Revolution (1966–1975) and perhaps beyond, was marked with rejection of "Western" or "bourgeois"—actually Russian— legal concepts and a striving for something indigenous and compatible with Chinese culture and custom. There was a considerable amount of experimentation with new forms of popular justice, such as teams of police, prosecutors and judges going into the countryside, and investigating, prosecuting, and disposing of cases "on the spot."[30] Public trials of the Russian kind were all but forgotten. They were replaced with administrative "trials," in which a judge would be assigned a case, would review the file prepared by the police, and might conduct his own supplementary ex parte investigation by questioning the defendant and witnesses. If questions remained, he would make his decisions to affirm or contradict the police and prosecutor's conclusions as to defendant's guilt, and then would discuss his decision with his superiors, the president of the court, or the chief judge of the court's criminal division. If, in the unlikely event there was disagreement between the judge and the police who investigated the case or the prosecutor, discussions and consultations between officials of these agencies took place to smooth out the differences. If the decision was to convict, the judge would prepare a draft judgment for the approval of his superiors. Once approved, the judgment was announced to the defendant, who was at the same time informed of his right to appeal and the time for doing so.[31] In the whole process there was no active participation by the defendant, except to answer the judge's questions if interviewed, and certainly none by defense counsel. If the case had educational potential, a public trial might be staged after the defendant's guilt had been administratively determined to publicize the nature of the evil and to decide upon an appropriate sentence with input from members of the community attending the trial.[32]

After the death of Mao Zedong in September of 1976 and the arrest of the "Gang of Four" a few weeks later, China entered yet another phase of her revolution, this time turning away from the lawlessness which had prevailed in governmental and judicial administration since the Cultural Revolution and toward a restoration of some of the legal rights and procedures enjoyed under the 1954 Constitution. The 1978 Constitution, for instance, resurrected the right of the accused to a defense and to a public trial; it re-established the office of the procuracy abolished in the 1975 Constitution, and revived the requirement that police get court or procurator approval before making a formal arrest.[33] Recent accounts of American visitors of public trials, staged no doubt for their benefit, reveals an adjudication procedure approximating that which was observed in the mid fifties, with the exception of greater audience participation.[34]

Under the 1979 Procedure Law there has been a return to some of the trial procedures briefly followed during the years 1953–1957— namely, a public trial, presided over by three judges (one professional judge and two lay persons selected from a list of approved community members), in which the defendant is usually represented by a defender if the case is of sufficient seriousness.[35]

The first phase of the trial process consists of the administrative review of the prosecutor's case before the people's court accepts it for adjudication. If the court believes there is no need for criminal punishment, it may demand that the procuracy withdraw its prosecution; and, if it believes the prosecution's case is lacking in evidentiary proof, it may send the case back to the procuracy for further investigation.[36] If it decides to accept the case, as it usually does, it convenes the three-judge trial panel, informs the defendant at least seven days before the court session opens of the charges against him (by serving him with a copy of the bill of prosecution), and makes arrangements to see that the defendant selects his own defender or has one appointed for him if a defender is felt to be necessary. It likewise notifies the procuracy of the time and place of the court session, and summons the parties, defenders, witnesses, and interpreters to attend the session. If the trial is to be held in public, the name of the defendant, the subject matter of the case, and the time and place of the court session must be announced publicly in advance.[37] Article 111 states when a court session must be held in public and when not. It provides that cases involving state secrets or the intimate affairs of individuals shall not be heard in public; nor shall cases involving minors between the ages of fourteen and sixteen.[38] Finally, Article 111 provides that whenever a case is not heard in public the reasons for closing the session shall be announced in court.[39]

The court session opens with the presiding judge ascertaining whether the parties are present in court and ready to proceed. The presiding judge then announces the subject matter of the case, the names of the judicial panel members, the court clerk, and prosecutor, the defender or defenders, and the expert witnesses and interpreters if there are any. He should also inform the parties of their right under Articles 23 through 25 to demand the withdrawal (disqualification) of any of these officials if their relationship to the parties or to the subject matter of the case is of such a nature that it would prevent their serving with impartiality.[40] After this is done, the prosecutor reads the bill of prosecution outlining the charges, after which the examination of the defendant begins—first, with questioning by members of the trial panel, followed by questions from the procurator, the victim, the plaintiff in a supplementary civil action joined with the criminal proceeding if there is one, and finally questioning by defendant's own defender.[41] The testimony of witnesses is not given under oath but after a warning from the court or the procurator that giving false evidence or concealing evidence are criminally punishable offenses. The method of questioning witnesses, after the trial panel has finished questioning them, is for the parties to submit questions to the trial panel for asking or to request the panel's permission to pose questions to the witnesses directly. The presiding judge can always terminate any line of questioning he considers irrelevant.[42] Documentary and physical evidence are admissible, as are records and transcripts of witness testimony taken outside court and before trial,[43] conclusions of experts, and records of inspections.[44] During the proceedings the participants may request the court to subpoena new witnesses, obtain new evidence, and new expert evaluation or inspection, but the court always has the power to refuse such requests.[45]

When the judicial investigation of the facts of the case is completed, the procurator may comment on the facts from the state's viewpoint; thereafter the victim may address the panel, and, afterward, the defendant may make a statement and present any witnesses he may have. This is followed by a debate between the court and the defendant, the victim and the defendant, or the prosecution and the defendant. The presiding judge may terminate this debate when he feels it has gone on long enough. When he does so, the defendant has the right to make a final statement before the trial panel retires for deliberations.[46] The trial panel deliberates over the issues of both guilt and punishment. A majority verdict (two out of three) is sufficient for conviction; the opinion of the dissenting member of the panel is entered in the record but is not publicly announced.[47] In major or difficult cases, the case may be submitted to an adjudication committee of the people's court for discussion and decision. In this event the trial panel simply carries out the decision of the adjudication committee.[48]

The public announcement of the judgment and sentence of the trial panel is not always made at the end of deliberations or at the same court session in which the trial took place. Article 125 indicates that the court has one month after receiving the case to make this announcement, and no longer than one and a half months with extensions.[49] If the judgment is announced at the trial session, or if the judgment is announced at a fixed future date, Article 121 provides the time periods in which the judgment document must be delivered to the parties; the time to appeal or protest the judgment runs from the day after the judgment document is received.[50] Article 123 stipulates the circumstances which must exist in order for the trial to be adjourned before completion and postponed till a future date.[51] There is nothing in Chinese procedure which corresponds to the right American defendants enjoy of not being subjected to piecemeal (adjourned and resumed) trials because the prosecution has not adequately prepared its case or because its witnesses suddenly betray it and refuse to testify as they previously indicated they would.

It is impossible to say how many cases prosecuted since January 1, 1980 under the new procedural law have gone through a public trial of the kind just described, because statistics are not available to foreign scholars and observers. Prior to 1980 such trials were a rarity, but, then, there was no requirement that public trial be held prior to that date.[52] There are some reasons for believing that the situation has changed and that most cases not screened out of the system before trial are now going through a trial process which is at least minimally "public."[53]

## TRIAL PROCEEDINGS IN THE UNITED STATES

In the United States the adjudication task is performed in two ways: (1) in a brief hearing before a single judge in which the defendant pleads guilty to the charge or charges (which may have been reduced in order to induce the plea) after having been advised by the judge of his rights to a full adversary hearing and after a short examination of the defendant to determine whether his guilty plea is voluntary and informed; or (2) if defendant decides to plead not guilty, in a public trial before a judge and a panel of jurors,[54] or before a single judge if he decides to forego his right to a jury.

Jury trials begin with the selection of jurors who will hear the case (voir dire), a process which consists of the presiding judge or lawyers (prosecutor and defense counsel) asking prospective jurors questions to determine their fitness to serve as jurors and challenging or striking those who are deemed not fit. Immediately after the jury is sworn and impanelled, the prosecutor and defense lawyer are given the option of making opening statements to the jury describing the nature of the case and outlining what they expect to prove. (Because both sides like to keep each other in the dark as long as possible as to their trial tactics, this option is not often exercised.) The prosecutor then presents his evidence through witnesses who are sworn to tell the truth before testifying. After each prosecution witness has testified for the state, the defense lawyer is allowed to "cross-examine" the witness to clarify or attack statements the witness previously made on "direct" examination. If the prosecutor believes the witness's credibility has been severely damaged by the defense lawyer's cross-examination, he may attempt to "rehabilitate" the witness (that is, restore his credibility) by asking him additional questions on "redirect." The defense lawyer may then counterattack, and so on until both lawyers have exhausted their questions (and probably the witness also). When the prosecutor has presented his witnesses, his experts, and any real or documentary proof he may have, he "rests" or closes his case, subject to being re-opened for rebuttal testimony after the defendant presents his case. The defense lawyer is then permitted to make motions to the court for dismissal of the case if he believes the state has not produced sufficient evidence of guilt to warrant submission of the case to the jury. This motion is judged solely on the sufficiency of the prosecutor's proof, there being no obligation in adversarial procedure for the defendant to dispel inferences of guilt which the prosecutor's case has raised or to clear up matters which are still vague. The presiding judge then rules on the motion, denying it in most cases since the prosecutor's proof is usually adequate to raise questions which only the jury can determine. The denial leaves the defendant in the position of deciding whether to present his own evidence, or "rest" at the close of the state's case and run the risk that the jury will agree that the state has proved him guilty "beyond a reasonable doubt." It is unlikely, however, that the defendant will take the chance of presenting no evidence on his own behalf, even if he himself maintains his silence throughout the trial.[55] Thus, after the close of the prosecutor's case-in-chief, the defendant will present his witnesses, who will be questioned "on direct" by his counsel and cross-examined by the prosecutor. When defendant has presented all his witnesses and other evidence, he closes his case, and may renew his motions to the court for a dismissal or directed verdict of acquittal. These motions are often pro forma and are made simply to preserve rights to be asserted on appeal if the verdict later goes against the defendant, and are usually swiftly denied by the presiding judge.

In most states the close of defendant's case may be followed by the prosecutor re-opening his case to offer rebuttal witnesses to controvert testimony given by defense witnesses. If no rebuttal witnesses are offered, both sides rest. Thereafter, the prosecutor, then the defense attorney, then the prosecutor again, addresses the jury, summarizing the evidence and arguing for conviction or acquittal. No arguments with respect to the sentence are usually made because it is rare in the United States that juries have the power to decide the sentence as well as the issue of guilt or innocence.[56] When the prosecution and defense have concluded their summations, the judge instructs the jury as to the applicable law, having reviewed these instructions with counsel beforehand. The jury then retires to deliberate its verdict, which in the United States will be a general verdict of guilty or not guilty on each charge, without any findings of fact or reasons given to explain the verdict. Most states and the federal government require unanimous verdicts, whether for guilt or innocence, and a failure to reach unanimity requires a mistrial be declared with retrial at a later date if the prosecutor chooses to pursue this course. Some states permit less-than-unanimous verdicts but greater-than-simple-majority verdicts in non-capital cases.[57] When, and if, the jury reaches agreement on the verdict, it returns to the courtroom where the verdict is announced by the foreman of the jury. It is not customary for judges to sentence the defendant immediately after the return of the verdict. Today this usually occurs at a separate sentencing hearing conducted several days or weeks after the adjudication proceeding.

"Bench trials" (trials held before a single judge when the jury has been waived by the defendant) are only slightly different. There is, of course, no voir dire; opening statements are extremely rare, as are lengthy summations or remarks made to the judge at the close of the evidence, except that the lawyers may argue the law and how it should be applied. The judge in this case is the adjudicator of both the law and the facts.

In both kinds of trials, jury and non-jury, the judge presides as a kind of referee during the presentation of the evidence by the trial lawyers, ruling on their objections to evidence: as to the form of the questions addressed to the witnesses by the other side, the admissibility of various kinds of evidence (for example, hearsay, opinion, immaterial, and privileged evidence), and the competency of witnesses to testify in the case. The judge is not supposed to ask questions himself, although he may do so, and he is expected to allow each attorney considerable latitude in directing the proof into avenues which are most advantageous to his client's case. Thus, one of the most noteworthy and characteristic attributes of American trial procedure is the extent to which the proceedings are controlled by the adversary lawyers. Both can, within ethical limits, shape the proof as they deem tactically beneficial. The judge is under no obligation, nor expected, to fill in the gaps left by the prosecutor and the defense lawyer, nor to elucidate vague points by summoning witnesses the parties have neglected to call. If the lawyers leave the proof in a confused or uncertain state, that is the condition in which the trier-of-fact will have to deal with it when the time comes to decide the case.

Another significant feature of American trial procedure is the power given to the person or persons who have to decide guilt or innocence. Neither the judge in a bench trial nor the jury in a jury trial has to explain the verdict. Because only judgments of conviction are appealable, this means that acquittals in defiance of the law and the evidence presented at the trial can occur without any remedy or method of correction. Americans justify this peculiar aspect of their criminal procedure on the grounds that justice and law are not perfectly congruent, and that some escape valve should be provided for the situation where the strict application of law to the facts would result in an injustice.[58] Other nations recognize this danger, but believe that it is more appropriately dealt with at the screening stage before a technically guilty offender is put through the ordeal of a public trial.[59] Unfortunately, the result of both of these unique aspects of American trial procedure is often just the reverse of what is intended: defendants are convicted on the basis of inadequate and confusing proof and acquitted on the basis of the amount of emotion and extraneous issues which the lawyers can pump into the case.

# 7

## SANCTIONING

All criminal justice systems are involved in the application of punishments and other sanctions to law violators, and therefore all must have procedures governing their execution. These procedures are likely to govern such matters as sentencing, the administration of prisons and jails, judicial or administrative supervision of correctional administration, early release from confinement, and collateral consequences of conviction, such as loss of status and civic rights. In the discussion which follows I intend to concentrate on two aspects of sanctioning and two sets of questions: (1) how great a variety of punishments and other sanctions is provided by the penal law and how much flexibility is given the sentencing authority in choosing among them? (2) after sentences are put into effect, how are sentences modified and by what officials?

### SANCTIONING IN FRANCE

France's penal code provides a somewhat limited range of alternative penalties for the sentencing judge.[1] For felonies the following punishments are available:

1. two different regimes of life imprisonment;[2]
2. two different regimes of imprisonment for a term;[3]

3. banishment;[4] and

4. loss of civic rights.[5]

For serious misdemeanors the following sanctions are provided:

1. incarceration (*emprisonnement*) for terms varying from two months to five years;[6]

2. fine;[7]

3. loss of certain civic, civil, and family rights;[8]

4. loss of the right to practice certain professions for a period of time;[9]

5. suspension of license to operate a motor vehicle, as well as confiscation or immobilization of owned vehicles;[10]

6. loss of the right to carry licensed weapons, including hunting licenses and confiscation of such weapons;[11]

7. community service (*un travail d'intérêt générale*);[12] and

8. day fines (not to exceed 360 days).[13]

For petty misdemeanors the penalties are: incarceration from one day to two months, fine, and confiscation of certain seized items of property.[14] For both felonies and serious misdemeanors there are certain additional sanctions which may be imposed when authorized by law and appropriate: confiscation of property involved or used in the commission of the crime, and exclusion of the offender from certain forbidden places and locales (*l'interdiction de séjour*) for a period of up to five years in the case of misdemeanors and up to ten years in the case of felonies.[15] There are also provisions for increasing the regularly prescribed penalties, especially imprisonment, in the case of recidivists.[16]

In France, sentences are usually not executed until the time limits for taking an appeal have expired or, if an appeal is taken, until the appeal has been decided, unless the court specifically orders the sentence to commence forthwith.[17] The execution of sentences is under the control of the public minister or the civil party if civil damages have been awarded in addition to criminal penalties.[18] Fines, however, are subject to collection by an official of the Ministry of Finance, called a *percepteur*, and sentences of imprisonment, once imposed, are under the control of a magistrate known as the judge for the application of punishments (*le juge de l'application des peines*). This magistrate, whom I shall refer to as the "sentence judge," is a judicial official appointed for three-year renewable terms "to assure the individualization of the execution of sentences by orienting and controlling the conditions of their application."[19] Although prior to 1975 the sentence judge had broad powers to supervise the process of rehabilitation carried out in prisons (*régimes progressifs*), a 1975 law terminated the progressive regime and with it also terminated the sentence judge's power to determine prison routines.[20] Nevertheless, the sentence judge still possesses considerable powers to release prisoners from confinement before their terms have expired under the various arrangements soon to be discussed; these powers he enjoys relatively free from external administrative or judicial control.[21]

The provisions of French law for the modification of sentences by sentencing judges and by the "sentence judge" are almost as manifold and complicated in their operation as provisions in the United States law for changing the punishment after it has been imposed. They are (1) suspension of sentence, in whole or in part, by the sentencing court (*sursis simple*, Articles 734–1 to 737, *CPPD*), which is subject to revocation if the condemned is convicted of a felony or serious misdemeanor during a five-year period thereafter;[22] (2) probation (*sursis avec mise à l'épreuve*, Articles 738 through 747, *CPPD*), where the sentenced offender is placed for a period of from three to five years under the control of a sentence judge who may impose conditions authorized by the penal code and who may revoke probation for failure to observe these conditions;[23] (3) conditional liberty (*la libération conditionnelle*, Articles 729 through 733–1, *CPPD*), or parole, which can be granted most convicts after serving one-half their sentences, recidivists after serving two-thirds, and "lifers" after fifteen years, by the sentence judge when the offender is serving a sentence of three years or less and by the Minister of Justice if the term is longer than three years;[24] (4) sentence reductions granted prisoners by the sentence judge on affirmative proof of good conduct in prison;[25] (5) temporary suspension, or "fractioning" of sentences, by the sentence judge who may temporarily suspend a misdemeanor prison sentence for up to three months for "medical, family, professional, or social" reasons or order it to be served on weekends or during vacation periods, and may do so for longer periods with the approval of the correctional or police courts;[26] (6) work release (*semi-liberté*) and outside placements (*le placement à l'extérieur*) which consist of permission granted the prisoner to work outside the prison, either under surveillance or not, to pursue his studies, or to undergo medical treatment, during the day and to return to prison at night;[27] (7) regular furloughs in preparation of final release and special leaves under escort from prison granted to prisoners for emergencies, such as death or serious illness in the family, by the sentence judge;[28] and, finally, (8) executive pardons and sentence commutation granted by the President of the Republic.

Many of these legal provisions for early release from prison are recent and reflect a growing disenchantment with imprisonment as an effective method of rehabilitation. Nevertheless, one gets the impression

that they have been motivated, not so much from a belief that rehabilitation can be more effectively accomplished by the community outside the prison, as by a desire to avoid the cost of expanding prison
facilities to accommodate the growing number of offenders. France,
like many Western nations, has few non-governmental institutions in
the community which can exercise coercive social control over offenders
entrusted to their care and supervision, and therefore it has limited
capacities for dealing with offenders outside its criminal justice apparatus. This lack renders "community treatment" a sham and pro-
duces the familiar "revolving door" phenomenon, where large numbers
of offenders are processed through the courts, only to be released after
short periods of incarceration into the community with very little surveillance or supervision and with scant motivation to reform their
behavior.

## SANCTIONING IN THE SOVIET UNION

The Soviet Union has a wider range of punishments, although not
all of them are available to the sentencing court as sentencing options
for every offense. They are: (1) deprivation of freedom, (2) exile, (3)
banishment, (4) correctional tasks without deprivation of freedom, (5)
deprivation of the right to occupy certain offices and to engage in
certain activities, (6) fine, (7) dismissal from office, (8) restitution, (9)
social censure, (10) confiscation of property, (11) deprivation of military
or special rank, and (12) assignment of persons in the military to a
disciplinary battalion.[29] In addition, the death penalty is provided as
an optional, "exceptional," measure of punishment for persons over the
age of eighteen years and non-pregnant women in the case of twenty-
seven crimes.[30] Punishments numbered 1, 4, 9, and 12 above are "basic"
measures of punishment; those numbered 2, 3, 5, 6, 7, and 8 may be
applied as basic or supplemental punishments; and those numbered
10 and 11 may only be used as supplemental punishments. Although
the Penal Code mentions only basic punishments in connection with
specific crimes, the sentencing court has available to it the supplemental punishments if it wishes to increase the penalty or shape it to
conform to its idea of the most suitable one for the particular offender.

Deprivation of freedom is the most usual basic punishment for serious crimes. Terms of confinement run from three months to ten years
depending on the crime; for especially grave crimes or for "especially
dangerous recidivists" the penalties may be increased to fifteen years.[31]
They may be served in correctional labor colonies of general, reinforced,
strict, and special regimes or in a prison, and also in educational labor
colonies of general and reinforced regimes, whichever the sentencing
court indicates in its judgment. Exile constitutes the removal of a

person from his place of residence and obligatory resettlement in another part of the USSR.[32] Banishment differs from exile in merely
requiring that the banished person not reside in certain localities,
including the place of residence, for a certain number of years; it does
not require obligatory resettlement in a specific place.[33] Both banishment and exile can be imposed for terms of from two to five years either
as a basic or supplemental punishment when the Code provisions so
indicate. Correctional tasks without deprivation of freedom are "assigned for a term of one month to one year and ... [are] served, in
accordance with the judgment of the court, either at the place of work
of the convicted person or in any other place determined by the agencies
in charge of application of correctional tasks, but in the convicted
person's district of residence."[34] From 5 percent to 20 percent of the
offender's wages may be deducted and transferred to the state. For
those who intentionally evade correctional tasks imposed by the court
there is a separate penal provision authorizing deprivation of freedom
for the remainder of the sentence.[35] Punishments such as deprivation
of office or of the right to engage in a specific activity (Article 29),
dismissal from office (Article 31), social censure (Article 33), and deprivation of military or special rank (Article 36) have their counterparts
in Western, non-Communist nations,[36] but in Communist countries
have, and are meant to have, a humiliating and exemplary function
in addition to their utilitarian purpose of preventing repetition of the
crime by exposure of the criminal and reducing his opportunities.[37]
The deliberate verbal chastisement of criminal offenders in full view
of friends and neighbors, persons whose good opinion the criminal still
might cherish whatever his attitude toward the impersonal state, is a
characteristic of punishment in Communist countries, one which seems
to have departed from the administration of punishments in the West.

Russian law also provides a variety of means of relieving offenders
of the consequences of conviction, although not as great a variety as
France or the United States. Article 43 of the Penal Code permits the
sentencing court to consider the exceptional circumstances of the case
and the personality of the offender and to mitigate the punishment
described by law by assigning a milder punishment than the minimum,
provided it sets forth its reasons for doing so. Under the same conditions
Article 44 allows the sentencing court to suspend a sentence of deprivation of freedom or correctional tasks and to place the offender on
probation for a period of one to five years. The condition of probation
is that the convicted person not commit a new intentional crime during
the probationary period; no other conditions are imposed. When conditional sentences are granted, supplemental punishments other than
fines may not be assigned. Also, the court may transfer a person on
probation to a social organization or collective for supervision, re-

education and correction, if it petitions the courts to be allowed to serve in this capacity or if it consents to a court assignment. If the probationer violates the conditions of the conditional sentence during the probationary term, the court may restore the original punishment and order that the remainder of it be served, in whole or in part, before the sentence imposed for the new crime.[38] Article 47 permits the court to deduct time spent in pretrial confinement from the term of punishment prescribed, allowing a full credit when the sentence is deprivation of freedom or assignment to a disciplinary battalion but only one-third credit (one day for three days) when the sentence is to correctional tasks, exile, or banishment.[39]

Article 53 of the Penal Code gives the court the power to revise the judgment in the case of persons sentenced to deprivation of freedom, exile, banishment, correctional tasks, or assignment to a disciplinary battalion when the convict has demonstrated by "exemplary conduct and an honorable attitude toward labor" that he has reformed. Conditional relief is in the form of early release from confinement, exile, banishment, correctional tasks or assignment to a disciplinary battalion, replacement of the unserved part of the punishment with another milder punishment, and elimination of any supplemental punishments which may also have been imposed. Applications for such relief must be made jointly by the agency charged with the execution of the punishment and the supervisory commission of the executive committee of the local soviet of working people's deputies, or, in the case of a soldier serving time in a disciplinary battalion, by his battalion commander.[40] Such applications may not be made in most cases before one-half the sentence has been served, and in the case of certain recidivists, not before the expiration of two-thirds of the sentence. Conditional early release is not available for "especially dangerous recidivists," persons who have previously violated conditional release, and persons convicted of various dangerous political crimes.[41] Like probation under Article 44, the condition of release is non-repetition of intentional criminal behavior during the probationary period, and the unexpired portion of the sentence may also be spent under the supervision of a social organization or collective assigned that task.[42]

Finally, brief mention should be made of a provision of the Penal Code which allows for the expunging of a criminal conviction records of persons who have been relieved of punishment or indicated complete reformation during service of their punishments,[43] and also a provision of the procedural code which gives the court the power to transfer prisoners from one type of prison or labor colony to another type (either maximum to minimum security or vice versa) upon the joint proposal of the administrator of the penal colony and the supervisory commission of the executive committee of the local soviet of working people's deputies.[44]

One should not be misled by these provisions which ostensibly give courts considerable authority over the ways criminal sentences are served in the Soviet Union. In point of fact, the administration and execution of punishments is largely, if not completely, in the hands of the agents of the Ministry of Internal Affairs (MVD) who operate secretly, administratively, and beyond the control of independent judicial organs. If courts are involved in the process of bringing a convict's sentence to an early end or of rehabilitating him and his record, it is merely as the passive instruments of executive officials who have already made the decision to do so for one reason or another.[45] Thus, although Soviet courts have some tasks assigned them, which have no counterparts in Western nations such as the United States,[46] these tasks are performed ministerially with little discretion vested in the court itself.

## SANCTIONING IN CHINA

Until recently a discussion of the sanctioning process in China was complicated by the fact that for many crimes specific penalties were not provided and the police had the discretionary power to evade the criminal process by applying administrative sanctions which were sometimes just as severe as criminal sanctions.[47] Today under the 1979 Criminal Law specific punishments are provided for specific crimes in the articles defining those crimes.[48] As Harold J. Berman, Susan Cohen, and Malcolm Russell have pointed out, whereas in the Soviet penal codes the emphasis is placed on the punishment of specific wrongful *acts*, in the Chinese penal code the emphasis is on the punishment of various kinds of wrongdoers.[49] This aspect of Chinese criminal law reflects its highly moralistic and reformative tone.

Sanctions for wrongful and illegal behavior are divided into those which are "administrative" (these may be formal and informal) and those which are "criminal." Since "informal" administrative sanctions, such as warnings and criticism ("censure") are measures of social control rather than controls exercised by organs of the criminal justice system according to legal prescription, I will pass them by. The "formal" administrative sanction of "rehabilitation through labor," which has been discussed in a previous chapter,[50] will also be passed over here. Criminal sanctions provided for in the new code are divided into five classes of "principal" punishments and three classes of "supplementary" punishments.[51] The five principal punishments are (1) "control," or "public surveillance," which consists of a kind of supervised probation in the community and can last from three months to two years;[52] (2) "criminal detention," which is short-term imprisonment lasting from fifteen days to six months;[53] (3) "fixed-term imprisonment," which involves imprisonment from six months to fifteen years;[54] (4) life imprisonment;[55] and (5) the death penalty, which is only applied to offenders who commit the most heinous crimes and which is subject to suspension for a two-year period during which reform through labor is carried out and the results observed.[56] The three "supplementary" punishments, which may be applied in addition to, or instead of, principal punishments are: (1) fines;[57] (2) deprivation of political rights, such as the right to vote or hold office or a leading position in "any enterprise, public institution, or people's organization";[58] and (3) confiscation of property.[59] Additional penalties mentioned in other provisions of the criminal code are deportation abroad, which applies only to foreigners, and enforced economic restitution made to a victim who has suffered financial loss from the crime.[60] Article 32 of the Criminal Law provides that, where the circumstances of the crime are minor and do not require the imposition of punishment, the offender may instead be officially reprimanded or ordered to make a statement of repentence or apology or be subjected to administrative sanctions. Thus, although Chinese penal law does not provide as many criminal sanctions as the Soviet criminal law does—for instance, there is no Chinese equivalent of the Russian punishments "exile," "banishment," or "correctional tasks without deprivation of freedom"[61]—Chinese law would seem to have an ample variety of sanctions sufficient to afford the sentencer a wide latitude to exert the force necessary to bring about a change in the offender's behavior and avert the recurrence of misbehavior.

Methods of relieving convicted offenders of the full consequences of their convictions are: (1) sentencing the offender to a milder punishment than the minimum set by law, if the adjudication committee of the people's court feels that such a sentence would inflict too heavy a punishment given the circumstances of the case;[62] (2) suspension of the sentence of an offender sentenced to criminal detention or to a fixed-term imprisonment of not more than three years, according to the circumstances of the crime, when the offender demonstrates sincere repentence and presents no further danger to society; when this is done the offender is placed on probation for a term not less than the original term of his imprisonment or detention, nor more than five years or one year, depending on whether the sentence was for fixed-term imprisonment or detention;[63] (3) exemption from punishment where the circumstances of a person's crime are minor and do not require sentencing to punishment and also where the offender voluntarily surrenders after committing a minor crime or demonstrates "meritorious service"; [64] (4)

reduction of the sentence of a person sentenced to control, detention, fixed-term or life imprisonment, if during his punishment the offender truly repents or demonstrates meritorious service;[65] and (5) parole for persons sentenced to fixed-term imprisonment of which not less than half has been served, or persons sentenced to life imprisonment where at least ten years have been served and where the offender demonstrates true repentence and his release will not endanger society.[66] During the remainder of the sentence, or for ten years (in the case of paroled "lifers") on parole, the parolee must remain under the supervision of the police.[67]

The Chinese manner of administering sanctions is heavily influenced by their ideology and particularly by their view of themselves as engaged in a continuous war against foreign subversion and domestic counterrevolution, although recently the intensity of this feeling has somewhat abated. Chinese law still recognizes "crimes of counterrevolution"[68] and places persons convicted of such crimes in a special category as far as application of some punishments and alternatives to punishment are concerned.[69] Probably no distinction is more fundamental to an understanding of the Chinese use of sanctions than the distinction Mao Zedong made in 1957 between cases involving "contradictions between the enemy and us" and cases involving "contradictions among the people."[70] These phrases used to have a social class significance and implied that crimes committed by family members of former ruling groups had counterrevolutionary implications and could be punished with greater severity than crimes committed by ordinary workers and peasants or by their sons and daughters. This is no longer true. In early 1979 the Chinese government abandoned its policy of discriminating against former landlords, rich peasants, or their descendants "as long as they support socialism."[71] Today, the discriminations which legally apply to "counterrevolutionary elements" are supposedly based on the counterrevolutionary nature of the acts committed rather than the social status of the offender. Nevertheless, these discriminations, whether embodied in law or in official custom, still exist. Ordinary offenders, if they are repentent, can be treated with leniency, and efforts are made to reform them. Counterrevolutionary elements and professional criminals ("recidivists") are removed from harm's way, usually by very long-term imprisonment at hard labor, but occasionally by the death penalty.

## SANCTIONING IN THE UNITED STATES

The laws of the several states of the United States differ as to what punishments may be imposed and how they may be modified later, but certain patterns exist which permit generalizations to be made. Typical punishments for felonies and misdemeanors under state laws are:

1. the death penalty (felonies only);[72]
2. life imprisonment or imprisonment for a term in a state or federal penitentiary or other correctional facility (felonies only in most states);
3. incarceration for a term in a county jail (misdemeanors usually, but sometimes felony conviction where term of incarceration is less than one year);
4. fines (both felonies and misdemeanors); and
5. forfeiture of property used in the commission of the crime (both felonies and misdemeanors).

In addition to these punishments there are certain collateral consequences of a criminal conviction, that is, certain judicial or administrative actions which can be taken to impose additional sanctions provided by another statute than the criminal statute violated and the loss of civil rights which may automatically occur without the action of anyone but by operation of law once the offender is legally deemed to be "convicted."[73] Without intending to provide a complete list, I shall mention the following as among these:

1. enhancement of punishment for offenders previously convicted of similar crimes or crimes of similar seriousness;
2. deportation of alien offenders by the federal government;
3. commitment for a definite or indefinite term in a specialized treatment institution;
4. sterilization or castration;[74]
5. suspension or revocation of certain licenses, such as the right to operate a motor vehicle or own, possess, or control firearms;
6. dishonorable discharge from the armed forces;
7. registration requirements;[75] and
8. civil disabilities, such as the loss of the right to vote; to hold public office; to sit on a jury; to hold a position of trust; to obtain or continue to hold an occupational license; to obtain public employment; to contract; to sue; to hold, transfer, or inherit property; to make a will or execute a power of attorney; to act in a fiduciary capacity as trustee or guardian; to receive insurance, pension, or workmen's compensation benefits; to have custody of one's children; to serve in the armed forces; and so forth.[76]

These collateral consequences, which greatly expand the penalties which may be suffered as a consequence of criminal conviction, are usually not contained in the criminal code of the states or the federal government but are scattered through their other statutes and thus "hidden," in a sense, from public awareness. Sometimes automatic and mandatory on conviction and sometimes discretionary with the agency enforcing the penalty, their application is both uncertain and sometimes totally unexpected.

The reader will note several significant differences between American sanctions and those of France, the Soviet Union, and China. First, the United States does not permit banishment of convicted offenders beyond the territorial limits of the sentencing jurisdiction as France does,[77] and also abstains from compulsory resettlement to a specific location within the territorial limits of the state ("exile" in the Soviet Union) and exclusion from certain areas within those territorial limits ("banishment" in the Soviet Union and *interdiction de séjour* in France).[78] Second, although enforced labor for little or no compensation is sometimes a consequence of imprisonment in a penitentiary or prison farm and holding a job is sometimes a condition of probation and parole, the states of the United States never impose compulsory labor outside prison as a punishment.[79] Third, the states and the federal government rarely use the sanctioning power as a tool for public education or indoctrination and they are hesitant about involving private organizations in correctional work, although this hesitancy has shown signs of relaxation within recent years.[80]

The major devices in the United States for relieving validly convicted offenders of the full consequences of conviction are probation and parole. Other measures employed with less frequency are: (1) executive pardon and commutation of the sentence; (2) suspension of the sentence, in whole or in part, without probation; (3) credit applied to a sentence of imprisonment for time already spent in pretrial confinement; (4) credit applied to a sentence of imprisonment for time spent in prison without disciplinary infraction ("good time"); (5) subsequent revision of the sentence by the court;[81] (6) partial release from prison for daytime work in the community ("work release"); (7) partial release from prisons to "half-way houses"; (8) special furloughs allowed to prisoners for emergencies; and (9) restoration of civil rights lost by reason of conviction and expungement or sealing of criminal records.[82]

Depending on the jurisdiction involved, between 40 percent and 70 percent of all convictions in the United States result in the suspension of the sentence imposed (usually to a term of imprisonment) and placement of the offender on probation.[83] The court approves a list of conditions which the probationer must abide by during the term of his probation, and the probation office supervises the observance of these conditions.[84] The conditions vary and sometimes consist of any condition which the sentencing judge thinks would be appropriate in protecting the public and advancing the offender's rehabilitation; they usually go far beyond the single condition of non-repetition of criminal conduct which is the condition of conditional release in Europe.[85] The violation of any one of these conditions, as well as the repetition of criminal conduct, may lead to the revocation of probation by the sentencing court and execution of the original sentence.[86] Under the laws of many states a convicted offender may be placed on probation even before a sentence has been imposed. If the court chooses this alternative (the "deferred sentence"), the successful completion of the probation without infraction will result in the dismissal of the case and the avoidance of a record of criminal conviction. On the other hand, an unsuccessful probation may lead to a more severe penalty than the offender would have received if his sentence had been imposed before probation and then suspended.

Most of the states of the United States still have laws which permit early release from prison on parole.[87] Often there are provisions which exclude a few types of offenders from eligibility for parole and others which establish minimum periods which must be served before the prisoner becomes eligible for release on parole.[88] Whether a prisoner obtains an early release from prison and when he does so is usually decided by an executive agency, known as a parole board. It makes its decisions after brief hearings which the prisoner under consideration attends for interviewing. The decision of the parole board is discretionary and subject to few legal constraints.[89] Once placed on parole, the parolee is supervised in much the same way as persons on probation. He must abide by the conditions of his parole and report to his parole officer. If he violates these conditions or commits a new crime, his parole may be revoked and he may be returned to prison to serve the unexpired portion of his sentence, determined usually from the date of his release on parole instead of from the date of violation. If he has committed a new crime and has been sentenced to a new term of imprisonment, how the new sentence and the unexpired part of his old sentence will be served—whether concurrently or consecutively—depends on the statutes of the particular state or the exercise of sentencing discretion by the court.

Thus, in actuality, there are three principal punishments which an average offender can look forward to if he violates a criminal law in the United States and is convicted. They are supervised probation, imprisonment for a period of time less than that provided by law or by his sentence, and fine. None of these punishments has proved to be remarkably effective in preventing crime, either by way of deterrence, incapacitation, or rehabilitation.[90]

# 8

# APPEAL

Of all the essential tasks of criminal procedure, providing for appellate review of decisions in courts of first instance is the most problematical. It is not immediately obvious *why*—given that sufficient care has been taken to make the determinations of fact and law by the trial court as reliable as possible—there should be such review, or indeed, *what* review by judges one step further removed from the controversy and less acquainted with the facts and the witnesses than the trial court lends to the credibility of the process. This apparent lack of essentiality may explain why rights of appeal, historically, are a late development, and, further, why they are not found in all parts of a modern procedural system.[1]

In Anglo-American legal history appellate review of criminal cases is not of great antiquity. Less than one hundred years ago it did not exist in Great Britain, although review of cases in lower courts was occasionally achieved by other methods.[2] In the United States the history of appellate review is only slightly older.[3] This may account for the fact that the United States Supreme Court has not yet held that appeals in criminal cases are constitutionally necessary for fairness (due process) in criminal proceedings,[4] notwithstanding the fact that they are universally available in the states and a state eliminating them entirely can hardly be imagined. However, review of criminal proceedings by higher courts is still usually available only for errors of law and not for determinations of fact in both the United States and England. The situation on the continent of Europe and other parts of the world where inquisitorial procedures prevail is quite different. There, review of the entire proceedings below, of the determination of guilt, of the conduct of the proceedings, and of the sentence imposed, is provided for by law and is felt to be an integral and essential part of the process.

The question presented by this contrast is how essential are appellate proceedings to the central tasks of criminal procedure. Most practitioners know that appellate proceedings are rarely successful, and that if a correct and satisfactory resolution of the case is not obtained by the time of adjudication and sanctioning, most likely it will not be obtained at all. Thus, wherever he happens to be in the world, a criminal defendant or his defender should concentrate on achieving a satisfactory result at the trial and sentencing stage or before and not depend too greatly on officials who review these proceedings. Does this observation imply that appellate proceedings are unnecessary—mere window dressing to forestall criticism but not significantly altering the nature of the process? I believe a negative answer to this question is required by correct analysis. First, although it is true that no procedural system can eliminate the possibility of error or arbitrariness on the part of persons who administer justice, a procedural system can provide checks upon both by providing review. Theoretically, such checks might be achieved by criminal or civil penalties assessed against officials who wrongfully administer justice. Such remedies are unlikely to be applied, however, in the absence of review and are of no great benefit to the person who has suffered the injustice. He would much prefer reversal of the decision and remand of the case for a correct disposition. Therefore, appeals provide a necessary deterrent to the arbitrary exercise of discretion at lower levels of the process. Second, there is the question of public confidence in the process. Citizens are aware that mistakes are made and that officials are sometimes capricious, and they enjoy a greater sense of security when they know the state provides a method of correcting error. Third, there is the requirement that the law be applied uniformly. Without appeal and review by higher authority there is too great a chance that official action at the local level will reflect the peculiar viewpoints and needs of the locality and will depart from the law of the state whenever a conflict arises between local policy and state policy. Basically, then, appeal is a procedural device whose function is more psychological than it is actual; it acts as a deterrent from abuses of and deviations from official policy and it bolsters confidence. It is not less necessary, however, by reason of this fact.

The question is also raised whether the inquisitorial method of providing review of both the factual and the legal decisions of the lower courts is preferable to the adversarial method of limiting review to errors of law. It is arguable that providing a second, third, or fourth level of fact determination to a process which has already undergone a thorough sifting by police, prosecutors, professional judges, and lay jurors is unnecessary because it does not greatly increase the chances that mistakes will be uncovered. Procedures do exist in adversarial systems for obtaining new trials on the basis of newly discovered evidence of innocence, and executive pardons are a final resort for reversing the effects of an unjust conviction. It is also arguable that the one sphere where appellate judges can exercise their particular professional competence is in reviewing legal rather than factual decisions made at a lower level and that they are not manifestly superior to their predecessors in the determination of facts. But, here too, arguments made in the preceding paragraph should be kept in mind. Errors of fact made in the investigation and determination of guilt at earlier stages of the proceeding gain a certain momentum and tend to become compounded as they pass through the hands of various officials. In the excitement of the investigation and trial, this momentum may dissuade witnesses from coming forward with facts contradicting the prevailing opinion of guilt. There should be at least one opportunity for a second trial of the facts when the excitement has subsided and errors of fact determination come to light. With these considerations in mind, let us now turn to a comparative study of the appellate procedures of France, the Soviet Union, China, and the United States.

## APPEALS IN FRANCE

In France the accused enjoys certain limited rights of appeal before trial from arbitrary or improper acts of the investigating magistrate concerning pretrial custody, refusal to employ experts, allowing intervention of a civil party (*partie civile*), and conducting an investigation which he had no authority to conduct. He may not appeal the magistrate's decision to remit the case for trial when the magistrate has jurisdiction. Appeals at this stage are taken to the indicting chamber of the local appeals court (the *chambre d'accusation*).[5]

With certain minor exceptions the defendant, once convicted, has two basic methods of appealing the verdict and sentence of the trial court. If he was tried in the *tribunal correctionnel* for serious misdemeanors (*délits*) or in the *tribunal de police* for a petty misdemeanor (*contravention*), provided that his sentence exceeds five days' imprisonment or a fine of sixty francs, he may appeal both the verdict and the sentence or either to the appeals court (*cour d'appel*). There he will receive a review of both the facts (based on the dossier, a summary of testimony prepared by a member of the court, and whatever additional witnesses are produced before the appeals court) and the law. At the conclusion of the hearing the appeals court may uphold the original verdict, modify it by reducing the charge or the sentence, retry the case if there was a procedural defect in the proceedings below, or reject the appeal.[6] If the defendant was tried and convicted of a felony in the *cour d'assises* or the *cour d'appel*, he must appeal to the Court of Cassation (*cour de cassation*), France's highest appellate court, where he will receive a review only on points of procedural law. This court of review may not consider whether the evidence was sufficient to justify conviction or whether the sentence imposed was excessive, but solely whether legal error was committed by the court or courts below. If it decides that it was, the Court of Cassation must return the case for retrial in the lower court, specifying the error committed but not mandating its correction. Unlike the appeals court, it is without the power to enter a revised judgment.[7]

## APPEALS IN THE SOVIET UNION

The right to appeal capricious and illegal acts of agencies of inquiry, investigators, and prosecutors before trial and those of criminal courts after trial is provided by various provisions of the RSFSR procedure code (see Articles 22, 218 through 220, 325 through 355, 371 through 383, CCP, RSFSR [1960]).[8] The major defect in Russian law dealing with pretrial appeals is that they are made to and are entirely within the control of the procuracy, an agency which is interested in the accused's conviction and therefore unlikely to be completely impartial.[9]

In the case of appeals taken from trial verdicts and sentences there is one appeal, called a "cassation" (*kassatsiia*). (The appeal when taken by the procurator is called a "cassational protest.") This appeal, similar to the French appeal from misdemeanor convictions, is in effect a reconsideration of the facts and the law. The procurator and defense attorney argue the evidence and the law and new written testimony may be presented. There is also a second method of obtaining review, called "supervisory review," where the higher court or courts may consider both facts and the law but will confine itself to the case record and will not hear the defendant or his counsel except at its own option.[10] Unlike the "appeal" procedure (*kassatsiia*), supervisory review is only granted on the protest of a procurator or court official, and can be pursued by them beyond the level of the court next higher in the court structure, conceivably all the way to the Supreme Court of the USSR.[11] If the defendant wishes to appeal a decision beyond the single cassational appeal allowed by law, he must persuade the procuracy to act on his behalf and file a protest.

There are also limitations imposed on how judgments and sentences may be affected on supervisory review: (1) procuratorial protests regarding the leniency of the sentence, termination of the case, or acquittal must be brought within a year (Article 373); (2) the punishment may not be increased nor may the supervisory court apply a law carrying a greater punishment than the one of which defendant was convicted (Article 380); (3) the supervisory court may not alter the findings of fact, the rulings on the weight of the evidence, the decision as to guilt or innocence, the application of the law, or the sentence, but may only remand the case for retrial or new investigation, reduce the sentence, or dismiss the protest (Article 380). Finally, Russian criminal procedure provides for the reopening of criminal cases after conviction by the courts on the procurator's petition on the basis of newly discovered "circumstances."[12] If the defendant or someone acting on his behalf wishes to avail himself of this remedy, he must persuade the procurator to initiate proceedings for the vacation of the judgment of conviction.

## APPEALS AND SUPERVISORY REVIEW IN CHINA

In China there are two methods of having the action of the trial court reviewed and corrected if erroneous. The first is by appeal or protest and involves the retrial of the case by the next-higher-level people's court at the request of the defendant or someone acting for him or at the request of the procurator.[13] The time limit for taking an appeal or protest is ten days in the case of a judgment and five days in the case of a judicial order, computed from the day after receipt by the aggrieved party.[14] An appeal may be based on any ground: error by the trial court in its determination of facts, erroneous application of the law to the facts, violation of litigation procedures prescribed by law, and an inappropriate sentence (too lenient or too severe) given the facts of the case and the character of the defendant.[15] After hearing the appeal, the appellate court (court of the second instance) has the power of rejecting the appeal and upholding the original judgment or order, or of revising the original judgment if there is merely an erroneous application of the law to facts correctly determined or an inappropriate sentence, or in the last resort, it may remand the case to the people's court of first instance for a new trial.[16] Since, as has been previously noted, the defendant-appellant no longer runs the risk of receiving a more severe sentence after appeal than he received from the court of first instance, appeals are now more frequent than they were in the past.[17]

The second method of having a case reviewed by other courts is "adjudication supervision" which is similar to "supervisory review" in the Soviet Union.[18] Under this procedure parties to a criminal action (the state and the defendant, but also the civil plaintiff if one has intervened), victims and their family members, and even interested third parties may go to the people's courts or people's procuracies and present petitions and supporting materials regarding judgments or orders that are final.[19] Three different kinds of action may be taken if the petition reveals definite error in the determination of facts or application of the law by whatever court adjudicated the case, whether in the first or second instance: (1) the court which committed the error may refer it to its adjudication committee for handling; (2) the Supreme People's Court may review the case itself or order people's courts at lower levels to retry it; and (3) the Supreme People's Procuracy or some higher-level procuratorate than the one which originally prosecuted the case, when it discovers error, may protest the judgment in accordance with the procedure established by law for adjudication at the court level at which the error was committed.[20] It should be pointed out that "adjudication supervision," unlike appeal, may be taken *any time* after criminal judgments or orders become final by a wide range of persons not limited to the party litigants. On the other hand, it is discretionary in the sense that there is no legal right to have one's case reviewed in this manner.

There is, in addition to these two methods of reviewing criminal judgments, a special review procedure for death penalty sentences.[21] Without going into detail, these provisions merely ensure that death penalty sentences and cases are reviewed by the Supreme People's Court or a high people's court for correctness and appropriateness.

## APPEALS IN THE UNITED STATES

In the United States appeals from criminal convictions are allowed by the laws of all the states and the federal government, even though, as stated earlier, the United States Supreme Court has never held such a right to be constitutionally guaranteed. Except for very minor crimes adjudicated in courts of non-record, appeals are made to higher courts only for errors of law and not to review the facts supporting the verdict or the fairness of the sentence.[22] States differ as to when interlocutory appeals may be made to review actions of officials or courts made prior to final judgment. They also differ regarding in what cases the defendant is entitled to more than one appeal (for example, whether a second appeal from an intermediate court of appeal to the state's highest appellate court is automatic, discretionary with high court, or disallowed altogether). The possibility always exists that the United States Supreme Court may itself review the decision of the state courts by way of appeal or certiorari when a federal law or constitutional provision is drawn into question. There is also an extremely elaborate and complex system of collateral review of decisions of the lower courts running parallel to the appellate process whereby federal courts can review the proceedings of state courts and state courts can review the proceedings of other state courts on writs of habeas corpus, mandamus, prohibition, and other ancient and extraordinary remedies.[23] Finally, it is always possible within a limited period after trial for a defendant to obtain some relief from the court which convicted him by moving for a new trial, entry of judgment of acquittal notwithstanding the verdict, or dismissal of the case.[24]

Although in the United States judgments of conviction become "final" within a certain time period following their entry whether or not appeals are taken,[25] the net effect of this extremely elaborate system of review is to render the finality of criminal judgments very uncertain and unfinal. By skillful manipulation of the review process, judgments can sometimes be kept in a state of suspended animation for years. Defendants are not, however, subjected to uncertainties they face in inquisitorial process from appeals taken by the state, since as a general rule such appeals are not permitted.[26]

## SUMMARY

Of the four nations compared here, the one which seems to provide the least appellate review is China and the one which provides the most, the United States (largely because of the provision of free counsel to indigent accused and convicted offenders). On the other hand, the United States provides so many opportunities for direct and collateral attack on convictions that a sense of finality and closure is never achieved, adding both to the public's and the litigant's frustration.[27] Perhaps it was this curious aspect of American criminal procedure which inspired the caustic comment of Mr. Dooley that "in this country a man is presoomed to be guilty ontil he's proved guilty an' afther that he's presoomed to be innicent."[28]

# 9

# USES OF THE ANALYTICAL
# MODEL

In this book I have attempted to show that there is a basic structure underlying the criminal procedural systems of four widely differing societies in the world today. In chapter 2 I argued that this similarity in structure is the result of a historical development which combined elements of two prior, philosophically opposed, systems—one emphasizing retributive (or substantive) justice and the other distributive (or procedural) justice. The first tends to have procedures which efficiently separate the wheat from the chaff as far as prosecutable and unprosecutable cases are concerned, which then ruthlessly, but still (for the most part) honestly, seek the truth of the matter through investigation and interrogation, which impose sentences mainly designed instrumentally to reduce the level of crime and restore the offender to his former place in society or isolate him from it, and which finally provide back-up to correct error in the form of appeals to higher authorities. The second views the criminal action essentially as a private dispute, which is litigated in a way which is likely to produce the maximum satisfaction for the persons who use it by fairly distributing favorable outcomes between them. This type of system is likely to emphasize procedure over substance and to transform the proceeding into a kind of game in which the litigants are players who use the law (especially procedural rules and rights) tactically to gain advantage or to act as a bargaining chip in the disposition of the case.

If I have succeeded in this endeavor, the analytical model presented here should prove useful for legal comparativists. It can aid in making more astute comparisons in different systems between procedural rules and practices which perform the same function, although, on first inspection, one would never guess this from their denomination. It can also help comparativists distinguish national differences in procedures and practices which are functional from those which are merely historical or cultural. For example, from a study of history one might come to understand how the English grand jury and the French investigation judge (*juge d'instruction*) developed in their separate ways into screening mechanisms to eliminate certain criminal complaints. But today the differences between these two mechanisms are more theoretical than practical. Neither performs the screening function in an efficient way, and both are falling into desuetude, except in special cases where they may offer peculiar advantages to the prosecutor or privacy to the investigation. To compare the grand jury institution in the United States with the investigating magistrate system in France, one must understand more than their origins, their development, and their justified functions; one must also appreciate the "task" each performs according to a theoretical model of the way criminal procedural systems must behave to accomplish their overriding goals.

I hope that the analytical model I have constructed will also prove beneficial to the reformer of criminal procedure, especially in the United States where comprehensive reform is badly needed. Theory helps to clear out the underbrush and permits one to see the forest in all its stark simplicity and beauty. When the tasks of criminal procedure are made clear and the focus is given to them rather than to the mechanisms a particular culture may favor to perform those tasks, the reformer is freed from the constraints of ethnocentricity in devising solutions to procedural problems which continually crop up in all modern procedural systems.

The procedural problems just referred to are: (1) how to stimulate reporting of crimes to authorities; (2) how to investigate these reports to ensure reliability and accuracy; (3) how to screen out unmeritorious claims so that the judicial, prosecutorial, and correctional machinery will not be overburdened with too much work; (4) how to do this in such a way that public interests will be served rather than merely the professional or political interests of the system managers; (5) how to protect the legitimate interests of suspects and accuseds so that the crime repression machinery does not become oppressive; (6) how to satisfy victims of crime that their claims are being attended to and their interests protected; (7) how to ensure public participation in the process so that organizational interests do not predominate and responsibility for doing justice is widely shared; (8) how to avoid error and bias in guilt determination; (9) how to prevent crime and correct offenders; (10) how to backstop the whole process so that error is caught and repaired; and so on. Of course, every nation must act within the constraints of its constitution in fashioning procedural solutions to these problems, and, realistically, every reformer is bound to a certain extent by the custom of his land in developing remedies. Nevertheless, within these limits and appreciative of the many different ways the tasks of criminal procedure have been performed in the past and are being performed today, the reformer will find it easier to start afresh in resculpturing criminal procedure if he detaches himself from specific procedural remedies and looks instead at the overall task.

Finally, it is possible that historians may find some value in the analytical model I have developed here. Just to give one example: historians studying the development of criminal procedure in Western Europe in the Middle Ages have noted the basic changes in criminal procedure that took place in the three hundred–year period between 1200 A.D. and 1500 A.D. both on the continent of Europe and on the island of Great Britain.[1] Many interesting questions have been explored, but a satisfactory explanation of the reasons for these changes has never been given. On the Continent and in England a system of private accusation resolved by oaths and oath-helpers (compurgators), ordeals, and trial by battle was supplanted by a system based on public or official inquisitions and accusations, resolved on the Continent by official inquests, torture, and confessions, and in England by jury trial. The role of the Church, the schools of law, and certain early European monarchs is well known and has been treated extensively,[2] but the reasons for their dissatisfaction with the system of private accusation have never been adequately explored.

The history of the era also suggests that a basic change occurred in the conception of the role authorities play in addressing and redressing complaints and grievances. In primitive legal systems authoritative intercessors are likely to see their role as basically arbitrating private disputes in order to achieve a satisfactory resolution—one which will preserve social harmony among all interests involved in the dispute.[3] This view changes in the Middle Ages to one of eradicating wrongdoing and sin and preserving the integrity and authority of legal principles. The conceptual revolution was a necessary precursor of the more forceful intervention in private disputes by kings and their officials which took place in the thirteenth and following centuries. In fact, it is hardly an exaggeration to state that this master change is the necessary predicate for the evolution from primitive to modern legal systems.[4] But the question remains: why did this change take place when it did?

The analytical model suggests a solution to this puzzle. First, when early monarchs are trying to form nations out of divided peoples who have only language and custom in common, and when a church is attempting to forge a universal spiritual community from ideological diversity, the administration of justice becomes a useful instrument for exerting authority and for unifying moral and religious beliefs. The proactive stance of secular and religious authorities is no longer satisfied merely to referee a private dispute or to sanction a resolution which depends on the manipulative skills of the litigating parties, the power of their adherents, or pure chance. A rational method of inculcating the desired moral point of view and of determining through investigation the factual predicate for a correct resolution becomes a necessity.

Second, it is possible that the Church and crown officials in Europe turned against the traditional manner of doing justice because it failed to stimulate crime reporting to the authorities. After all, there were considerable risks faced by complainants under the system of private accusation; if the accusation failed to result in a conviction, the accuser faced the penalties of perjury or civil suit.[5] A new system was needed to stimulate the reporting of crime to authorities in a way whereby the accuser would be protected from such liability in case the accusation failed.

Third, in time all systems which are based on producing optimal solutions for the parties immediately involved begin to betray interests which are more general—for example, the interest of the public in being protected from criminal wrongdoing or the public's interest in seeing abstract justice vindicated. Moreover, they do so more openly as the mystery surrounding these proceedings is penetrated by skeptics and social critics. It seems quite clear from the historical evidence available to us that not only the Church, whose priests officiated at trials and ordeals before 1215 A.D., but also secular authorities and the common people became all too conscious of the fact that these judicial ceremonies were being cynically abused and corrupted to serve exclusively private interests. "God's justice" became a mockery as its all-too-human nature became evident to all.

None of these ideas are offered as anything more than speculations, but they are speculations worthy of future historical research, guided, I hope, by a better understanding of criminal procedure and its functional requirements ("tasks") under two different conceptions as to its ultimate objective. If he understands this, the historian can, I believe, better appreciate the nature of the changes which have been introduced in criminal procedure over the ages. These changes all represent ongoing attempts to come to terms with problems caused by the malfunctioning of old procedures in changed circumstances. However, "malfunctions" can only be understood in the light of some theoretical model which first postulates the various tasks criminal procedure must perform if it is to accomplish its primary objective.

## CONCLUSIONS

In the preceding pages I have presented an analytical model of criminal procedure which I claim can be put to various scholarly and practical uses. To prove that the model has universal applicability, I analyzed highlights of the procedures of four nations in the world today whose politics, culture, and history differ considerably. The following conclusions can be drawn from the discussions heretofore:

1. The skeletal structure of criminal procedure in all modern systems is the same: intake, screening, charging the defendant and safeguarding his rights, adjudicating, sanctioning, and appeal.
2. Within this basic structure there is considerable room for difference, and the comparison of four nations has shown that there are significant differences between inquisitorial and adversarial systems and between non-Communist inquisitorial and Communist inquisitorial systems.
3. Some of the major differences between inquisitorial and adversarial procedures are:
    (a) *where the emphasis is placed.* In inquisitorial systems the emphasis is placed on the screening phase of the criminal process where a careful investigation ensures the correct determination of factual guilt. In adversarial systems it is placed on the adjudication phase where an active advocate manipulating complex rules of evidence to produce substantive results ensures the defendant a "fair fight."
    (b) *the extent to which courts try to control, or have the power to control, agencies of the criminal justice system.* Because of the separation-of-powers doctrine, observed in some form in most Western countries, the judiciary cannot directly control the acts of an executive enforcement agency, but it can legally nullify its acts and thus punish it for failing to abide by legal procedures. There is much less use of this indirect form of control in inquisitorial countries than in adversarial.
    (c) *the defendant's role in the proceedings.* In inquisitorial systems the defendant is expected to be more cooperative and forthcoming than in adversarial systems; although not required to do so, he is expected to furnish information to investigators and answer questions at his trial. In adversarial systems, on the other hand, the defendant is expected to maintain his silence until the state has produced sufficient proof of his guilt at his trial to shift the burden of persuasion to him; even then he continues to have this right if he chooses to exercise it.
    (d) *the court's role in the proceedings.* In adversarial systems the court is the custodian of the law but is supposed to leave fact determination to others—to the lawyers (prosecutor and defense counsel) to develop and present their respective cases for and against conviction and to the jurors

to decide between the contending versions of the facts. In inquisitorial systems the court is another investigator, different from previous investigators in also possessing the power to decide the case. There the presiding officer of the court asks most of the questions and develops the facts. Attorneys do not play a significant role in fact determination; their function is to argue the interpretation that should be placed on those facts by the fact-finder.

4. Some of the major differences found between Communist and non-Communist inquisitorial procedures are:

   (a) *the personnel performing the function.* In Communist countries different agencies are entrusted with tasks which in non-Communist inquisitorial countries (such as France) are entrusted to an independant judiciary.[6] For example, in the Soviet Union the "investigator" (*sledovatel'*) is not an investigation judge (a magistrate); he is an agent of the police or of the Procuracy. In China the pretrial investigation of the case is done by a police investigator working in conjunction with his colleagues in the procuratorate and the courts. In China the police used to issue themselves arrest warrants and search warrants rather than apply for them to the basic-level court of the district. In the Soviet Union appeals regarding pretrial errors and abuses in the investigation are made to the procurator's office and not to the court, and so on.

   (b) *public participation.* Communist nations are most adept at involving the public at all levels of the process: in generating complaints and increasing intake; by allowing intervention in criminal proceedings by the victim and other concerned members of the community; by permitting public representation in the adjudication process and public advice as to the nature of the sanction; and by involving the public in the sanctioning process, especially with regard to the application of lesser sanctions (for example, supervision of correctional labor).

   (c) *educative-rehabilitative function of the process itself.* Generally speaking, criminal procedure in Communist nations emphasizes to a much greater degree than is found in non-Communist inquisitorial countries the educative-rehabilitative function of the process itself, as opposed to that function applied only to sanctions. Criminal procedure is designed to begin the process of reforming the offender into a new man with a new outlook long before sanctions are applied and to demonstrate "lessons" to a public audience. While it is true that rehabilitation of the offender and general deterrence have always been goals of Western criminal law, these objectives have been connected with the exercise of the sanction rather than the process which precedes the application of the sanction. Also, the goals of rehabilitation and deterrence in the non-Communist West have never been as *explicitly* associated with the moral and political objectives of the state as they are in Communist countries. Communist nations do not look upon the punishment of the offender and the process by which this is brought about as ends in themselves but as one means of developing a new society. Whether the criminal process is an effective instrument of inducing this kind of personal and social reformation is open to argument, but in the use of criminal law for these purposes, Communist nations are further advanced than non-Communist nations.

I close this book by stating directly something which must have occurred to the reader by now: that the author's conception of an underlying structure of criminal procedure resembles the Renaissance conception of natural law: a fundamental order of society and of nature which commands all human laws to conform to its norms. That such an order exists is the basic assumption of all social scientists, although few would be so bold as to claim all human laws must conform to it. Therefore, I will close my essay by quoting an eminent representative of this ancient school, one who advises us that, if the senses are properly formed and the conditions necessary for perception present, one cannot help but perceive the underlying principles as manifest and clear as natural objects:

Primum mihi cura haec fuit, ut eorum quae ad jus naturae pertinent probationes referrem ad notiones quasdam tam certas, ut eas nemo negare possit, nisi sibi vim inferat. Principia enim ejus juris, si modo animum recte advertas, per se patent atque evidentia sunt, ferme ad modum eorum quae sensibus externis percipimus; qui et ipsi bene conformatis sentiendi instrumentis, et si cetera necessaria adsint, non fallunt. Ideo in Phoenissis Euripides sic loquentem facit Polynicen, cujus aperte justam vult fuisse causam:

> Haec sum profatus, mater, haud ambagibus
> Implicita, sed quae regulis aequi et boni
> Suffulta rudibus pariter et doctis patent.
> — Hugo Grotius, *De Jure Belli et Pacis*
> Prolegomena, para. 39.[7]

# NOTES

## CHAPTER 1

1. See Barney G. Glaser and Anselm L. Strauss, *The Discovery of Grounded Theory: Strategies of Qualitative Research* (Chicago: Aldine, 1967), 24–26; Henry W. Ehrmann, *Comparative Legal Cultures* (Englewood Cliffs, N.J.: Prentice-Hall, 1976), 11.

2. Glaser and Strauss, *Discovery of Grounded Theory*, 28; Raoul Naroll, "Some Thoughts on the Comparative Method in Cultural Anthropology," in H.M. Blalock and A.B. Blalock, eds., *Methodology in Social Research* (New York: McGraw-Hill, 1968), 236–77.

3. Charles Darwin, *The Origin of Species* and *the Descent of Man* (New York: Modern Library, n.d.), 23.

4. There are many ways that adversarial and inquisitorial procedures, so-called, can be distinguished and perhaps it is a mistake to emphasize any one to the exclusion of others, but for brevity's sake I will make the easiest and most obvious distinction between them: inquisitorial procedure leaves the development of evidence to official investigators who conduct an inquest and produce an official file (dossier) on which the case will be litigated; adversarial procedure leaves it to the litigants to develop the facts and the evidence in support of their respective positions and then leaves it to them to adduce as much of this evidence as they want for the neutral and passive fact-finder/adjudicator to consider in deciding the case.

5. Ehrmann, in his notable comparative study of legal cultures (*Comparative Legal Cultures*), identifies four major "families" of legal systems: the

Romano-Germanic family; the family of common law; the family of socialist law; and non-Western legal families. The present study contains one representative from each family—France from the Romano-Germanic family; the United States of America from the common law family; Soviet Russia from the socialist law family; and the People's Republic of China, arguably from the non-Western group as well as the socialist law group. Ehrmann is somewhat undecided as to how to classify China (ibid., 19); the present author is also hesitant to place it into the family of non-Western legal systems, notwithstanding China's Confucian cultural tradition, because its legal codes are so obviously modeled on the Soviet codes.

6. The term is Ehrmann's (ibid., 6).

7. See John Griffiths, "Ideology in Criminal Procedure or a Third Model of the Criminal Process," *Yale Law Journal* 79 (1970): 359–417.

8. Harold J. Berman, Susan Cohen, and Malcolm Russell, "A Comparison of the Chinese and Soviet Codes of Criminal Law and Procedure," *Journal of Criminal Law and Criminology* 73 (Spring, 1982): 238–39.

9. See D. Holloway, "Foreign and Defence Policy," in A. Brown and M. Kaser, eds., *Soviet Policy for the 1980's* (Bloomington: Indiana University Press, 1982), 35–64; Antonio Carlo, "Structural Causes of the Soviet Coexistence Policy," in Egbert Jahn, ed., *Soviet Foreign Policy: Its Social and Economic Conditions* (New York: St. Martin's Press, 1978), 57–90. For a different view of a somewhat more ambitious Soviet foreign policy, see Roger E. Kanet, "East-West Political Relations: The Challenge of Détente," in Roger E. Kanet, ed., *Soviet Foreign Policy and East-West Relations* (New York: Pergamon Press, 1982), 39–55.

10. The constitutions of both the USSR and the PRC not only protect *rights* but also impose civic duties. See 1977 USSR Constitution, Arts. 59–69, *Great Soviet Encyclopedia*, vol. 31 (Macmillan Education Co., 1982), 13; Constitution of the People's Republic of China, adopted December 4, 1982, arts. 42, 46, 49, 51–56, *Beijing Review* 25 (December 27, 1982): 16–18.

11. Harold J. Berman, "The Use of the Law to Guide People to Virtue: A Comparison of Soviet and U.S. Perspectives," in J.L. Tapp and F.J. Levine, eds., *Law, Justice, and the Individual in Society: Psychological and Legal Issues* (New York: Holt, Rinehart and Winston, 1977), 75–84.

12. Harold J. Berman, *Justice in the USSR: An Interpretation of Soviet Law*, rev. ed. (Cambridge, Mass.: Harvard University Press, 1966); Shao-chuan Leng, *Justice in Communist China* (Dobbs Ferry, N.Y.: Oceana, 1967); Timothy Gelatt, "The People's Republic of China and the Presumption of Innocence," *Journal of Criminal Law and Criminology* 73 (Spring, 1982): 259–316.

13. Ehrmann, *Comparative Legal Cultures*, 27.

14. Courts in Communist countries—as well as courts in most nations of the world—do not enjoy the judicial review power of American courts of striking down legislation and executive orders on the basis of their unconstitutionality. See Dina Kaminskaya, *Final Judgment: My Life as a Soviet Defense Attorney*, trans. Michael Glenny (New York: Simon and Schuster, 1982); Konstantin Simis, *USSR: The Corrupt Society*, trans. Jacqueline Edwards and Mitchell Schneider (New York: Simon and Schuster, 1982); Shao-chuan Leng, "Criminal Justice in Post-Mao China: Some Preliminary Observations," *Journal of Crim-*

*inal Law and Criminology* 73 (Spring, 1982): 204–37. [Hereinafter cited as "Preliminary Observations."]

15. Article 155 of the 1977 USSR Constitution states: "Judges and people's assessors are independent and subject only to law." *Great Soviet Encyclopedia*, 31: 18; Article 126 of the 1982 Constitution of the People's Republic of China states: "The people's courts shall, in accordance with the law, exercise judicial power independently and are not subject to interference by administrative organs, public organizations or individuals." *Beijing Review* 25 (December 27, 1982): 28.

16. Kaminskaya, *Final Judgment*, 38, 193; Simis, *Corrupt Society*, 106, 108; Leng, "Preliminary Observations," 218–21.

17. George P. Fletcher, "The Presumption of Innocence in Soviet Law," *Criminal Justice Ethics* 3 (Winter/Spring, 1984): 69–75; Gelatt, "Presumption of Innocence."

18. Harold J. Berman, *Law and Revolution: The Formation of the Western Legal Tradition* (Cambridge, Mass.: Harvard University Press, 1983).

19. René David, *French Law: Its Structure, Sources, and Methodology*, trans. Michael Kindred (Baton Rouge: Louisiana State University Press, 1972), 76–78.

20. Law (especially constitutional law) may be an external constraining force limiting government in its administration and in its policy making, but the judiciary need not be. The American practice of allowing ordinary courts (engaged most of the time in everyday civil and criminal litigation) to pass on the consitutionality of acts of the legislature and the executive and to declare them unconstitutional is not widely imitated in the world and is not found in France. France has two special courts—the *Conseil Constitutionnel* (Constitutional Council) and the *Conseil d'État* (The Council of State)—which have the power to declare acts of government invalid which violate constitutional principles. But neither, strictly speaking, is a judicial court. Henry J. Abraham, *The Judicial Process*, 2d ed., rev. and enl. (New York: Oxford University Press, 1968), 268–72, 295–99. West Germany also has a special court for handling constitutional questions, the *Bundesverfassungsgericht* (Federal Constitutional Court). The United Kingdom (Great Britain and Northern Ireland) allows its courts to declare governmental acts as ultra vires (beyond the power vested in them by Parliament) but not as "unconstitutional," since no court has the power to strike down any law of Parliament on that ground. Abraham, *Judicial Process*, 294–95, 299–301.

21. The fact that some supportive case authority for even the most farfetched argument can be found, if one searches long enough through the case reports of fifty states, probably results in part from the fact that judicial holdings are as restricted as they are to the particular facts of the case and partly from the fact that there is such a large amount of uncorrected judicial error in these decisions. By "uncorrected judicial error" I mean clear misinterpretations of past judicial decisions, clear misreadings of legislative intent and purpose, and totally illogical judicial reasoning in applying law to facts. Notwithstanding both of these inherent shortcomings, United States courts are receptive to case law from any common law jurisdiction and, therefore, there is a rich source of "law" on which to base arguments, both bizarre and customary.

22. Richard Neely, *How Courts Govern America* (New Haven: Yale University Press, 1981); Raoul Berger, *Government by Judiciary: The Transformation of the Fourteenth Amendment* (Cambridge, Mass.: Harvard University Press, 1977).

23. Neely, *How Courts Govern America*, chap. 1.

24. Steven Landsman, *The Adversary System: A Description and Defense*, American Enterprise Institute Studies in Legal Policy (Washington, D.C.: American Enterprise Institute for Public Research, 1984), 9–10; Charles Evans Hughes, *The Supreme Court of the United States* (New York: Columbia University Press, 1936), 186.

25. Charles L. Black, Jr., *The People and the Court: Judicial Review in a Democracy* (New York: Macmillan, 1960), 32; Hugo Black, majority opinion in *Chambers v. Florida*, 309 U.S. 227, 241 (1940).

26. Herbert Wechsler, "Toward Neutral Principles of Constitutional Law" [1959], reprinted in Herbert Wechsler, ed., *Principles, Politics, and Fundamental Law: Selected Essays* (Cambridge, Mass.: Harvard University Press, 1961), 3–48.

27. Abraham, *Judicial Process*, 100–101.

28. Ibid.

29. American Bar Association, *ABA Project on Standards for Criminal Justice: Standards Relating to the Prosecution Function and the Defense Function* (New York: Institute of Judicial Administration, 1970), 3.

30. John H. Langbein, "The Criminal Trial Before the Lawyers," *University of Chicago Law Review* 45 (Winter, 1978): 263–316; R. Carter Pittman, "The Colonial and Constitutional History of the Privilege against Self-Incrimination in America," *Virginia Law Review* 21 (1935): 763–82.

31. Abraham S. Blumberg, "The Practice of Law as a Confidence Game: Organizational Cooptation of a Profession," *Law and Society Review* 1 (1967): 15–39; Malcolm M. Feeley, *The Process is the Punishment: Handling Cases in Lower Criminal Court* (New York: Russell Sage Foundation, 1979); Milton Heumann, *Plea Bargaining: The Experiences of Prosecutors, Judges, and Defense Attorneys* (Chicago: University of Chicago Press, 1978).

32. Barry S. Martin, "The Razor's Edge of Conflicting Duties," *California Lawyer* 4 (January, 1984): 15–16; Anne Strick, *Injustice For All* (New York: Penguin Books, 1978). Compare Roscoe Pound, *The Causes of Popular Dissatifaction with the Administration of Justice* (first published in 1906; reprint. Chicago: American Judicature Society, 1963), 12–14.

33. The problem is one which confronts the modern legislator in successfully regulating and preventing corruption and publicly deleterious behavior by officials in public and private organizations. J.W. Doig, D.E. Phillips, and T. Manson, "Deterring Illegal Behavior by Officials of Complex Organizations," *Criminal Justice Ethics* 3 (Winter/Spring, 1984): 27–56.

34. Frank H. Easterbrook, "Criminal Procedure as a Market System," *Journal of Legal Studies* 12 (June, 1983): 289–332.

35. John Thibault and Laurens Walker, "A Theory of Procedure," *California Law Review* 66 (1978): 541–66; id., *Procedural Justice: A Psychological Analysis* (Hillsdale, N.J.: Lawrence Erlbaum Assoc., 1975).

36. Easterbrook, "Criminal Procedure," 290.

37. Ibid., 331.

38. In discussing Rule 11 of the Federal Rules of Criminal Procedure and similar state court rules requiring the court to satisfy itself, before accepting a plea bargained plea of guilty, that the defendant has entered into it "knowingly, voluntarily, and intelligently," Easterbrook remarks and inquires: "There is nevertheless a puzzle. Why is it necessary for the court to satisfy itself, before taking the plea, that there is evidence of guilt?" (ibid., 320). He answers his own question in contract law terminology: to ensure the court that the bargain is "reasonable," that it does not represent the unconscionable overreaching by one of the parties who is in a superior bargaining position with respect to the other.

39. See, e.g., Donald J. Black, *The Behavior of Law* (New York: Academic Press, 1976).

40. See Thibault and Walker, "Theory of Procedure" and their *Procedural Justice*.

41. Thibault and Walker, "Theory of Procedure," 542.

42. Ibid.

43. Ibid.

44. Ibid., 548:

> This conception of distributive justice is empirical and relativistic; it is not a philosophical ethic. It is grounded in the *perceptions* that justice has been done or has not been done, according to the cultural or subcultural standards that define the values of contributions or inputs and of rewards and outcomes.

45. Ibid., 545. Thibault and Walker seem to argue in this part of their article that facts established in a legal proceeding have no "enduring significance" beyond the role they play in furnishing the legal basis or the division of outcomes. Once facts established in legal proceedings serve this purpose, they lose *all* significance: "... typically determinations of fact are subordinate to the justice objective ... in a criminal case the question of whether the defendant fired the pistol has no significance after the determination of guilt or innocence and the resulting distribution of outcomes." It is difficult to conceive why Thibault and Walker are unwilling to accord to judicial fact finding the establishment of facts which have "enduring significance," when it seems obvious that judicial fact finding may establish the historical truth of certain past facts in particular instances, which may have very significant impacts on later events. What this view probably represents is the scientists' bias against any non-scientific method, such as judicial fact finding, as being incapable of establishing generally true propositions which may be relied upon in guiding the future conduct of people who find themselves in like circumstances.

46. Ibid., 546–47.

47. Ibid., 547–48.

48. Ibid., 548–52. See also, *Procedural Justice*, 81–96. Thibault and Walker do not argue merely that such procedure should be preferred over "autocratic decision-making" because it leads to greater litigant satisfaction. They also point to the following "objective" advantages which process control by the disputants has over process control by the decision-maker, which their con-

trolled experiments are claimed to reveal: (1) the capacity of adversarial procedure ("arbitration") to stimulate advocates who encounter facts unfavorable to their side to search more diligently for more favorable evidence; (2) its greater effectiveness in moderating pre-existing bias in decision makers and in causing them to reserve judgment until all the facts have been presented; and (3) its ability to correct potential distortions of judgment arising from the manner and temporal sequence in which the evidence is presented to the decision maker. *Procedural Justice*, 118.

49. The evidence, which is presented in *Procedural Justice*, 52–53, 77–80, only weakly supports Thibault and Walker's very tentative conclusion that their results are not culture-bound. In one cross-national replication the responses of University of Paris students paralleled those of students at the University of North Carolina at Chapel Hill, whereas another replication conducted among West German university students at Mannheim did not. In another experiment (ibid., 78–80) conducted with these same university students, in which four types of hearing procedure were presented (two of which were designed to "match" adversarial and inquisitorial modes of procedure), French and West German students seemed to prefer the adversarial to the inquisitorial procedure by significant margins, although neither procedure was identified as such. The main shortcomings of these experiments were (1) that the procedure-types were so briefly described that only certain apsects of inquisitorial and adversary procedures were tested, and (2) that the outcome of the dispute which was to be decided by these procedures was never made clear. Was the outcome of the altercation between Adams and Zemp to be the award of compensation to the plaintiff or the punishment of the defendant? Since the amount of process control exercised by lawyers in civil proceedings in inquisitorial countries differs substantially from the amount of control they exercise in criminal cases, the fact that the experimental subjects may have been unclear as to the kind of proceeding they were dealing with could have influenced their responses or could affect the way their responses should be interpreted. In other words, if they thought they were dealing with a civil dispute (a tortious assault), it is possible that the procedure they expressed a preference for more closely resembled the way such proceedings are handled in their countries than the mode of procedure Thibault and Walker characterized as being "autocratic decision–making."

50. Lon L. Fuller, "The Adversary System," in Harold J. Berman, ed., *Talks on American Law* (New York: Random House, 1961), 30–43; Herbert L. Packer, *The Limits of Criminal Sanction* (Stanford Calif.: Stanford University Press, 1968), 151–246; Griffiths, "Ideology in Criminal Procedure"; Abraham S. Goldstein, "Reflections on Two Models: Inquisitorial Themes in American Criminal Procedure," *Stanford Law Review* 26 (1974): 1009–25; Landsman, *The Adversary System*.

51. Thurman Arnold, *The Symbols of Government* (New Haven: Yale University Press, 1935); Barton L. Ingraham, *Political Crime in Europe, 1770–1970* (Berkeley and Los Angeles: University of California Press, 1979), 9.

52. Alfred Friendly and Ronald F. Goldfarb, *Crime and Publicity: The Impact of News on the Administration of Justice* (New York: Vantage Books, 1968), 35.

53. Pound, *Causes of Popular Dissatisfaction*.

54. One almost has to go back to Edward Livingston (1764–1836) in the early part of the nineteenth century to find an American lawyer reconceptualizing criminal procedure.

## CHAPTER 2

1. See, for example, Gerhard O.W. Mueller and Fré Le Poole-Griffiths, *Comparative Criminal Procedure* (New York: New York University Press, 1969); Claude R. Sowle, ed. *Police Power and Individual Freedom* (Chicago: Aldine, 1962); R.T. Farrar, "Aspects of Police Search and Seizure without Warrant in England and the United States," *University of Miami Law Review* 29 (Spring, 1975): 491–558; A.L. Del Russo, "Prisoners' Right of Access to the Courts: A Comparative Analysis of Human Rights Jurisprudence in Europe and the United States," *Journal of International Law and Economics* 13 (1978): 1–39; A.S. Goldstein and M. Marcus, "The Myth of Judicial Supervision in Three 'Inquisitorial' Systems: France, Italy, and Germany," *Yale Law Journal* 87 (December, 1977): 240–83.

2. Alexander H. Pekelis, "Legal Techniques and Political Ideologies: A Comparative Study," *Michigan Law Review* 41 (February, 1943): 665–92; M. Damaška, "Evidentiary Barriers to Conviction and Two Models of Criminal Procedure: A Comparative Study," *University of Pennsylvania Law Review* 121 (1973): 506–89; M. Damaška, "Structures of Authority and Comparative Criminal Procedure," *Yale Law Journal* 84 (January, 1975): 480–544. Two recent works are not really comparative studies of different justice systems but merely descriptions of the justice systems of different nations laid side-by-side so that comparisons may be made by the reader. George F. Cole, Stanislaw J. Frankowski, and Marc Gertz, eds., *Major Criminal Justice Systems* (Beverly Hills, Calif: Sage, 1981); Richard J. Terrill, *World Criminal Justice Systems: A Survey* (Cincinnati: Anderson Publishing Co., 1984).

3. Griffiths, "Ideology in Criminal Procedure," 365–67.

4. Gary T. Marx, "Undercover Police Tactics," *Encyclopedia of Crime and Justice*, ed. Sanford Kadish, 4 vols. (New York: The Free Press, 1983), 3: 1154–60.

5. E. Adamson Hoebel, *The Law of Primitive Man* (New York: Atheneum, 1970), ch. 12; A.S. Diamond, *Primitive Law, Past and Present* (London: Methuen, 1971), chs. 14 and 15; Barbara Yngvesson and Lynn Mather, "Courts, Moots, and the Disputing Process," in K. O. Boyum and L. Mather, eds., *Empirical Theories about Courts* (New York: Longman, 1983), 51–83; R.F. Barton, *Ifugao Law* (Berkeley and Los Angeles: University of California Press, 1969); A.L. Kroeber, "Law of the Yurok Indians," *Proceedings of the 22nd International Congress of Americanists* 2 (1926): 511–16.

6. Diamond, *Primitive Law*, calls this the period of the Early Codes.

7. Ibid., ch. 5.

8. Ibid., 61–62. Law during the European early Middle Ages (roughly 500 A.D.–1000 A.D.) provides evidence of both third-party *arbitration* (both disputants consent to third-party resolution of their dispute) and third-party *ad-*

*judication* (one disputant forces third-party resolution by unilaterally invoking its intervention in the dispute). See Berman, *Law and Revolution*, 56.

9. Berman, 53–54. Compensation, however, tended to be punitive, in the sense that it was not measured according to the value of the material loss suffered by the person or thing injured but was usually a multiple of that value. Significantly, compensatory payments were pre-established by law and custom at fixed reparations which differed according to the status of the individual wrongfully injured. This indicates that they were really punitive reparations to restore the lost honor of the injured person or his family rather than damages designed to make good the economic loss. Ibid., 55–56. See also Daniel H. Kaiser, *The Growth of the Law in Medieval Russia* (Princeton, N.J.: Princeton University Press, 1980), 64–65; Diamond, *Primitive Law*, 66–67, 75–77.

10. A[démar] Esmein, *A History of Continental Criminal Procedure with Special Reference to France*, trans. John Simpson (South Hackensack, N.J.: Rothman Reprints and New York: Augustus Kelly, 1968), 3–4; Sir Frederick Pollock and Frederic Maitland, *The History of English Law Before the Time of Edward I*, 2 vols. (Cambridge: University Press, 1968), 2: 604–10 (appeal of felony); Kaiser, *Growth of the Law*, 128; Compare contemporary African tribal societies: L.A. Fallers, *Law Without Precedent: Legal Ideas in Action in the Courts of Colonial Busoga* (Chicago: Chicago University Press, 1969), 22–23; Max Gluckman, *The Judicial Process among the Barotse of Northern Rhodesia* (Manchester: University of Manchester Press for the Rhodes-Livingston Institute, 1955), 80–81.

11. Berman, *Law and Revolution*, 57–60; Kaiser, *Growth of the Law*, 13, 148–52; Hoebel, *Law of Primitive Man*, 266; Diamond, *Primitive Law*, ch. 21; Pollock and Maitland, *History of English Law*, 2: 598–601.

12. (Emphasis on procedure) Sir Henry Maine, *Dissertations on Early Law and Custom* (London: Murray, 1883), 389–90. By "distributive justice" I mean the fair distribution of outcomes according to some principle other than merit. Compare Thibault and Walker, *Procedural Justice*, 3. Distribution of outcomes (i.e., wins and losses) according to the merit of the position of the litigants is, by my terminology, referred to hereafter as either "retributive justice" or "substantive justice." I assume that on most occasions in most legal systems merit is usually to be found in the plaintiff's position because had he not been seriously injured by the defendant he would not have taken the trouble or the risk of involving third parties and of setting often irreversible legal machinery into motion, machinery which could end up injuring the accuser rather than the accused. That being the case, plaintiffs or criminal complainants should usually win if cases are to be decided according to the merits. However, a game or contest in which one side usually wins and the other usually loses is not considered fair because wins and losses are not distributed fairly. The odds favor one side too much. Therefore, the balance must be redressed so that those in the wrong have a fair chance of escaping justice, or at least of exerting sufficient influence on the outcome to win a partial victory by way of compromise or leniency. Morally correct retributive justice all the time would be insufferable for the average man and is especially intolerable for men in primitive societies. Thus, whenever the average man has any say in the justice system which intrudes into his disputes with others, he will prefer that system

which provides him with an even chance of winning, in whole or in part, and of escaping the full consequences of his wrongful behavior. Fixed, rigid rules of law, especially when they are procedural and do not address the merits of the case, introduce an element of chance and luck into the proceedings and provide both an escape route from retributive justice and bargaining chips to trade for compromise or leniency. Compare, R.H. Mnookin and L. Kornhauser, "Bargaining in the Shadow of the Law: The Case of Divorce," *Yale Law Journal* 88 (1979): 950, 968; Marc Galanter, "The Radiating Effects of Courts," in K. O. Boyum and L. Mather, eds., *Empirical Theories about Courts*, (New York: Longman, 1983): 121.

13. On the "magical" efficacy of extremely formal procedure and its substantive effects, see Max Weber, *Max Weber on Law in Economy and Society*, ed. Max Rheinstein and trans. Edward Shils and Max Rheinstein (Cambridge, Mass.: Harvard University Press, 1954), 51–52, 77–78, 81, 89. Pollock and Maitland (*History of English Law*, 2: 599) indicate that the procedure of oath-taking followed by ordeal by no means always favored the accuser. There are many indications from that period that tricks and connivance with those administering the ordeals were common, were well-known, and eventually brought this method of "divine proof" into disrepute. Ralph J. Hexter, *Equivocal Oaths and Ordeals in Medieval Literature* (Cambridge, Mass.: Harvard University Press, 1975). Trial by battle favored the accused if the accused could obtain a better champion than his accuser. Pollock and Maitland, *History of English Law*, 2:632–634. It was a system that could be manipulated by procedural statagem and maneuver. Kaiser, *Growth of the Law*, 149.

14. Berman, *Law and Revolution*, 57–59. Hoebel, *Law of Primitive Man*, 266 says:

> The law, for its part, consistently turns to religion when its techniques are not up to the problem of eliciting adequate evidence on which to settle a trouble case. Appeal to the supernatural to determine facts through divination, conditional curse, oath, and ordeal appears to be universal.

Besides alleviating the burden of responsibility of the third-party adjudicator for the result, "magical" methods of proof, with all the uncertainties that accompany them, reinforce the disposition of the disputants to resolve their dispute by negotiation. Procedural mistakes, omissions, defaults, and contumacy are within the control of the party litigant who makes them. If they result in a loss, he has no one to blame but himself. He has had his chance; he does not have to concede what he did was wrong; he just pays with his punishment. "Magical" methods of proof are particularly well attuned to people who believe in fate and accepting the consequences of voluntary choices, whatever they may be.

15. Screening usually involves officials who can investigate the facts underlying the dispute or criminal incident and make a judgment whether it involves a matter worthy of government intervention. In a system which regards serious interpersonal wrongs and injuries as private disputes and which leaves the policing thereof to private action, there is little occasion to have such officials. Since facts are not what determine the outcome, there is also

no occasion to investigate the facts. Moreover, far from wanting to turn away or weed out disputes submitted to the court for adjudication or arbitration, there is often a desire to encourage the filing of such suits in royal tribunals (fees and fines become substantial sources of revenue). Hoebel, *Law of Primitive Man*, 233; Pollock and Maitland, *History of English Law*, 1: 48–49, 566. Both appeal and screening are hallmarks of a system of bureaucratic justice—one which distinguishes sharply between private and public wrongs and which arrogates for itself the task of searching out and rectifying public wrongs, while rejecting or diverting merely private controversies to other methods of resolution.

16. Berman, *Law and Revolution*, 55–56; Diamond, *Primitive Law*, 61–67; Hoebel, *Law of Primitive Man*, 318; Kaiser, *Growth of the Law*, 13, 63, 69.

17. Berman, *Law and Revolution*, 50:

> In the late eleventh and early twelfth centuries all this changed "with marvelous suddenness," to use Maitland's phrase. In every country of the West there were created professional courts, a body of legislation, a legal profession, a legal literature, a "science of law." The primary impulse for this development came from the assertion of papal supremacy over the entire Western church and of the independence of the church from secular control.
>
> In the following centuries the folklaw of the peoples of Europe seemed to disappear almost completely. New sophisticated legal systems were constructed, first by the church, and then for the secular political order.

See also John H. Langbein, *Prosecuting Crime in the Renaissance: England, Germany, France* (Cambridge, Mass.: Harvard University Press, 1974), 133–39.

18. Berman, *Law and Revolution*, 171, 179–85.

19. Ibid., 250–54. John H. Langbein, *Torture and the Law of Proof* (Chicago: University of Chicago Press, 1977), 4–8.

20. Kaiser, *Growth of the Law*, 15–17.

21. Henri Maspero, "Le serment dans la procédure judiciaire de la Chine antique," in *Mélanges chinois et bouddhiques*, 3 vols. (Brussels: 1934–1935), 3: 257–317; A.F.P. Hulsewé, *Remnants of Han Law*, 2 vols. (Leiden: E.J. Brill, 1955), 1: 10–11; Derk Bodde and Clarence Morris, *Law in Imperial China: Exemplified by 190 Ch'ing Dynasty Cases* (Philadelphia: University of Pennsylvania Press, 1973), 48–51 and n. 95.

22. See Max Radin, *Handbook of Roman Law* (St. Paul: West, 1927), 83–87. During Republican Rome (500 B.C.–33 B.C.) criminal procedure was more accusatorial than it was inquisitorial. See A.H.M. Jones, *The Criminal Courts of the Roman Republic and Principate* (Totowa, N.J.: Rowman and Littlefield, 1972).

23. M. Cherif Bassiouni, "A Survey of the Major Criminal Justice Systems in the World," in Daniel Glaser, ed., *Handbook of Criminology* (Chicago: Rand McNally College Publishing Co., 1969), 529. Pierre Montet, *Everyday Life in Egypt in the Days of Ramses the Great*, trans A.R. Maxwell-Hyslop and M.S.

Drower (Westport, Conn.: Greenwood Press, 1974), 267–268; Adolf Erman, *Life in Ancient Egypt*, trans. H.M. Tirard (London: Macmillan, 1894), 141.

24. Esmein, *History*, 8; Langbein, *Prosecuting Crime*, 130–31. In France the concept of official responsibility to initiate and carry forward the prosecution became entrenched during the 14th century. Ibid., 221. In Germany *offizialprinzip* emerged in the 14th and 15th centuries. Ibid., 146–47. In Russia this process did not occur until the 16th century. Kaiser, *Growth of the Law*, 15.

25. Langbein, *Prosecuting Crime*, 131–32; Berman, *Law and Revolution*, 251, 423–24. Although England failed to pursue the inquisitorial course that other European nations took and remained basically accusatorial in its civil and criminal procedure, it too abandoned primitive methods of accusation and proof (the appeal of felony, trial by battle, ordeal, wager of law, etc.) in favor of a system which stimulated public reporting, accusation, and trial of criminal wrongdoing: the grand and petit juries of Henry II and his royal successors. At first the grand jury was not an investigative body but rather a body of witnesses and accusers. Theodore Plucknett, *A Concise History of the Common Law*, 5th ed. (Boston: Little, Brown, 1956), 107. China's criminal procedure during the Ch'ing (Manchu) Dynasty (1644–1912) contained many inquisitorial elements. Although Sybille Van der Sprenkel (*Legal Institutions in Manchu China: A Sociological Analysis* [London: Athlone Press, University of London, 1966], 69) characterizes criminal proceedings as accusatorial, the existence of an elaborate judicial/administration bureaucracy, the use of torture to extract confessions, the sole control over the proceedings of the local magistrate who not only directed out-of-court investigations but conducted the judicial inquest as well, suggest that proceedings were more inquisitorial than accusatorial. See also Bodde and Morris, *Law in Imperial China*, 119.

26. Esmein, *History*, 9; Langbein, *Prosecuting Crime*, 221–22; Berman, *Law and Revolution*, 251–53. In Russia the church predilection for written evidence probably preceded the switch from accusatorial to inquisitorial procedure. Kaiser, *Growth of the Law*, 158. Curiously, considering the Chinese genius for administration, written evidence was not used much at proceedings at the local magistrate level. Written records on a case first began to be compiled at the provincial level where the case received its first appellate review. Bodde and Morris, *Law in Imperial China*, 119.

27. Langbein, *Prosecuting Crime*, 185; Langbein, *Torture*, 12–16; Esmein, *History*, 155–56, 374–79. It may strike the modern reader as odd, but many of the procedural rules and practices of medieval and Renaissance European criminal procedure which we regard as grossly unbalanced in favor of the prosecution (including the infamous use of judicial torture) were defended on the grounds that they protected the rights of truly innocent defendants, while rightly denying escape routes for the wily and devious accused who in fact was guilty but knew how to dissemble innocence.

28. Magna Carta (1215 A.D.) is a good example of the earlier conception of rights as status-based and non-utilitarian entitlements. Such rights may not be taken from a free man at the king's discretion, although they might be voluntarily surrendered or lost in lawful proceedings conforming to the customary way of doing justice ("the law of the land"). Under the law the accused had a fair chance of defeating "justice," even if in the wrong, because luck,

God's grace, his own strength, or the strength of his powerful friends, could save him where the truth would surely condemn him.

29. Berman, *Law and Revolution*, 251 (greater emphasis on facts as establishing guilt and of legal rules to ensure reliability of evidence necessary to establish those facts). Discretion to depart from procedural rules was rarely, if ever, acknowledged in the statutes and ordinances which established those rules. However, discretion to depart from them when it was felt to be necessary was the natural result of the limited right of appeal which addressed mainly substantive issues rather than procedural error. Esmein, *History*, 239–44, 245–48 (note the remarks of Attorney General Séguier in reference to the extraordinary appeal to the Crown known as "reserved justice" which seeks to annul a judgment on the ground of procedural error, which Esmein accounts as "amounting to nothing" in practical usefulness).

30. See Fuller, "The Adversary System," 35–36.

31. Appeals are characteristic of inquisitorial systems of justice but not of accusatorial, at least originally. Esmein, *History*, 10. The assistance of legal counsel for the accused is more common in accusatorial than in inquisitorial systems. Just as appeals are late in developing in accusatorial systems, so are procedural provisions for assistance of counsel for the accused late in entering inquisitorial systems; they are originally viewed as interfering with and obstructing the determination of truth. Nevertheless, the necessity of defense counsel, even in inquisitorial systems, is acknowledged when the imbalance between an increasingly effective police and prosecutorial apparatus and an isolated and often friendless accused becomes so striking and poignant that it endangers public confidence in the validity of the outcome of the proceedings.

32. Landsman, *The Adversary System*, 45.

33. Langbein, *Torture*, ch. 1; Esmein, *History*, 112–13, 128–33; Pollock and Maitland, *History of English Law*, 2: 659–60; Berman, *Law and Revolution*, 252. Judicial torture to extract confessions was a feature of Chinese justice under the emperors (Van der Sprenkel, *Legal Institutions*, 74) and also was in common use during the last centuries of the Roman Empire in the West. Esmein, *History*, 9, 107–08.

34. Langbein, *Torture*, 6.

35. Ibid., 77–78. Sir Edward Coke, *The Third Part of the Institutes of the Law of England* (London: 1797 edition), *35. Langbein's efforts to explain why the English never adopted judicial torture as a standard technique for gathering evidence by arguing that "the jury standard of proof made it unnecessary to provide for extensive and refined evidence-gathering. An English jury could still convict on whatever evidence persuaded it..." fails to explain why the English refused to adopt a system of strict legal proofs which commended itself to church canonists elsewhere in Western Europe. It can hardly be argued that English churchmen were not involved in the same intellectual movement that brought about the adoption of this system in Italy, France, Spain, Portugal, and later Germany. See Berman, *Law and Revolution*, 161.

36. Langbein, *Prosecuting Crime*, 132, quoting Eberhard Schmidt, *Inquisitionsprozess und Rezeption* (Leipzig: Weicher Verlag, 1940), 9. Measures were taken to ensure the reliability of confessions produced by torture: (1) suggestive (leading) questions were to be avoided; (2) the accused had to repeat his confes-

sion in court long after the torture had ceased; (3) in some codes—for example, the *Carolina*, Articles 54 and 60—confessions had to be verified and corroborated by subsequent investigation. Langbein, *Torture*, 15.

37. In a society without bureaucratic organization in which private disputants bring their complaints to court where they are resolved, both screening of complaints and appeal are scarcely possible since the functionaries to perform these tasks do not exist. Esmein, *History*, 10; Pollock and Maitland, *History of English Law*, 2: 664–65. Although they were not appeals in the strict sense, procedures did exist before the 12th century for reviewing through private suit the "false judgments" of courts by suing them and their judges. Ibid., 666–67. Esmein, *History*, 51–52. Likewise, there were ways in which a plaintiff's criminal complaint could fail under the old procedure: he could fail in the utterance of his oath or in supporting it with pledges, or his oath helpers might fail in their oaths. Pollock and Maitland, *History of English Law*, 2: 604–10; Esmein, *History*, 56-57. But "screening," as the term is used herein, means pretrial review of the sufficiency of a complaint *by a public official* and the decision to eliminate it or reduce it to a lesser charge; it does not refer to the attrition in the number of cases submitted to the court for adjudication either by reason of dismissal for failure of pleading or because of voluntary withdrawal of complaints by litigants.

38. Diamond, *Primitive Law*, 97–98. Kaiser, *Growth of the Law*, 12–13; Graeme Newman, *The Punishment Response* (Philadelphia: J.B. Lippincott, 1978), chap. 5.

39. Landsman, *The Adversary System*, 15:

> Reliance on a small group of elite judges also had the effect of inhibiting the establishment of any sizable judicial bureaucracy. Such a bureaucracy in several European countries had facilitated the adoption of methods dependent on extensive judicial inquiry rather than on party presentation. Its absence in England made inquisitorial methods impractical.

As to prosecutorial officials in Renaissance England, see Langbein, *Prosecuting Crime*, 43–44, 206.

40. For example, see the description of Sir Thomas Smith of the typical felony trial of his day (1565 A.D.) in *De Republica Anglorum*, L. Alston, ed. (1906; reprinted edition, New York: Barnes and Noble, 1972), Book 2, ch. 23.

41. Ibid.; see also Langbein, *Prosecuting Crime*, 45–54.

42. For example, felony defendants were not entitled to the assistance of counsel in England in all cases until 1837; up till the end of the 17th century defendants were not permitted to call witnesses in their defense, nor to conduct any real cross-examination, nor to develop an affirmative case. Many kinds of evidence—irrelevant, immaterial, and incompetent—were admitted, and judges not only freely commented on the evidence, as they do to this day, but also attempted by various means to pressure the juries into bringing in convictions. Landsman, *The Adversary System*, 17; Langbein, "Criminal Trial before the Lawyers," 263–316. Concerning techniques of evading conviction on procedural technicality or lessening the amount of punishment, see William

Blackstone, *Commentaries on the Laws of England*, 4 vols. (Chicago: University of Chicago Press, 1979), 4: 326–82.

43. Concerning the long struggle during the 17th and 18th centuries in England to provide assistance of counsel for felony defendants, see Langbein, "Criminal Trial before the Lawyers," 263–316.

44. The story is told in Esmein, *History*, 356–69.

45. Ibid., 462–606.

46. Ibid., 11–12, 629–30 (Appendix B).

47. Landsman, *The Adversary System*, 50; Inga Markovits, "Law and Order—Constitutionalism and Legality in Eastern Europe," *Stanford Law Review* 34 (February, 1982): 513–613. The process of gradual adversarialization of European criminal procedure has not been even and steady; it has suffered setbacks, as during the Hitler regime in Germany (1933–1945) and during the early Bolshevik and Stalin eras in Russia (1917–1953).

48. Prosecutors have had the power to initiate misdemeanor prosecutions on the basis of an information (a criminal accusation which does not require the approval of a grand jury) in the United States since colonial times, since it was a power that existed at common law in England at that time. *Ex parte Wilson*, 114 U.S. 417 (1885); *Weeks v. United States*, 216 Fed. 292 (2d Cir., 1914), cert. den. 235 U.S. 697 (1914). In the last one hundred years many states have extended this power to include the prosecution of felony cases. In England, the Director of Public Prosecutions has a similar power as to all cases over which he exercises statutory jurisdiction (the grand jury having been abolished in England in 1948); however, most prosecutions in England are in fact entrusted to the police who act through regularly retained or specially retained solicitors and barristers. Michael McConville and John Baldwin, *Courts, Prosecution, and Conviction* (Oxford: Clarendon Press, 1981), 83–84; Terrill, *World Criminal Justice Systems*, 48.

49. As will be noted subsequently, preliminary investigation and screening of criminal cases in the United States and England are done, as is true everywhere else, by police and prosecutors. See citations in preceding footnote.

50. See, for example, Rule 16 of the Federal Rules of Criminal Procedure, *Federal Rules of Civil—Appellate—Criminal Procedure*, as amended to April 30, 1984, law school edition (St. Paul: West, 1984). See also Illinois Supreme Court Rules 412–415, Ill. Rev. Stat., ch. 110A, secs. 412–415 (1971), and Florida's Rules of Criminal Procedure 1.200 and 1.220, upheld in *Williams v. Florida*, 399 U.S. 78 (1970).

51. Goldstein, "Inquisitorial Themes," 1022.

52. See, e.g., Rule 11(f) of the Federal Rules of Criminal Procedure, *Federal Rules (1984)*. Usually, judicial supervision of plea bargained "deals" merely ensures that the plea has not been coerced and was voluntarily accepted by a defendant aware of the rights he is surrendering by pleading guilty. Some inquiries may be made as to the factual basis for the plea, but only rarely is much care taken to ensure that public interests beyond the convenience of the court (its docket load) or of the prosecutor's office are not being betrayed.

53. Appeals (including novel methods of collateral review of criminal judgments) are an aspect of inquisitorial procedure which Americans have embraced with a passion. The President's Commission on Law Enforcement and

Administration of Justice, *Final Report: The Challenge of Crime in a Free Society* (Washington, D.C.: U. S. Government Printing Office, 1967), 139. Although procedural issues still predominate, substantive issues (the evidentiary support for findings of guilt) are more frequently raised than in the past. *New York Times Co. v. Sullivan*, 376 U.S. 254, 284–85 (1964); *In re Primus*, 436 U.S. 412, 434 (1978).

54. Goldstein, "Inquisitorial Themes," 1016, 1019.

55. R.B. Schlesinger, "Comparative Criminal Procedure: A Plea for Utilizing Foreign Experience," *Buffalo Law Review* 26 (Spring, 1977): 361–85.

56. The adjective "totalitarian," always used in a highly pejorative sense, is a word which implies almost total control by a central government over every aspect of human life. Theoretically, *and in actuality*, there are no limits to what it can prescribe or proscribe. Certainly, the Soviet Union and the People's Republic of China possess far greater powers over their people than either France or the United States. However, it is doubtful that either society is "totalitarian" in the strict sense. Both seem extremely sensitive to public opinion and expend enormous efforts to maintain the good opinion of the masses. Thus, however much power either society could wield in the face of widespread opposition if that condition was ever allowed to arise, the leaders of both societies do not feel secure enough in their positions to ignore public opinion. For this reason, strictly speaking, neither society is "totalitarian."

57. Damaška, "Structures of Authority," 487–509 (discussion of hierarchical model).

58. Ibid., 526–29.


# CHAPTER 3

1. *Criminal Victimization in the United States, 1973*, A National Crime Panel Survey Report (Washington, D.C.: U.S. Government Printing Office, 1976); *Criminal Victimization in the United States: A Comparison of 1973 and 1974 Findings*, A National Crime Panel Survey Report (Washington, D.C.: U.S. Government Printing Office, 1976); *Criminal Victimization in the United States: A Comparison of 1974 and 1975 Findings*, A National Crime Panel Survey Report (Washington, D.C.: U.S. Government Printing Office, 1977); see also Charles E. Silberman, *Criminal Violence, Criminal Justice* (New York: Random House, 1978), 451–52.

2. Article 40, *Code de Procédure Pénale* (Paris: Dalloz, 1983–84) [hereafter abbreviated as *CPPD*].

3. Articles 54–63, *CPPD. Les délits flagrants* (crimes openly committed) is a concept which has expanded beyond its statutory definition of being caught in the act of committing a crime or immediately thereafter (see Article 53). It includes being found with the fruits, instrumentalities, or evidence of the crime in one's possession and also cases where offenses are committed within a house and the head of the household requests police investigation. Thomas Weigend, "Continental Cures for American Ailments: European Criminal Procedure as a Model for Law Reform," in Norval Morris and Michael Tonry, eds., *Criminal Justice: An Annual Review of Research* (Chicago: University of Chicago Press,

1980) 2: 391; Roger Merle and André Vitu, *Traité de droit criminel: Procédure pénale*, troisième édition (Paris: Éditions Cujas, 1977), 323–25.

4. Articles 63 and 77, *CPPD*.

5. A. V. Sheehan, *Criminal Procedure in Scotland and France* (Edinburgh: Her Majesty's Stationery Office, 1975), 32–33, paras. 39 and 40; Weigend, "Continental Cures," 389–95.

6. Article 79, *CPPD*. See also Goldstein and Marcus, "Myth of Judicial Supervision," 250. As Weigend ("Continental Cures," 390, 392–93) points out, there are only two situations in which the *juge d'instruction* has to be involved —(1) when the accused is charged with a serious felony before the *cour d'assises*, and (2) when it is necessary to detain a criminal suspect during the investigation for longer than the short period allowed by the *garde à vue* procedure. Statistics from the Ministry of Justice during the mid seventies (1974) indicate that of 513,176 *crimes* and *délits* (felonies and serious misdemeanors) processed and not dismissed by the prosecutor, only 14 percent were referred to the *juge d'instruction* for investigation. Ministère de la Justice, *Compte Général, 1974*, 2 vols. (Paris: La Documentation Française, 1977) 1: 16.

7. Goldstein and Marcus, "Myth of Judicial Supervision," 255. Weigend, "Continental Cures," 393. Articles 151–155, *CPPD* give the investigation judge the power to delegate his investigative functions to the judicial police on rogatory commissions (*commissions rogatoires*).

8. Jean-Jacques Gleizal, "Police, Law, and Security in France: Questions of Method and Political Strategy," *International Journal of the Sociology of Law* 9 (November, 1981): 373–74.

9. Harold J. Berman, *Soviet Criminal Law and Procedure*, 2d ed., trans. Harold J. Berman and James W. Spindler (Cambridge, Mass.: Harvard University Press, 1972), 99–100.

10. *Code of Criminal Procedure of the RSFSR* (Russian Soviet Federated Socialist Republic) in Berman, *Soviet Criminal Law*, 206–333 (hereafter cited as "CCP, RSFSR").

11. Article 109, CCP, RSFSR.

12. Article 118, ibid.

13. Article 119, ibid.

14. Article 126, ibid.

15. Articles 120 and 121, ibid.

16. Articles 97 and 122, ibid. See also Berman, *Soviet Criminal Law*, 53.

17. Article 214, ibid.

18. In the 1960 Code of Criminal Procedure the term "investigator" is defined as an "investigator of the procuracy, investigator of agencies of internal affairs [i.e., the police], investigator of agencies of state security [i.e., secret police]." See Article 34(7), CCP, RSFSR; cf. Article 125.

19. See Article 127(2), ibid. This is one of those highly idealistic provisions which is almost impossible to implement in a hierarchical bureaucracy. If the investigator happens to be one from the KGB (agency of internal security), however, he is truly independent of the local procurator.

20. See Articles 211 and 212, ibid.; see also Berman, *Soviet Criminal Law*, 55.

21. Articles 119(4) and 127(4), ibid.

22. See "Seven PRC Laws Adopted at the Fifth NPC Second Session, Part II," *FBIS Daily Report [People's Republic of China]*, vol 1. no. 147, supp. 020 (July 30, 1979): 1–30; see the English translation in J.A. Cohen, T.A. Gelatt, and F.M. Li, "The Criminal Procedure Law of the People's Republic of China," *Journal of Criminal Law and Criminology* 73 (Spring, 1982): 171–203. (Hereafter, all references to the 1979 Procedure Law will be to the Cohen, Gelatt and Li translation and will be abbreviated as "CPL, PRC").

23. See "NPC Promulgates New Regulations on Arrests, Detentions," *FBIS Daily Report [People's Republic of China National Affairs]* (February 26, 1979): E2–E5.

24. The Criminal Law of the People's Republic of China of July 1, 1979; see, "Seven PRC Laws Adopted at the Fifth NPC Second Session, Part I," *FBIS Daily Report [People's Republic of China]*, vol. 1, no. 146, supp. 019 (July 27, 1979): 33–62; see also J.A. Cohen, T.A. Gelatt, and F.M. Li, "The Criminal Law of the People's Republic of China," *Journal of Criminal Law and Criminology* 73 (Spring, 1982): 138–70 (hereafter, all references to the 1979 Penal Code will be to the Cohen, Gelatt and Li translation and will be abbreviated as "CL, PRC").

25. Jerome A. Cohen, *The Criminal Process in the People's Republic of China, 1949–1963* (Cambridge, Mass.: Harvard University Press, 1968), 8–9; Leng, *Justice in Communist China*.

26. Victor H. Li, *Law Without Lawyers* (Stanford: Portable Stanford, 1977); George W. Crockett, Jr. and Morris Gleicher, "Teaching Criminals a Lesson," *Judicature* 61 (January, 1978): 278–88. Jerome A. Cohen, "Will China Have a Formal Legal System?" *American Bar Association Journal* 64 (October, 1978): 1510–15; Ruth Bader Ginsburg, "American Bar Association Delegation Visits People's Republic of China," *American Bar Association Journal* 64 (October, 1978): 1516–25.

27. Among the significant changes which have been introduced in the new procedural code are: (1) the reintroduction of the procuracy at all levels of judicial administration and the supervisory role given procuratorates over arrests, the filing of formal charges, the judgments and punishments handed down by people's courts, and, in general, the legality of the actions taken by its two partners in the administration of justice, the police and the courts (Arts. 39, 95, 130, 152); (2) the emphasis now placed on public trials conducted openly by a mixed panel of lay and professional judges before an audience of observers (Arts. 8 and 9); (3) the emphasis now placed on legality and equal treatment of all citizens before the law, regardless of beliefs or social origins (Art. 4); and (4) the greater role assigned to lawyers, especially in acting as defenders of people accused of crime (Arts. 26–30). See Zhang Zipei, "Basic Principles of the Law of Criminal Procedure," *Beijing Review* 23 (June 9, 1980): 23–26. If one discounts the brief period, 1954 to 1957, during which some of the above were features of Chinese criminal procedure, these provisions are innovative in a judicial system which either did not allow for them, or, if it did, ignored them. Nevertheless, there is a tendency on the part of Chinese exegetes to pretend that these are not so much innovations as they are a return to previous policies and pure "Mao Zedong thought" after a period of turmoil caused by

the arch traitor, Lin Biao, and later by the criminal "Gang of Four" (Mao's widow, Jiang Qing, Yao Wenyuan, Zhang Chunqiao, and Wang Hongwen).

28. See Leng, "Preliminary Observations," 226–28.

29. See also Articles 1 and 5 of the Organic Law of the People's Procuratorates, *FBIS Daily Report [People's Republic of China]*, vol. 1, no. 146, supp. 019 (July 27, 1979): 27–33. However, as Leng indicates, this supervisory power is significantly curtailed by provisions in the same law (Arts. 5 and 6) which restrict the power of the procuracy to deal with noncriminal violations by state functionaries; and its independence from other state organs, supposedly assured by Article 9 of said law, is limited by the fact that the procuracy itself is accountable to the standing committees of the people's congresses at its level of government, as well as being accountable to supervisors within its hierarchy. Leng, "Preliminary Observations," 210.

30. Li Yuchang, "The Role of Chinese Lawyers," *Beijing Review* 23 (November 17, 1980): 24; Leng, "Preliminary Observations," 207–08.

31. Cohen, *Criminal Process*, 22; Stanley Lubman, "Form and Function in the Chinese Criminal Process," *Columbia Law Review* 69 (1969): 535–75.

32. Cohen, *Criminal Process*, 20–25.

33. For example, regarding mediation, Article 13 of the Procedure Law provides in its first paragraph, "Minor criminal cases that may be handled only upon complaint [of private complainants] and others that do not require the conducting of an investigation shall be accepted directly by the people's court, and *mediation may be carried out*." (Cohen, Gelatt, and Li, "CPL, PRC," 174; emphasis added). This, of course, is without prejudice to mediation activities carried out independently by other social organizations under the control of local officials.

For the present law with respect to administrative punishment ("rehabilitation through labor"), see "Supplemental Regulations of the State Council on Rehabilitation Through Labor, Approved at the Twelfth Meeting of the Standing Committee of the Fifth Session of the National People's Congress, November 29, 1979, promulgated by the State Council, November 29, 1979," *FBIS Daily Report [People's Republic of China]* (February 26, 1980): L5. The major change from the past law has been that a top limit (four years) has been placed on the amount of time the sanctioned offender can be subjected to forced labor. Regarding this sanction Timothy A. Gelatt writes:

> More fundamental is the extent to which the criminal process, with the protections it theoretically provides, is being bypassed for such "non-criminal," "administrative" methods as "rehabilitation through labor." The latter sanction, which involves a stay in a labor camp, is to be meted out ex parte by a committee of public security, civil affairs, and labor officials for, among others, "those who do not engage in proper employment, those who behave like hoodlums and those who engage in theft, swindling and other conduct but whose criminal responsibility is not pursued." Although the Chinese have passed measures limiting the period of rehabilitation through labor to a maximum of four years and curbing the use of a variety of other administrative methods such as "forced

labor" and "taking in for investigation," the fact remains that up to four years of treatment that apparently is not appreciably different from that accorded real "criminals" may be prescribed without any clear standard for when this non-criminal method is to be employed instead of the criminal process.

Gelatt, "Presumption of Innocence," 313–14.

34. Cohen, Gelatt, and Li, "CPL, PRC," 183–84.

35. Article 59, ibid. Article 13 of the Procedure Law sets forth the respective jurisdictions of the three recipient agencies. Basically, the people's courts have jurisdiction to receive and to act directly upon minor criminal complaints which do not require pretrial investigation; procuratorates may investigate cases involving crimes of corruption, violation of the democratic rights of citizens, dereliction of duty, and other cases they consider necessary to accept themselves; public security organs (police) are vested with the authority to investigate all other complaints.

36. Article 60, ibid.

37. Article 61, ibid.

38. Investigative detention and arrest are covered in Articles 38–52 of the Procedure Law (CPL, PRC).

39. See, infra, chapter 5, "Protection from illegal searches and seizures," (China).

40. Both the citizen and the policeman have the right to apprehend and take into custody anyone who is committing or who has just committed a crime; however, only the policeman has this right as to a person suspected of "being in the process of preparing to commit a crime." Compare Articles 41(1) and 42(1), CPL, PRC.

41. Only the policeman has the right to detain a suspect on one of these bases (see categories two through seven). Compare Articles 41(2)–(7) and Article 42, ibid.

42. Article 42 mentions these as being bases for a citizen detention (Art. 42[2]-[4]), but obviously a police officer would also have the right to detain, if not to arrest, any person falling in the eighth category.

43. There is no provision in the 1979 Chinese Criminal Law comparable to Articles 88(1) (failure to report crimes against the state) and 190 (failure to report crimes) of the Criminal Code of the RSFSR. Berman, Cohen, and Russell, "A Comparison of the Chinese and Soviet Codes," 253.

44. Article 138, Cohen, Gelatt, and Li, "CL, PRC," 161–62.

45. Articles 53 and 54, Cohen, Gelatt, and Li, "CPL, PRC," 182.

46. Efforts have been made recently to increase the amount of citizen reporting. See Robert K. Yin, et al., *Patrolling the Neighborhood Beat: Residents and Residential Security* (Santa Monica: Rand, March 1976); Gerald D. Robin, *Introduction to the Criminal Justice System*, 2d ed. (New York: Harper and Row, 1984), 119–24.

47. Probable cause has been defined as "... more than bare suspicion: [it] ... exists where 'the facts and circumstances within their [the officers'] knowledge [are] sufficient in themselves to warrant a man of reasonable caution in

the belief that' an offense has been or is being committed." *Brinegar v. United States*, 338 U.S. 160, 175–76 (1949).

48. For other methods of obtaining release from detention before trial, see, infra, chapter 5, "Protections against prolonged and unnecessary pretrial detention," (United States).

49. See *Dunaway v. New York*, 442 U.S. 200 (1979); *Pennsylvania v. Mimms*, 434 U.S. 106 (1977); *United States v. Place*, 462 U.S. 696 (1983).

## CHAPTER 4

1. Kenneth Culp Davis, *Discretionary Justice: A Preliminary Inquiry* (Urbana, Ill.: University of Illinois Press, 1973), 81–83; Joseph Goldstein, "Police Discretion Not to Invoke the Criminal Process: Low-Visibility Decisions in the Administration of Justice," *Yale Law Journal* 69 (March, 1960): 543–94.

2. Screening by magistrates and grand juries is provided only in cases of felonies and serious misdemeanors in the United States.

3. American Bar Association, *ABA Project on Standards for Criminal Justice*, 18 vols. (New York: Institute of Judicial Administration, March 1969); National Advisory Commission on Criminal Justice Standards and Goals, *Reports*, 6 vols. (Washington, D.C.: U.S. Government Printing Office, 1973).

4. Goldstein and Marcus, "Myth of Judicial Supervision," 247.

5. Article 79, *CPPD*.

6. Ministère de la Justice, *Compte Général, 1974*, 2 vols. (Paris: La Documentation Française, 1977), 1:16.

7. Reducing a serious crime (*crime*) to a misdemeanor (*délit*) means that the offense will be tried in a different court. *Crimes* are tried in the assize court (*cour d'assises*), *délits*, in the *tribunal correctionnel*—hence, the derivation of the term, "correctionalizing" a case. See Goldstein and Marcus, "Myth of Judicial Supervision," 251; Sheehan, *Criminal Procedure in Scotland and France*, 6; Weigend, "Continental Cures," 407–09.

8. See Merle and Vitu, *Traité de droit criminel*, 682–84.

9. Goldstein and Marcus, "Myth of Judicial Supervision," 271, 276; R. Vouin, "The Protection of the Accused in French Criminal Procedure," *International and Comparative Law Quarterly* 5 (1956): 9; Weigend, "Continental Cures," 400.

10. Sheehan, *Criminal Procedure in Scotland and France*, 42.

11. Goldstein and Marcus, "Myth of Judicial Supervision," 276–77. Sheehan, *Criminal Procedure in Scotland and France*, 41–43.

12. Sheehan (ibid., 21–22) reports that in Parisian courts (1970) victims intervene in approximately 20 percent of criminal actions but institute such proceedings themselves in only .2 percent of the cases.

13. Sheehan, ibid., 42, 43. Subtracting the check-bouncing cases, one arrives at a dismissal rate closer to 30 percent, which happens to be close to the national average of cases marked *classer sans suite*: 25.9 percent.

14. See Articles 40 and 54, *CPPD*.

15. J. Bernat de Celis, "Police et victimisation: Réflexions autour d'une main-courante," *Archives de politique criminelle* (Paris: Pedone, 1983), no. 6, 147–68.

16. Sheehan, *Criminal Procedure in Scotland and France*, 33, 42.
17. Ibid.
18. See Articles 177–181, *CPPD*.
19. Sheehan, *Criminal Procedure in Scotland and France*, 63–64.
20. Vouin, "Protection of the Accused," 24–25.
21. Goldstein and Marcus, "Myth of Judicial Supervision."
22. The distinction which American lawyers make between "explicit" and "implicit" forms of plea bargaining is revealed in this recent survey of American plea bargaining practices:

> in some situations defendants (through their lawyers) negotiate for explicit considerations from the state such as charge reduction; a specific sentence recommendation; a promise by the prosecutor that he will not oppose a request for probation; or some other specific consideration. This kind of bargaining has been referred to by Newman as "explicit." On other occasions defendants do not negotiate in the sense of requesting or discussing certain kinds of concessions. Instead they learn that if they go to trial they will be punished more severely than if they plead guilty. There is nothing to discuss. That is simply the pattern of judicial sentencing based on policy statements by judges or years of sentencing practices. Newman calls this "implicit" bargaining.

Herbert S. Miller, William F. McDonald, and James A. Cramer, *Plea Bargaining in the United States*, National Institute of Law Enforcement and Criminal Justice, Department of Justice, (Washington, D.C.: U.S. Government Printing Office, September 1978), 6–7. See also Donald Newman, *Conviction: The Determination of Guilt or Innocence without Trial* (Boston: Little, Brown, 1966), 60.

23. Goldstein and Marcus, "Myth of Judicial Supervision," 264–69.
24. Ibid., 270.
25. Ibid., 269–79.
26. Weigend, "Continental Cures," 409.
27. Ibid., 418–23.
28. For a discussion of administrative penalties which can be imposed by the police directly or after summary proceedings, see Berman, *Soviet Criminal Law*, 7–11. Two Russian criminologists have estimated that from 20 percent to 25 percent of all adult offenders escape criminal responsibility through decisions not to initiate formal prosecution or through termination of cases in progress. N. Kondrashkov, "Mery nakazaniia v zakone i na praktike," *Sotsialisticheskaia zakonnost'*, No. 2 (1968): 24–25; M. M. Babaev, *Individualizatsiia nakazaniia nesovershennoletnikh* (Moscow: Iuridicheskaia literatura, 1968): 84. These figures probably represent the percentage of cases which are formally rather than informally terminated or diverted.

29. Berman, *Soviet Criminal Law*, 206. See also Article 112, CCP, RSFSR.
30. Ibid., 207.
31. Comrades' courts are "informal, nonprofessional tribunals staffed by neighbors or fellow workers in housing units, enterprises or institutions, collective farms, etc., with power to issue warnings, reprimands, recommenda-

tions of eviction from an apartment or demotion in a job, fines up to 50 rubles, and transfer to menial work for fifteen days." Their sanctions are termed "measures of social pressure" to distinguish them from criminal punishments and administrative sanctions. Ibid., 9.

32. Ibid., 209.

33. See Harold J. Berman, *Justice in Russia* (Cambridge, Mass.: Harvard University Press, 1963), 286–98.

34. Article 113, paras. 3 and 4, CCP, RSFSR. Article 116 gives the procurator the right to countermand a decision by an investigator or agency of inquiry refusing to initiate a criminal case.

35. This right of appeal is less significant than it appears, since in most cases the appeal from such decisions must be made to the procurator's superior in the office of the Procuracy. See Article 220, CCP, RSFSR.

36. Article 29(2), ibid.

37. Article 208, ibid.

38. Article 209(5), ibid.

39. Article 210, ibid.

40. Article 211(2) (i), ibid.

41. Berman, *Soviet Criminal Law*, 57–62.

42. The Procuracy was eliminated in the 1975 Chinese Constitution (Article 27 (2)), but was restored in Articles 129–33 of the 1982 Constitution. See *Beijing Review*, 25 (December 25, 1982): 29.

43. Article 61, CPL, PRC. See discussion in chapter 3, supra, with regard to the decision to "file a case." There is no provision in the Procedure Law of 1979 corresponding to Article 3 of the Code of Criminal Procedure Law of the RSFSR, which states: "A court, procurator, investigator, and agency of inquiry *shall be obliged*, within the limits of their competence, to initiate a criminal case in every instance in which indicia of a crime are disclosed and to take all measures provided by law for ascertaining the event of the crime and the persons guilty of committing it, and for punishing them." (Berman, *Soviet Criminal Law*, 206; emphasis added.) In other words, there is no provision imposing an obligation on the police to investigate and prosecute, if the facts support the accusation, every criminal incident of which they are made aware. Nevertheless, the ignoring of major infractions of the criminal law by police would risk public and official criticism if the facts become publicly known. Thus, regardless of the exact state of the law, the discretion *the police* exercise to screen cases is always limited.

44. Article 45, CPL, PRC.

45. Gelatt, "Presumption of Innocence," 290.

46. See Article 61, CPL, PRC. The cases over which the procuracy has original investigative jurisdiction are stipulated in Article 13 of the 1979 Procedure Law, which is discussed in n.35 in chapter 3, supra.

47. Concerning prosecutorial review of the "arrest" decision, see Articles 39, 45–47, CPL, PRC; concerning the prosecutorial decision to "initiate a prosecution," see Articles 95–104, ibid.

48. This standard for evaluating the factual sufficiency of criminal complaints would seem, at least on the face of things, to be more rigorous than that which exists in most Western legal codes, including the procedural codes

of the other three countries compared in this work. See discussions in Gelatt, "Presumption of Innocence," 293 and accompanying footnotes. Whether there is much practical difference between the various standards of legal and factual sufficiency, however, must remain a matter for speculation until empirical studies are conducted.

49. Cohen, Gelatt, and Li, "CPL, PRC," 190.

50. Article 102, CPL, PRC.

51. Article 99, ibid.

52. There are very few statistics available to indicate with what frequency the prosecutor approves applications for arrest, decides to initiate a prosecution, or decides not to prosecute, "exempt a case," or remand it for further investigation. However, in December of 1979 it was reported that in the first ten months of 1979 (January to the end of October), which was before the new procedural code went into effect, the capital city's (Beijing) procuratorates approved 867 police applications for arrest out of 933 submitted (approximately 93 percent), turned down 60 (6.4 percent), and returned 6 (.6 percent) for further investigation. In the same time period, city, district, and county procuratorates in the same municipality examined 1,351 cases submitted by police for criminal prosecution. Of these they decided to prosecute 1,042 (77.1 percent), decided 132 (9.8 percent) were non-prosecutable, and exempted 56 cases (4.1 percent); 121 cases (9 percent) were referred back to police for further investigation. "Procuratorates in Beijing," *Beijing Review* 22 (December 28, 1979): 18.

53. Article 108, CPL, PRC.

54. Marvin E. Frankel and Gary P. Naftalis, *The Grand Jury: An Institution on Trial* (New York: Hill and Wang, 1977), 100; majority opinion of Justice Stanley Mosk in *Hawkins v. Superior Court*, 22 Cal. 3d. 584, 586 P. 2d. 916, 150 Cal. Reptr. 435, 438 (1978). Early and more recent statistical studies have usually shown that grand juries refuse to follow the prosecutor's recommendation to indict in a very small percentage of cases—usually less than 10 percent. See Wayne Morse, "A Survey of the Grand Jury System," *Oregon Law Review* 10 (1931): 101, 151–52; Dallin Oaks and Warren Lehman, *A Criminal Justice System and the Indigent: A Study of Chicago and Cook County* (Chicago: University of Chicago Press, 1968), 44–45. Even in those jurisdictions where larger percentages are no-billed, the prosecutor may have a hand in the grand jury's decision. See note, "An Examination of the Grand Jury in New York," *Columbia Journal of Law and Social Problems* 2 (1966): 98–99.

55. *Bracy v. United States*, 435 U.S. 1301, 1302 (1978); *United States v. Kysar*, 459 F. 2d 422, 424 (10th Cir., 1972); *Anderson v. Sills*, 56 N.J. 210, 265 A. 2d 678 (1970).

56. See citations in n. 54, supra, and in L. Hall, Y. Kamisar, W.R. La Fave, and J.H. Israel, *Modern Criminal Procedure*, 3d. ed., American Casebook Series (St. Paul: West, 1969), 791–94.

57. Morris, "Grand Jury System."

58. Hall, Kamisar, La Fave, and Israel, *Modern Criminal Procedure*, 850–51. The statistics here, as to dismissals at the preliminary hearing stage, vary more greatly according to jurisdiction than in the case of the grand jury dismissals (no-bills). However, more often than is true of grand jury hearings, no screening has been done by the prosecutor's office prior to submission and, in

effect, the prosecutor allows the magistrate the privilege of dismissing "junk cases" which he himself would have rejected in his own screening. See Oaks and Lehman, *Criminal Justice System*, 44.

59. *Coleman v. Alabama*, 399 U.S. 1, 9 (1970); *Gerstein v. Pugh*, 420 U.S. 103, 119–20 (1975).

60. Melvin P. Stein, "Preliminary Hearings in Pennsylvania: A Closer Look," *University of Pittsburgh Law Review* 30 (Spring, 1969): 481–99; Gary L. Anderson, "The Preliminary Hearing—Better Alternatives or More of the Same?" *Missouri Law Review* 35 (1970): 281–93.

61. If one defines as "screening" all decisions by police (for whatever reason) not to go further with an investigation or prosecution once having received a complaint, then approximately 80 percent of all reported crimes are screened out by the police before an arrest is made. See 1977 Uniform Crime Reports: difference between total number of reported index crimes [10,935,777] and total number of index crime arrests [1,986,043]. This ratio of arrests-to-total-reported-index-offenses has remained fairly steady over the last ten years.

62. See Joseph Goldstein, "Police Discretion," 543–94.

63. A recent survey conducted by INSLAW (the Institute of Law and Social Research) of felony case processing in a number of cities and counties in the United States of varying population size indicates that about half the felony cases in most of the jurisdictions studied were dropped by prosecutors before plea or trial. Kathleen B. Brosi, *A Cross-City Comparison of Felony Case Processing* (Washington, D.C.: INSLAW, 1979). If one counts as "screening" by the prosecutor only his decision to drop the case before filing a formal charge, his decision to "nolle" the case after charging, and his agreeing to, and perhaps moving for, a dismissal of the case before plea or trial, the statistics for the first six months of 1977 were:

| | | |
|---|---|---|
| Cobb County, Georgia | (n = 632) | 29% |
| District of Columbia | (n = 3,141) | 49% |
| Salt Lake City, Utah | (n = 1,402) | 44% |
| New Orleans, Louisiana | (n = 3,167) | 55% |
| Los Angeles, California | (n = 19,418) | 52% |

If one includes in "screening" the prosecutor's decision to refer the felony complaint to misdemeanor court after reducing the charge, the above statistics become 31%, 49%, 45%, 64%, and 76% respectively. The rate of attrition resulting from *post-filing* screening by prosecutors is much less (14 percent, 35 percent, 38 percent, 17 percent, and 34 percent respectively). These statistics are not greatly different from those revealed by surveys conducted in various U. S. cities during the 1920s by a number of different municipal crime commissions. See Brosi, ibid., 3, 4, 7.

64. Ibid., 11–13. Pre-charge screening seems to be the type of screening contemplated by Standard 3.4 of the American Bar Association's *ABA Standards: The Prosecution and the Defense Function*, 83–87.

65. See George F. Cole, "The Decision to Prosecute," *Law and Society Review* 4 (February, 1970): 313–43; Frank Miller, *Prosecution: The Decision to Charge a Suspect with a Crime* (Boston: Little, Brown, 1969).

66. Using Brosi's data (*Cross-City Comparison*, 9) comparing percentage of

post-filing dispositions represented by nolles and dismissals versus those represented by guilty pleas and estimating that 80 percent of the guilty plea dispositions were negotiated, it would appear that in the jurisdictions listed above in n. 63 the percentage of non-trial dispositions resulting from negotiated guilty pleas outnumbered the percentage of non-trial dispositions resulting from nolles and dismissals in every case:

|  |  | % Nolled or<br>Dismissed |  | % Negotiated<br>Guilty Plea |  |
| --- | --- | --- | --- | --- | --- |
| Cobb County, Georgia | (n = 507) | 14% | 61.1% | (80% of 77%) |
| District of Columbia | (n = 3,441) | 35% | 41.6% | (80% of 52%) |
| Salt Lake City, Utah | (n = 1,497) | 38% | 44.0% | (80% of 55%) |
| New Orleans, Louisiana | (n = 1,354) | 17% | 49.6% | (80% of 62%) |
| Los Angeles, California | (n = 7,064) | 34% | 37.6% | (80% of 47%) |

67. See Miller, McDonald, and Cramer, *Plea Bargaining in the United States*; Lynn M. Mather, "Some Determinants of the Method of Case Disposition: Decision-Making by Public Defenders in Los Angeles," *Law and Society Review* 8 (Winter, 1974): 187–216.

68. Milton Heumann, *Plea Bargaining*; D.C. Dodge, "Plea Bargaining Revisited," *State Court Journal* 2 (Fall, 1978): 13–18, 38–40.

## CHAPTER 5

1. *Palko v. Connecticut*, 302 U.S. 319 (1937). Justice Cardozo asked whether a procedural right was essential to anyone's conception of "ordered liberty," not viewed narrowly or parochially, but according to principles of justice recognized in the traditions of all civilized nations.

2. Articles 63 and 77, *CPPD*. For drug trafficking the 24-hour *garde à vue* may be extended by the prosecutor or investigation judge an additional 48 hours and again for another 24 hours (for a possible total of four days). Art. L 627–1 of the *Code de la santé publique* (See *Code pénal* [Paris: Dalloz, 1985–1986], Appendix, 1020.)

3. See Articles 137, 144–146, *CPPD*.

4. Article 145–1, ibid.

5. Mueller and Le Poole-Griffiths, *Comparative Criminal Procedure*, 24.

6. Articles 146–148, *CPPD*.

7. Sheehan, *Criminal Procedure in Scotland and France*, 51. See Articles 138–143, *CPPD*. Judicial supervision is not used as much as it should be. As a result French prisons and jails are overflowing with "temporary detainees" who often outnumber persons convicted of crimes and serving their sentences. *Contrôle judiciaire*, instituted to remedy this situation, has not been very successful in doing so.

8. Article 122, CCP, RSFSR.

9. Based on personal conversation with a former Russian defense attorney who practiced in the Moscow district.

10. Article 89, CCP, RSFSR.

11. Article 97, ibid.

12. Articles 218 and 219, ibid.

13. Article 220, ibid.

14. Cohen, *Criminal Process*, 28.

15. Article 48, CPL, PRC. See also Berman, Cohen and Russell, "Comparison of the Chinese and Soviet Codes," 243; Gelatt, "Presumption of Innocence," 293.

16. Article 92, CPL, PRC. This time limit, as well as the time limits imposed in other procedural sections (Articles 97, 125 and 142), have been extended by special action of the Standing Committee of the National People's Congress at least once. Shao-chuan Leng and Hongdah Chiu, *Criminal Justice in Post-Mao China: Analysis and Documents* (Albany: State University of New York Press, 1985), 87.

17. Some suggestion of when guaranteed release or house arrest under surveillance is appropriate is found in Article 40, which states that the accused should be immediately arrested when the facts of his crime have already been clarified, when he could be sentenced to imprisonment, and "where adopting such measures as allowing him to obtain a guarantor and await trial out of custody or to live at home under surveillance would be insufficient to prevent the occurrence of danger to society...." Cohen, Gelatt, and Li, "CPL, PRC," 179. The negative implication is that release on either or both of these conditions should be granted when the offender presents no danger to society. "Danger to society," however, is probably broad enough to include the case of a nondangerous offender whose crime is so scandalous that his release from custody before trial would have a negative moral impact on community sentiments. Article 40 also prescribes that these two alternatives to pretrial detention may be granted to a gravely ill accused person or a pregnant or nursing mother, even in a case where arrest would be appropriate.

18. *Terry v. Ohio*, 392 U.S. 1 (1968); *United States v. Brignoni-Ponce*, 422 U.S. 873 (1975); *Pennsylvania v. Mimms*, 434 U.S. 106 (1977).

19. *Davis v. Mississippi*, 394 U.S. 721 (1969); *Dunaway v. New York*, 442 U.S. 200 (1979); *Delaware v. Prouse*, 440 U.S. 648 (1979); *United States v. Place*, 462 U.S. 696 (1983).

20. Pretrial detentions of from six months to a year are not uncommon.

21. Articles 54 and 56, *CPPD*.

22. Article 76, ibid. Sheehan, *Criminal Procedure in Scotland and France*, 40.

23. The French exclusionary rules are exceedingly narrow by American standards.

> Under the French exclusionary rule, the violation of certain rights of the accused in the course of the judicial investigation can lead to the striking in the *cour d'assises* of the tainted part of the *dossier* from the record. The exclusionary rule does not apply, however, to the preliminary inquiry conducted by the police before or instead of the judicial investigation....Thus, the *garde à vue*, warrantless searches, and other critical confrontations between the citizen and the executive are effectively exempt from the purview of the rule ....Finally, French law knows no equivalent of the "fruit-of-the-poisonous-tree" doctrine. If part of the record is stricken the pros-

ecution can easily be reinstituted and the tainted part of the investigation be repeated in accordance with the law.

Weigend, "Continental Cures," 393–94.

24. See Articles 169–171, CCP, RSFSR.

25. Article 168(3), ibid.

26. See Articles 166–177, ibid.

27. The Soviet Union, like most inquisitorial nations, has no exclusionary
rule for illegally seized evidence and no criminal punishment provided for the
conduct of illegal searches.

28. Arrest and Detention Act of the PRC, December 20, 1954, *FKHP* (*Fa-
kuei hui-pien*) 1:239–242; Cohen, *Criminal Process*, 360–62.

29. "NCP Regulations Governing Arrest and Detention," *FBIS Daily Report [People's Republic of China]* (February 26, 1979): E2–E5, Arts. 2–8; Cohen,
*Criminal Process*, 28.

30. See pages 62–66 of the text, "Protection Against Prolonged and Unnecessary Pretrial Detentions" (China).

31. Ibid.

32. See n. 29, supra, for citations.

33. Article 37(2) of the 1982 Constitution provides: "No citizen may be
arrested except with the approval or by decision of a people's procuratorate or
by decision of a people's court and arrests must be made by a public security
organ." *Beijing Review* 25 (December 27, 1982): 16 (English translation). The
predecessor provision (Article 47 of the 1978 Constitution) varied only slightly
and not significantly in its language.

34. Article 45, CPL, PRC.

35. Articles 46 and 47, ibid. The chief procurator of the procuratorate
makes the decision to arrest, except in major cases where the decision is made
by a procuratorial committee.

36. Article 49, ibid.

37. Article 50, ibid.

38. Article 41, ibid.

39. Illegal searches of the person and home of the citizen are prohibited
by Articles 37(3) and 39 of 1982 Constitution. The privacy of correspondence
is given very limited protection in Article 40:

> The freedom and privacy of correspondence of citizens of the Peo-
> ple's Republic of China are protected by law. No organization or
> individual may, on any ground, infringe upon the freedom and
> privacy of citizen's correspondence, except in cases where, to meet
> the needs of state security or of investigations into criminal offen-
> ses, public security or procuratorial organs are permitted to censor
> correspondence in accordance with the procedures prescribed by
> law.

See English translation, *Beijing Review* 25 (December 27, 1982): 16–17.

40. Article 82, CPL, PRC.

41. Articles 83–85, ibid.

42. Articles 167–177, CCP, RSFSR.

43. United States Constitution, Amendment IV:

The right of the people to be secure in their persons, houses, papers, and effects, against unreasonable searches and seizures, shall not be violated, and no Warrants shall issue, but upon probable cause, supported by Oath or affirmation, and particularly describing the place to be searched, and the person or things to be seized.

44. *Payton v. New York*, 445 U.S. 573 (1980).

45. *United States v. Watson*, 423 U.S. 411 (1976).

46. *Terry v. Ohio*, 392 U.S. 1 (1968); *Adams v. Williams*, 407 U.S. 143 (1972); *United States v. Mendenhall*, 446 U.S. 544 (1980).

47. *Steagald v. United States*, 451 U.S. 204 (1981); *Warden v. Hayden*, 387 U.S. 294 (1967).

48. *Coolidge v. New Hampshire*, 403 U.S. 443 (1971); *Johnson v. United States*, 333 U.S. 10 (1948); *Aguilar v. Texas*, 378 U.S. 108 (1964).

49. *Harris v. United States*, 390 U.S. 234 (1968); *Ker v. California*, 374 U.S. 23 (1963); *Colorado v. Bannister*, 449 U.S. 1 (1980).

50. *United States v. Salvucci*, 448 U.S. 83 (1980); *Rakas v. Illinois*, 439 U.S. 128 (1978).

51. *Ker v. California*, 374 U.S. 23 (1963); *Sabbath v. United States*, 391 U.S. 585 (1968).

52. *Marron v. United States*, 275 U.S. 192 (1927); *Michigan v. DeFillippo*, 443 U.S. 31 (1979) [search incident to a lawful arrest]; *Bumper v. North Carolina*, 391 U.S. 543 (1968), *Schneckloth v. Bustamente*, 412 U.S. 218 (1973) [consent]; *United States v. Martinez-Fuerte*, 428 U.S. 543 (1976), *Chambers v. Maroney*, 399 U.S. 42 (1970), *Harris v. United States*, 390 U.S. 234 (1968) [border, automobile, and inventory exceptions to the warrant requirements].

53. See Leonard W. Levy, *Against the Law* (New York: Harper Torchbooks, 1974), chap. 2; Wayne R. La Fave, "Fourth Amendment Vagaries (of Improbable Cause, Imperceptible Plain View, Notorious Privacy, and Balancing Askew)," *Journal of Criminal Law and Criminology* 74 (Winter, 1983): 1171–1224.

54. See dissent of Chief Justice Warren Burger in *Bivens v. Six Unknown Agents*, 403 U.S. 388 (1971); see also Judge Malcolm R. Wilkey, "The Exclusionary Rule: Why Suppress Valid Evidence?" *Judicature* 62 (November, 1978): 215–32.

55. See "Closing Arguments in the Debate over the Exclusionary Rule," *Judicature* 62 (February, 1979): 336–56.

56. See *Illinois v. Gates*, 462 U.S. 213 (1983); *Segura v. United States*, 468 U.S. 796 (1984); *United States v. Leon*, 468 U.S. 897 (1984); *Massachusetts v. Sheppard*, 468 U.S. 981 (1984).

57. See J. David Hirschel, "What We Can Learn fom the English Approach to the Problem of Illegally Seized Evidence." *Judicature* 67 (April, 1984): 427–29. For the situation in Canada, see Wilkey, "Exclusionary Rule," 216–18.

58. Article 114 (1), *CPPD*.

59. Sheehan, *Criminal Procedure in Scotland and France*, 70. See also Article 406, *CPPD*, which provides additional notice of the charges given to

the accused at the time he appears before the *tribunal correctionnel* for trial and Article 279 when he appears before the *cour d'assises* (assize court for the trial of felonies).

60. See Article 118(3), *CPPD*; Sheehan, *Criminal Procedure in Scotland and France*, 49, 58. When the investigation judge has completed his investigation, he must notify the accused and the civil party that he has sent the dossier to the prosecutor and must allow them an opportunity to study a copy of it.

61. Article 148(1), CCP, RSFSR.

62. Articles 47(1) and 201, ibid.

63. Robert H. Jackson, *The Nuremberg Case* (New York: Knopf 1947), vi-vii.

64. Article 110 (para. 2), CPL, PRC. Lawyers in China are organized into organizations or collectives. Whether requested to serve as counsel by the litigant or assigned to a case by the court acting in coordination with his organization, the individual lawyer cannot accept a request to handle a case himself; he is always appointed to a case by persons other than the client. His salary is paid by the state, and he sees himself as a government functionary, whose primary duty is to defend the defendant in strict accordance with state laws and not to attempt to bend them in his client's favor. See "China's Lawyers," *Beijing Review* 23 (June 9, 1980): 26.

65. Article 29, CPL, PRC:

> A defense lawyer may consult the materials of the case, acquaint himself with the circumstances of the case, and may interview and correspond with a defendant held in custody; other defenders, with the permission of the people's court, may also acquaint themselves with the circumstances of the case and interview and correspond with a defendant held in custody.

Cohen, Gelatt, and Li, "CPL, PRC," 177. It should be noted that Article 29 does not provide the defendant himself with the right of inspection in the event he is representing himself.

66. Criminal Procedure Teaching Group, Law Faculty of China People's University, *Basic Knowledge about the Criminal Procedure Law of the People's Republic of China* (Beijing: 1980), 103, 104; Gelatt, "Presumption of Innocence," 289.

67. Gelatt, ibid.

68. Cohen, Gelatt, and Li, "CPL, PRC," 184–85.

69. Cohen, *Criminal Process*, 31. André Bonnichon, *Law in Communist China* (The Hague: International Commission of Jurists, 1956), 26.

70. American Bar Association, *ABA Project on Standards for Criminal Justice: Standards Relating to Discovery and Procedure Before Trial* (New York: Institute of Judicial Administration, 1969), 25; J. H. Israel and Wayne R. La Fave, *Criminal Procedure in a Nutshell* (St. Paul: West, 1975), 48–51.

71. Part of the state's case may have been revealed during the preliminary hearing which is required in many states before formal felony charges may be filed, but preliminary hearings are often waived. Also, many states require prosecutors to list the witnesses they intend to call at the trial and notify the

defendant of this list in advance of the trial. This permits the defendant or his attorney to interview these witnesses before trial in order to learn the substance of their testimony. However, some witnesses are unwilling to talk to defense counsel and repeat the statements that were made earlier to police. There is no way that the defendant can force them to talk to him or his counsel before the trial commences if they refuse to be interviewed.

72. G.A. Pelletier, "Legal Aid in France," *Notre Dame Lawyer* 42 (June, 1967): 643; J.M. Snee and A.K. Pye, "Due Process in Criminal Procedure: A Comparison of Two Systems," *Ohio State Law Journal* 21 (1960): 484.

73. Pelletier, "Legal Aid," 644.

74. Article 114(3), *CPPD*. Note, "Developments in the Law: Confessions," *Harvard Law Review* 79 (March, 1966): 1114.

75. Article 116, *CPPD*.

76. Article 118(3), ibid.

77. Sheehan, *Criminal Procedure in Scotland and France*, 38, 39. There is one exception to this rule: Article 70, *CPPD*, which provides that if a person summoned before the *procureur* in the case of a flagrant felony *voluntarily* appears accompanied by his counsel the prosecutor may not question him except in his counsel's presence.

78. Technically, defense counsel is not permitted to cross-examine witnesses directly but may only question them through the court—i.e., by submitting questions to the president of the court. Article 312, *CPPD*.

79. Goldstein and Marcus, "Myth of Judicial Supervision," 265.

80. Note, "Confessions," *Harvard Law Review*, 1118–19.

81. Article 47(1), CCP, RSFSR, as amended by edicts of the Presidium of the Supreme Soviet of the USSR, dated August 31, 1970 and February 3, 1972. Berman, *Soviet Criminal Law*, 218. Earlier intervention of defense counsel is required in case of minors, deaf, dumb or blind persons, or persons suffering from physical or mental defects who cannot themselves exercise their right of defense.

82. Article 47(3), CCP, RSFSR.

83. See Articles 51, 63, 64, 67, 202, 217–20, 221–23, ibid. See also Berman, *Soviet Criminal Law*, 53–54 and Ivo Lapenna, *Soviet Penal Policy: A Background Book* (Westport, Conn.: Greenwood Press, 1968), 122.

84. Article 47(4), CCP, RSFSR (lay counsel). Article 50, ibid. (self-representation).

85. Berman, *Soviet Criminal Law*, 107; Kaminskaya, *Final Judgment*, 24–25.

86. Article 31 of the 1962 RSFSR statute on the Advokatura, cited in Berman, *Soviet Criminal Law*, 110; see also Article 51(1), CCP, RSFSR.

87. George Feifer, *Justice in Moscow* (New York: Simon and Schuster, 1964), 223–52.

88. See *Beijing Review* 25 (December 27, 1982): 28.

89. See Articles 29 and 110(2) of the 1979 Procedure Law. Cohen, Gelatt, and Li, "CPL, PRC," 117, 192.

90. See Articles 47 and 41, CCP, RSFSR; Berman, Cohen, and Russell, "Comparison of the Chinese and Soviet Codes," 241.

91. Article 115 of the 1979 Procedure Law (Cohen, Gelatt and Li, "CPL,

PRC," 193) states that "[p]arties and defenders may request the presiding judge to put questions to the witnesses or expert witnesses or may request permission from the presiding judge to put their questions directly." The presiding judge has the power to terminate such questioning, even when allowed, if he thinks the questioning bears no relation to the case. Thus, as in most inquisitorial systems, the defender is restricted in his ability to weaken the state's case through cross-examination of the state's witnesses.

92. Article 28, CPL, PRC.

93. Leng, "Preliminary Observations," 219–21; Leng and Chiu, *Criminal Justice in Post-Mao China*, 92–96.

94. Leng, "Preliminary Observations," ibid.

95. Article 25, CPL, PRC.

96. Article 27(2), ibid.

97. Article 26, ibid.

98. Article 30, ibid.

99. *Gideon v. Wainwright*, 372 U.S. 335 (1963).

100. *Argersinger v. Hamlin*, 407 U.S. 25 (1972). In *Scott v. Illinois*, 440 U.S. 367 (1979) the United States Supreme Court held that the right to appointed counsel for indigent defendants is based on the sentence *imposed*, rather than the sentence authorized, by the penal statute. Thus, a defendant may face a possible penalty of imprisonment, but, unless one is actually imposed, he is not entitled to appointed counsel at state expense. Imprisonment and death, apparently, are the only punishments that the Supreme Court so far has held warrant appointment of counsel, although there may be others.

101. *Faretta v. California*, 422 U.S. 806 (1975).

102. *Carnley v. Cochran*, 369 U.S. 506 (1962).

103. The following have been held to be "critical phases": (1) arraignment (proceeding at which formal response pleas are made to the formal charges), *White v. Maryland*, 373 U.S. 59 (1963); (2) preliminary hearing, *Coleman v. Alabama*, 399 U.S. 1 (1970); (3) during post-indictment line-up identification, *United States v. Wade*, 388 U.S. 218 (1967); (4) at trial, *Gideon v. Wainwright*, 372 U.S. 335 (1963); (5) at sentencing, *Mempa v. Rhay*, 389 U.S. 128 (1967); (6) on appeal, *Douglas v. California*, 372 U.S. 353 (1963).

104. *Escobedo v. Illinois*, 378 U.S. 478 (1964); *Massiah v. United States*, 377 U.S. 201 (1964); *Miranda v. Arizona*, 384 U.S. 436 (1966).

105. See citations in n. 103, supra.

106. *Gilbert v. California*, 388 U.S. 263, 267 (1967); *United States v. Ash*, 413 U.S. 300 (1973).

107. Monroe H. Freedman, *Lawyers' Ethics in an Adversary System* (Indianapolis: Bobbs-Merrill, 1975), 201–30; Lloyd L. Weinreb, *Denial of Justice: Criminal Process in the United States* (New York: The Free Press, 1977), 106–107.

108. In the adversary system of criminal justice found in the United States, it often appears that the "ancillary objectives" seem at times to displace the fundamental purpose of the privilege (i.e., protection against coerced cooperation in one's own conviction). The adversary system, it is true, discourages cooperation of the accused in the investigation and trial of his guilt by removing any prejudice that might result to him from maintaining silence in the face

of accusation. On the other hand, this system is so intent upon leaving to the accused the right to control his own defense that it tolerates his right to bargain with the prosecutor not only as to the existence but also as to the extent of his guilt. In order to make the bargaining situation workable, the system permits the prosecutor to raise the stakes by "stacking" charges in his indictment in order to bring increased pressure on the defendant to compromise on *his* (the prosecutor's) terms. See *Bordenkircher v. Hayes*, 434 U.S. 357 (1978). Thus, in effect, it allows the coercion of guilty pleas (judicial confessions) in derogation of the privilege against self-incrimination.

109. R. Vouin, "France," in C.R. Sowle, ed., *Police Power and Individual Freedom* (Chicago: Aldine, 1962), 258.

110. Ibid.

111. Manfred Pieck, "The Accused's Privilege Against Self-Incrimination in the Civil Law," *American Journal of Comparative Law* 11 (1962): 585–86.

112. Ibid., 598.

113. Article 114(1), *CPPD*.

114. Pieck, "Accused's Privilege," 596. See also S. Hrones, "Interrogation Abuses by the Police in France—A Comparative Solution," *Criminal Law Quarterly* 12 (1969): 68–90. The importance of this omission may be less grave than at first it appears. Sheehan, (*Criminal Procedure in Scotland and France*, 34, n. 16.) reports that it is not uncommon for criminal suspects questioned by police to refuse to answer by employing verbal formula: "I have nothing to say regarding that question," suggesting that many Frenchmen are well aware of this right. But see Weigend, "Continental Cures," 391; G. Stefani and G. Levasseur, *Procédure Pénale*, Dixième édition (Paris: Dalloz, 1977), 284.

115. Article 105, *CPPD*.

116. Ibid. ("... dans le dessein de faire échec aux droits de la défense").

117. Pieck, "Accused's Privilege," 591, 593–94. See also Goldstein and Marcus, "Myth of Judicial Supervision," 255, n. 36.

118. See Article 20(2) and (3), CCP, RSFSR; Berman, *Soviet Criminal Law*, 259:

> The court, procurator, investigator, and person conducting the inquiry shall not have the right to shift the obligation of proof to the accused. It shall be prohibited to solicit the accused's testimony by force, threats, or any other illegal measures.

119. At the commencement of defendant's trial, after the defendant is advised of the nature of the accusation and his understanding of it is confirmed, he is asked whether he acknowledges himself guilty, and may be allowed to explain his answer if the presiding judge permits (Article 278, CCP, RSFSR). This does not violate defendant's right to remain silent, and is of even less legal significance than the request for defendant's plea to charge at his arraignment in American criminal procedure, which also does not violate the privilege against self-incrimination. I say less legal significance, because in American criminal procedure a plea of guilty by the accused resolves all issues against him, avoids the need of a trial, and permits the entry of a judgment of conviction thereafter, whereas in Soviet criminal procedure the acknowl-

edgement of guilt by the defendant at the commencement of trial would not save the prosecutor the obligation of submitting independent proofs and the trial would proceed, albeit in abbreviated form.

120. Article 77, CCP, RSFSR.

121. Article 76, ibid.

122. Berman, *Soviet Criminal Law*, 65.

123. Article 72, CCP, RSFSR.

124. See Articles 32, 34, 37(1), 64, 114–18, CPL, PRC.

125. Cohen, Gelatt, and Li, "CPL, PRC," 178.

126. Ibid.

127. Ibid.

128. Wang Shunhua, Xu Yichu, Zhang Zhonglin, Xiao Xianfu, and Chuan Kuanzhi, *Annotation of the Criminal Procedure Law of the People's Republic of China* (Beijing: 1980), 40; see also Gelatt, "Presumption of Innocence," 290, n. 188.

129. Cohen, Gelatt, and Li, "CPL, PRC," 184–85.

130. Article 114(1), CPL, PRC.

131. Western observers have already been treated to one example of a defendant tried under the new law who chose to maintain a defiant silence in his trial—namely, Zhang Chunqiao during the recent "Gang of Four" trial. See David Bonavia, "Give them Rice and Circuses," *Far Eastern Economic Review* (December 5–11, 1980): 12.

132. Leng, "Preliminary Observations," 221–24.

133. Weinreb, *Denial of Justice*, 147–64; *Malloy v. Hogan*, 378 U.S. 1, 7 (1964).

134. The basic rule guaranteeing the privilege is the Fifth Amendment provision "...nor shall [any person] be compelled in any criminal case to be a witness against himself."

135. *Griffin v. California*, 380 U.S. 609 (1965).

136. *Bordenkircher v. Hayes*, 434 U.S. 357 (1978); *Blackledge v. Perry*, 417 U.S. 21 (1974); *North Carolina v. Pearce*, 395 U.S. 711 (1969).

137. See Pamela J. Utz, *Settling the Facts: Discretion and Negotiation in Criminal Court* (Lexington, Mass.: Lexington Books, 1978), 10–12.

138. *Bordenkircher v. Hayes*, 434 U.S. 357 (1978); *Brady v. United States*, 397 U.S. 742 (1970); *Parker v. North Carolina*, 397 U.S. 790 (1970); *North Carolina v. Alford*, 400 U.S. 25 (1970).

139. Sheehan, *Criminal Procedure in Scotland and France*, 69. On appeal of a misdemeanor conviction the appellate court cannot increase the gravity of the charges the appellant faces, nor increase the punishment already imposed if he is the sole appellant. See Article 515(2), *CPPD*; Sheehan, ibid., 92. However, if the public minister appeals, the appellate court may increase the punishment, although not the number of criminal charges. This increase in punishment at the appellate level is not considered retroactive because in civil law countries an appealed judgment is not considered final until the appeal is decided.

140. Article 5(1), subparas. 9 and 10, CCP, RSFSR.

141. See Article 353(2), ibid.

142. See Article 380(2), ibid.

143. Cohen, *Criminal Process*, 40.

144. Article 137(2), CPL, PRC. See Leng, "Preliminary Observations," 232; Berman, Cohen, and Russell, "Comparison of the Chinese and Soviet Codes," 245–46.

145. *North Carolina v. Pearce*, 395 U.S. 711 (1969). The Fifth Amendment provision as to double jeopardy states: " . . . nor shall any person be subject for the same offense to be twice put in jeopardy of life or limb." This right has been expanded by judicial decision to cover other rights besides the right to be protected against repetitious prosecutions for the same offense and retroactive increases in punishment—e.g., "a defendant's valued right to have his trial completed by a particular tribunal," once "jeopardy" has attached. See *Wade v. Hunter*, 336 U.S. 684, 689 (1949) and Note, "Fifth Amendment—Double Jeopardy and the Single Tribunal Rule," *Journal of Criminal Law and Criminology* 60 (Winter, 1978): 563–73.

146. *United States v. DiFrancesco*, 449 U.S. 117 (1980).

## CHAPTER 6

1. Lloyd L. Weinreb, *Denial of Justice*, 97–103; Landsman, *The Adversary System*, 3.

2. Compare W.C. Jones, "Possible Model for the Criminal Trial in the People's Republic of China," *American Journal of Comparative Law* 24 (Spring, 1976): 229–45.

3. The jurisidictional limits of the three courts are as follows: *tribunal de police*: up to two months imprisonment, up to 10,000 franc fine; *tribunal correctionnel*: imprisonment from two months to five years, fine in excess of 10,000 francs; *cour d'assises*: imprisonment for life or from five to twenty years, and any other punishment the court may award. Most correctional sentences do not exceed five years, but it is worth mentioning that for recidivists the maximum is doubled to ten years and for specific crimes it can reach twenty years and even forty years, as is the case for major drug trafficking offenses.

4. Articles 523 and 535, *CPPD*.

5. Articles 398(3) and 398–1, ibid. (law no. 72–122 of December 29, 1972, as modified by the law (no. 85–677) of July 5, 1985 regarding road accidents) provide that the *tribunal correctionnel* may be composed of a single judge when the misdemeanor charge relates to check violations, certain traffic offenses, road accidents, and hunting and fishing violations of the *Code Rural*.

6. Article 400, ibid.

7. See Sheehan, *Criminal Procedure in Scotland and France*, paras. 81 and 95 for circumstances permitting trials in defendant's absence.

8. Goldstein and Marcus, "Myth of Judicial Supervision," 266. The "principle of orality" requires that all evidence considered by the fact finder be presented through live witnesses testifying in open court. Since the jury in the assize court is not permitted to examine the dossier compiled by the examining magistrate the principle of orality is necessary. It is not necessary in the correctional court, where the judges have free access to the dossier during trial.

9. For a more detailed description of adjudication proceedings in the *tri-*

*bunal de police, tribunal correctionnel,* and *cour d'assises*, see Sheehan, *Criminal Procedure in Scotland and France*, 69–85.

10. Berman, *Soviet Criminal Law*, 50–51.

11. Ibid., 56.

12. Article 278, CCP, RSFSR. However, in special circumstances the presiding judge has discretion to close sessions to the public. Article 263, ibid.

13. Article 15(2), ibid. See also Article 10(2), Law on Court Organization, Berman, *Soviet Criminal Law*, 337.

14. Articles 306 and 307, ibid. In point of fact, dissenting votes are rare and the professional member of the court is never overridden by his lay associates.

15. Article 278, ibid.

16. Article 279, ibid.

17. Article 280, ibid.

18. Article 283, ibid.

19. Articles 291, 293, ibid.

20. Article 295, ibid.

21. Article 295 (para.5), ibid.

22. Article 296, ibid.

23. Article 297, ibid.

24. Article 298, ibid.

25. Articles 299 and 318, ibid.

26. See Berman, *Justice in Russia*, 288–291, concerning comrades' courts.

27. As to "social accusers" and "social defenders," see Article 250, CCP, RSFSR. See also Articles 228, 236, 251, 288, 291, and 293–98, ibid.

28. Berman, *Soviet Criminal Law*, 69–70. According to my informants this Kruschevian reform has actually not had the desired impact it was expected it would have.

29. However, non-public administrative adjudication was still common, even during this period. As Cohen (*Criminal Process*, 13), states:

> [f]or the most part adjudication continued to take place behind closed doors. The defendant, who was without counsel, was subjected to judicial interrogation in an effort to verify the evidence assembled by the investigative agencies. This procedure was supplemented by ex parte interrogation of witnesses in those cases in which the information in the file and the account of the defendant left important questions unanswered.

30. Ibid., 17.

31. Ibid., 36–38. Throughout there was constant consultation with the local Communist Party Secretary. Leng and Chiu, *Criminal Justice in Post-Mao China*, 23.

32. See David Fogel, "China: Trial by the Masses," *Corrections Magazine* 3 (December, 1977): 42–44.

33. See Articles 41 and 47, Constitution of the People's Republic of China, dated March 5, 1978. English translation in *Beijing Review* 21 (March 17, 1978): 5–14. See also 1982 PRC Constitution: Article 125 (right to a public trial and right of defense); Articles 129–133 (establishing people's procuratorates), and Article 37(2) (approval or order of procurator or people's court

required prior to formal "arrest") *Beijing Review* 25 (December 27, 1982): 16, 28, 29.

34. See Fogel, "Trial by the Masses"; Crockett and Gleicher, "Teaching Criminals a Lesson"; Cohen, "Will China Have a Formal Legal System?"; Ginsburg, "ABA Delegation Visits People's Republic of China"; Martin Garbus, "Justice without Courts: A Report on China Today," *Judicature* 60 (March, 1977): 395–402.

35. Articles 105–125 govern trial proceedings in the first instance where the prosecution is instituted by the procuracy. See Leng, "Preliminary Observations," 217–218; Berman, Cohen, and Russell, "Comparison of the Chinese and Soviet Codes," 244–45; Gelatt, "Presumption of Innocence," 295–99.

36. Article 108, CPL, PRC.

37. Article 110, ibid.

38. Criminal responsibility for crimes committed by minors *under* the age of fourteen does not exist under the 1979 penal code; see Article 14, CL, PRC. Cases involving crimes committed by minors between the ages of 16 and 18 are usually not heard in public but may be in special circumstances; Article 111, CPL, PRC. Leng and Chiu (*Criminal Justice in Post-Mao China*, 19) question the true publicity of Chinese trials. Those who attend public sessions of criminal trials are issued tickets by government organizations, and those whose presence may not be desired can be excluded by not being issued a ticket of admission.

39. Article 111 (para. 3), ibid.

40. Article 113, ibid.

41. Article 114, ibid.

42. Article 115, ibid.

43. Thus, the trial court may consider documentary hearsay evidence since there is no requirement in Chinese law that out-of-court witness testimony be taken and transcribed either in defendant's presence or subject to his opportunity to cross-examine. Notwithstanding Article 36 which states that "[t]he testimony of witnesses must be subjected in the courtroom to the questioning and verification of both sides—the public prosecutor and the victim, and the defendant and the defender—and only after the testimony of witnesses on all sides has been heard and has undergone examination for truth may it be used as a basis for determining a case..." (Cohen, Gelatt, and Li, "CPL, PRC," 178). Chinese legal commentary makes clear that a lack of cross-examination, past or present, is *not* what leads to the non-admission of out-of-court witness testimony; rather it is the unverifiability of that testimony at the time of trial which renders it inadmissible. Thus, verifiable out-of-court witness statements may be used in the trial regardless of whether the defendant has or had any opportunity of challenging the witness by cross-examining him. Criminal Procedure Teaching Section, Beijing Political-Legal Institute, *Lectures on the Criminal Procedure Law of the People's Republic of China* (Beijing: 1979), 47; Gelatt, "Presumption of Innocence," 297–98.

44. Article 116, CPL, PRC.

45. Article 117, ibid.

46. Article 118, ibid.

47. Article 106, ibid.

48. Article 107, ibid.

49. These time limits were temporarily relaxed in a decision rendered on September 10, 1981, by the 20th meeting of the Standing Committee of the Fifth Session of the National People's Congress. "Decision of the Standing Committee of the National People's Congress Regarding the Question of Time Limits for Handling Cases," *Renmin Ribao* (September 11, 1981): 1; see also Cohen, Gelatt, and Li, "CPL, PRC," 189 (footnote).

50. Article 131, CPL, PRC.

51. These circumstances are (1) need for new witnesses, new material evidence, or need for expert evaluation or inspection; (2) prosecutorial request for supplementary investigation; (3) panel's own felt need for supplementary investigation by the prosecutor; (4) delay necessitated by a party's application for disqualification and withdrawal of one or more of his adjudicators.

52. Jerome Cohen, who visited Beijing in January of 1978, reported that this large city of over eight million inhabitants had merely two or three public trials a month, "a claim that is credible if one understands that most criminal cases do not culminate in a public trial, but are informally processed behind closed doors." Cohen, "Will China Have a Formal Legal System?", 1514.

53. First, it is difficult to see how the Chinese can now legally avoid affording defendants a public trial, since there is no device, such as a guilty plea, in Chinese law by which a trial might be avoided. Article 35 of the Criminal Procedure Law states: "In cases where there is only the testimony of the defendant and there is no other evidence, the defendant cannot be found guilty and sentenced to criminal punishment . . . " (Cohen, Gelatt, and Li, "CPL, PRC," 178). This would seem almost to rule out guilty pleas even if the practice were known to the Chinese, which it is not. Secondly, there is the fact the Standing Committee of the National People's Congress has found it necessary almost from the start to grant police, prosecutors, and the courts extensions of time beyond the time limits imposed by Articles 92, 97, 125, and 142 of the Procedure Law. Gelatt, "Presumption of Innocence," 313 (fn. 339). Unless there was a commitment to carry through on the promise of public trials and other proceedings conducted in accordance with written law, these time extensions would hardly seem to be necessary.

54. The number of jurors varies from 6 to 12, depending on the state and sometimes on the seriousness of the criminal charges.

55. The tactical reasons why so many defendants choose to remain silent in the United States is not only their fear of committing perjury if sworn as a witness but also to avoid cross-examination by the prosecutor, a cross-examination which would reveal facts—for instance, defendant's prior criminal record—which would otherwise be inadmissible evidence. John Evart Tracy, *Handbook of the Law of Evidence* (New York: Prentice-Hall, 1952), 191–92; Spencer A. Gard, *Jones on Evidence: Civil and Criminal*, 6th ed., 4 vols. (Rochester, N.Y.: Lawyers Co-operative Publishing Co., 1972) 4: 219–24 (sec. 26.20).

56. Sol Rubin, *The Law of Criminal Correction*, 2d ed. (St. Paul, Minn.: West, 1973), 145–47. In the United States, by reason of constitutional law, juries do decide the question of death versus life imprisonment, but often in a separate phase of trial after the determination of guilt.

57. See, for instance, Louisiana where 9 votes out of 12 are sufficient for

criminal conviction or acquittal (upheld constitutionally in *Johnson v. Louisiana*, 406 U.S. 356 [1972]) and Oregon where 10 votes out of 12 suffice (upheld constitutionally in *Apodaca v. Oregon*, 406 U.S. 404 [1972]).

58. Roscoe Pound, "Law in the Books and Law in Action," *American Law Review* 44 (1910): 12, 18; *United States v. Dougherty*, 473 F.2d 1113 (D.C. Cir., 1972), concurring and dissenting opinion of Chief Judge Bazelon, at 1141–42; cf. Gary J. Simson, "Jury Nullification in the American System: A Skeptical View," *Texas Law Review* 54 (1976): 508.

59. For instance, in the Soviet Union, as we have already seen, cases may be terminated before trial and even before investigation if the act committed by the accused has lost "its socially dangerous character," or he has. See Articles 6 and 10 of the 1960 Code, CCP, RSFSR. In China cases involving mere technical violation of the law without injury to social or political interests are not likely to be prosecuted in the first place, but, if they are, it is possible that some lower official's excessive zeal would be checked by higher officials, local Party officials, or community leaders who superintend the process.

## CHAPTER 7

1. *Code Pénal* (Paris: Dalloz, 1983–84) [hereafter abbreviated as *CPD*] articles 6–58. In 1981 (law no. 81–908 of October 9, 1981) the death penalty was abolished, narrowing even further the range of available penalties.

2. *La réclusion criminelle à perpétuité* and *la détention criminelle à perpétuité.* See Article 7, *CPD*.

3. *La réclusion criminelle à temps* and *la détention criminelle à temps.* Article 7, ibid. The terms may be for any number of years between five and twenty, as the specific law may prescribe. Articles 18 and 19, ibid.

4. Banishment (i.e., exile beyond municipal limits of France) is only imposed for a few crimes. Article 8(1), ibid.

5. Loss of civil rights (*la dégradation civique*) is rarely imposed on the principal punishment; it is not automatic upon conviction, as is often true of civil disabilities in the United States; it must be imposed as part of the penalty; and it cannot last longer than ten years. Article 8(2), ibid.

6. See Articles 9 and 40, ibid.

7. See Articles 9 and 41, ibid.

8. See Articles 9 and 42, ibid.

9. See Article 43–2, ibid.

10. See Article 43–3(1–3), ibid., and law no. 83–466 of June 10, 1983.

11. See Article 43–3 (4–6), ibid.

12. See Article 43–3–1, ibid., (law no. 83–466 of June 10, 1983).

13. See Articles 43–8 to 43–10, ibid.

14. See Articles 464 and 465, ibid. Fines now run from 20 francs to 10,000 francs. Article 466, ibid.

15. See Articles 11 and 44, ibid.

16. See Articles 56–58, ibid.

17. See Article 506, *CPPD*; Sheehan, *Criminal Procedure in Scotland and France*, 86–87.

18. Article 707, *CPPD*.

19. Language of the authorizing statute quoted in Philippe Chemithe and Paul Strasburg, "France's 'Sentence Judge'," *Corrections Magazine* 4 (March, 1978): 39–45, 65.

20. Ibid., 43.

21. Chemithe and Strasburg (ibid., 44) point out that these discretionary powers of the sentence judge have brought him into frequent conflict with fellow judges, who feel that their sentences are being undermined, with prison administrators who do not appreciate judicial meddling in prison administration, and with the public who are shocked by the number of dangerous offenders who are released before the expiration of their sentence. Recently the power of the sentence judge to do many of the things hereinafter enumerated—suspend or fractionize the sentence, allow the prisoner to work outside the prison, grant semi-liberty and parole, grant furloughs, etc.—was eliminated in the case of convictions of certain crimes carrying a non-suspended imprisonment sentence in excess of five years during a "period of security" consisting of one-half of the term. In the case of convictions for other crimes carrying non-suspended prison sentences in excess of three years, courts are given the authority of fixing these "periods of security" for up to two-thirds of the sentence. For more on the sentence judge and his powers, see Jean Chazal, *Les magistrats* (Paris: Grasset, 1978), 257–59.

22. Simple suspension and probation account for the great majority of all criminal sentences given in France—probably in excess of 65 percent. See Chemithe and Strasburg, "France's 'Sentence Judge'," 42.

23. Most of the conditions by which the probationer must abide are set by administrative regulation and by the judgment of the court, but special conditions can also be set by the sentence judge. Article 739(2) and (3), *CPPD*.

24. Conditional liberty (parole) is granted by the sentence judge after consulting with a "punishment commission" (*la commission de l'application des peines*) in the prison, composed of the director of the prison, chief guard, social workers, doctors, other persons working in prison who might furnish information about the prisoner, and the public prosecutor. This commission acts in a merely advisory capacity and meets at least once a month with the sentence judge, during which time hundreds of cases may be disposed of in one sitting. Although the sentence judge usually talks with the prisoner and may confer with his lawyer and members of his family, it is generally felt that the press of business, the limited time for its performance, and the almost total reliance of the sentence judge on the information provided by prison personnel prevents careful consideration of paroling decisions. Chemithe and Strasburg, "France's 'Sentence Judge'," 44. Most imprisonment sentences in France are flat sentences imposed within sentencing ranges provided by law, and approximately two-thirds are for less than three years. Ibid., 40. Thus, the sentence judge, rather than the Minister of Justice, is the most important person in France as far as parole is concerned. The basis for granting parole is now "serious assurances of social readaption" (see Article 729, *CPPD*).

25. See Articles 721 and 721–1, *CPPD*, and law nos. 72–1226, dated December 29, 1972 and 75–624, dated July 11, 1975. Unlike statutory "good time" provisions in American law, judicial reductions in the sentence are not supposed to be granted automatically in the absence of bad behavior. In practice,

however, they often are. In 1976, out of 39,838 cases examined, 38,232 were granted some reduction. Chemithe and Strasburg, "France's 'Sentence Judge'," 40. They are also not permanent like executive pardons. Reductions granted in one year may be retracted by the sentence judge in a subsequent year, in whole or in part.

26. See Article 720–1, *CPPD*, law no. 75–624 of July 11, 1975. None of the time spent out of confinement counts toward completion of the sentence.

27. See Articles 723, 723–1 and 723–2, ibid. "While on work release, which rarely exceeds six months, offenders spend non-working hours in special segregated quarters in jails and prisons or in one of the thirteen halfway houses managed by the prison administration. From their salaries, the administration deducts seven francs (about $1.50) per day to cover the cost of lodging and meals." Chemithe and Strasburg, "France's 'Sentence Judge'," 41.

28. As to furloughs (*la permission de sortir*) and special leaves under escort (*l'autorisations de sortie sous escorte*), see Articles 722, 723–3, 723–4, 723–5 and 723–6, *CPPD*.

29. See Article 21, Penal Code of the Russian Soviet Federated Socialist Republic of October 27, 1960, as amended to March 1, 1972 [hereinafter abbreviated as "PC, RSFSR"]; Berman, *Soviet Criminal Law*, 130.

30. Article 23, PC, RSFSR.

31. Article 24, ibid. The term, "especially dangerous recidivist" is defined in Article 24–1.

32. Article 25, ibid.

33. Article 25, ibid.

34. Article 27(1), ibid.

35. Article 28, ibid.

36. For instance, the French *dégradation civique* and American civil disabilities.

37. I say this notwithstanding the fact that Article 20 of the Penal Code states that "lowering of human dignity" is not a purpose of punishment.

38. See Article 45, PC, RSFSR, in connection with Article 41; Berman, *Soviet Criminal Law*, 140, 141.

39. As to other sentences, the court is allowed to mitigate the punishment by reasons of pretrial confinement or completely relieve the convicted person of any additional punishment.

40. See Article 53(3), PC, RSFSR, and Article 353(1) CCP, RSFSR.

41. See Article 53(1), PC, RSFSR.

42. Special provisions for conditional early release exist for minors under the age of 18—see Article 55, ibid.

43. Article 57, ibid.

44. Article 364, CCP, RSFSR.

45. Aleksandr I. Solzhenitsyn, *The Gulag Archipelago: 1918–1956*, 4 vols. (New York: Harper and Row, 1973, 1974). Connor reports that, according to a more recent Soviet textbook on prison administration, *Ispravitel'no-trudovoe pravo*, Higher School of the RSFSR Ministry for the Maintenance of Public Order (Moscow: Iuridicheskaia literatura, 1960), 84, the supervisory commissions of the executive committee of the local soviets share with the courts and the Procuracy the responsibility of seeing that labor colony administration

and staff operation operate within the bounds of legality. Walter D. Connor, *Deviance in Soviet Society: Crime, Delinquency, and Alcoholism* (New York: Columbia University Press, 1972), 215. He also reports, however, the court supervision of punishment is minimal. Recommendations for conditional early release tend to be rubber-stamped and post-release supervision of the parolee receives very little judicial attention. Connor, ibid., 226–227. For an account of conditions in the labor camps in post-Stalinist times, see Anatoly Marchenko, *My Testimony* (London: Pall Mall, 1969), and Avraham Shifrin, *The First Guidebook to Prisons and Concentration Camps of the Soviet Union* (New York: Bantam Books, 1982).

46. For example, in the United States the granting of parole (conditional early release) is left by most states to the unregulated discretion of parole boards. H. Kerper and J. Kerper, *Legal Rights of the Convicted* (St. Paul: West, 1974), 490–91, 495; Sol Rubin, *Law of Criminal Correction*, 631–33. Also, courts do not usually determine what kind of prison a prisoner will be assigned to once he is sentenced to imprisonment, and prisoners may be shifted from one to another without judicial interference. See *Meachum v. Fano* 427 U.S. 215 (1976).

47. Cohen, *Criminal Process*, 20–25; Lubman, "Form and Function," 558–60.

48. See Special Part of the 1979 Criminal Law, Arts. 90–192; Cohen, Gelatt, and Li, "CL, PRC," 153–70; see also Berman, Cohen, and Russell, "Comparison of the Chinese and Soviet Codes," 250.

49. Berman, Cohen, and Russell, "Comparison of the Chinese and Soviet Codes," 251.

50. See chapter 3, supra.

51. Articles 27–29, CL, PRC.

52. Articles 33–36, CL, PRC. A person sentenced to "control" is required during the period of probation to abide by all laws and decrees, submit to the supervision of the masses, actively participate in productive work, report regularly on his activities to the group supervising his probation, and obtain approval from said group before changing his residence or departing the area. See Article 34, ibid.

53. Articles 37–39, ibid.

54. Articles 40–42, ibid., which also cover life imprisonment. A person sentenced to fixed-term or life imprisonment is usually sentenced to confinement in a prison or camp, where he is subject to compulsory labor ("reform through labor"). See Article 41, ibid.

55. See n. 54, supra.

56. Articles 43–47, ibid. According to a recent revision by the Standing Committee of the National People's Congress (June 10, 1981), Article 43, which provides that death penalty sentences for immediate execution (i.e., without suspension for two years) must be submitted to and approved by the Supreme People's Court, has been modified so that for years 1981–1983 death penalty sentences, whether suspended or not, need only be approved by a high people's court and not by the Supreme People's Court, in cases of murder, robbery, rape, bombing, arson, poisoning, breaching of dikes, or sabotage of communications and power facilities. See *FBIS Daily Report [People's Republic of*

*China]* (June 11, 1981): K4. The death penalty when carried out is by firing squad. It is usually suspended for two years, after which the sentence is customarily commuted to life imprisonment or imprisonment for a fixed term of years (15 or 20 years). See Articles 45 and 46, CL, PRC.

57. Articles 48 and 49, ibid. There is no top limit to the amount of the fine which may be imposed. The sentence should indicate whether the fine is to be paid in a lump sum or in installments.

58. Articles 50–54, ibid. Of whichever political rights the convicted offender is deprived in his sentence, the minimum and maximum term for this deprivation is from one to five years, except in the case of persons sentenced to life imprisonment or to death or to control. Articles 51 and 53, ibid.

59. Articles 55 and 56, ibid.

60. Articles 30 and 31, ibid.

61. Berman, Cohen and Russell "Comparison of the Chinese and Soviet Codes," 255.

62. Article 59 (para. 2), CL, PRC.

63. Articles 67–70, ibid. Suspension of sentence is an alternative not available to "counterrevolutionary criminals" or recidivists; Article 69, ibid.

64. Articles 32 and 63, ibid.

65. Articles 71 and 72, ibid. For those sentenced to control, detention, or fixed term imprisonment, the term actually to be carried out may not be, after one or more reductions, less than half of the term originally decided upon and in the case of life imprisonment, it may not be less than ten years.

66. Articles 73–75, ibid.

67. Revocation of parole is always a possibility if the offender commits further crimes. Article 75, ibid. It is not clear from the penal code whether parole could be revoked if the parolee merely violated the terms and conditions of his supervision or refused to be supervised. The question may be academic since there are so many other actions the police could take against a person merely considered dangerous or unmanageable. If a parolee's parole is revoked, he is not necessarily required to serve the entire balance of the unexpired part of his first sentence in addition to the punishment he receives for the new offense. See Articles 75 and 64, ibid.

68. See Articles 90–104, ibid.

69. Capital punishment is most frequently authorized for counterrevolutionary crimes. Article 103, ibid.; Leng, "Preliminary Observations," 212. Deprivation of political rights is *always* a supplementary punishment to be imposed on counterrevolutionary offenders, whereas it is optional as to others. Article 52, ibid. If, after completing his sentence or receiving a pardon, a counterrevolutionary offender commits another counterrevolutionary crime, he must be punished as a recidivist; ordinary repeat offenders are not subject to treatment as recidivists unless they have been sentenced to fixed-term imprisonment or more and within three years of completing the sentence or receiving a pardon, they commit a crime for which they could receive another fixed-term imprisonment sentence or more. Articles 61 and 62, ibid. Criminal sentences may not be suspended in the case of counterrevolutionary offenders or recidivists. Article 69, ibid.

70. Mao Zedong, "Problems Relating to the Correct Handling of Contradic-

tions among the People" (Address at the Eleventh Enlarged Meeting of the Supreme State Conference, February 27, 1957), *FKHP* 5 (1957): 13.

71. "Policy Toward Descendants of Landlords and Rich Peasants," *Beijing Review* 22, no. 4 (1979): 8.

72. The death penalty is authorized in 37 states. Its constitutionality as a penalty for intentional homicide (murder) was upheld by the United States Supreme Court in 1976. *Gregg v. Georgia*, 428 U.S. 153 (1976); *Proffit v. Florida*, 428 U.S. 242 (1976); *Jurek v. Texas*, 428 U.S. 262 (1976).

73. Kerper and Kerper, *Legal Rights*, 8–15.

74. Provisions for asexualization of certain offenders exist in 9 states, but are seldom used and of doubtful constitutionality. Rubin, *Law of Criminal Correction*, 413–415.

75. A person convicted of a sex or narcotics offense may be required to register with the police of the place where he resides.

76. Kerper and Kerper, *Legal Rights*, 20–21.

77. "The courts of this country have universally held banishment to be an improper punishment implicitly prohibited by public policy. While some courts have qualified this by declaring it void in the absence of legislative authorization, it is doubtful that the Supreme Court would uphold such legislation today . . . " Gerald R. Miller, "Banishment —A Medieval Tactic in Modern Criminal Law," *Utah Law Review* 5 (Spring, 1957): 367. See also *Rutherford v. Blankenship*, 25 C. Law Reptr. 2034 (W.D. Va., 1979).

78. Both kinds of restrictions might violate the Constitutional prohibition on restricting freedom of movement. See *Crandall v. Nevada*, 73 U.S. (6 Wall.) 35 (1868); *Edwards v. California*, 314 U.S. 160 (1941). Conditions applied to both probation and parole customarily require persons on parole or probation to notify the supervising agencies of any contemplated movements beyond the jurisdiction of these agencies, but do not otherwise restrict their movements. Although imprisonment necessarily entails compulsory resettlement of a person in a specific location, it does not follow under United States law that compulsory assignment to residence in the absence of imprisonment would be constitutional. See n. 77, supra.

79. Compulsory labor performed outside prison would require the states to provide jobs for convicted offenders who were unable to secure one for themselves. Providing jobs for *any* citizen is something the states are very reluctant to do. No state can force private industry or business to employ convicted persons, although they may encourage them to do so, and providing public employment for them would necessitate offering similar employment for all unemployed persons, which could not be done without disturbing effects on the free market economy.

80. See F. Dell'Apa, W.T. Adams, J.D. Jorgensen, and H. R. Sigurdson, "Advocacy, Brokerage, Community: The ABC's of Probation and Parole," *Federal Probation* 40 (December, 1976): 37–44; D. Epstein, et al., "Volunteers in Corrections: An Effective Resource," *International Journal of Offender Therapy* 18, no. 2 (1974): 171–77.

81. Few states allow subsequent revision of the sentence by the court, since that would interfere with the system of parole.

82. Kerper and Kerper, *Legal Rights*, ch. 15.

83. Edwin H. Sutherland and Donald R. Cressey, *Criminology*, 9th ed. (Philadelphia: J.B. Lippincott, 1974), 465.

84. The supervision of probation in the United States is often very lax, amounting to no more than a monthly visit or written report to the probation office.

85. Common conditions of probation are: restitution to be paid to the victim, abstention from liquor or drugs, non-operation of a motor vehicle without probation officer's consent, keeping probation officer informed about activities, whereabouts, and so forth. Kerper and Kerper, *Legal Rights*, 252.

86. In some states the probationer is allowed a credit for time spent on probation without violation, but in most states he is not. Ibid., 270. Rubin, *Law of Criminal Correction*, 243.

87. The sentencing statutes of the states which permit parole are said to be "indeterminate," because it cannot be determined with certainty when the prisoner will be released once the sentence has been passed (the court sentence merely imposes an outer limit beyond which the prisoner may not be confined). A growing number of states in the United States have changed to "determinate" sentencing by eliminating parole or by fixing the conditions under which it is granted.

88. Kerper and Kerper, *Legal Rights*, 491–93. The minimum non-eligibility periods are a fixed number of years set by statute or a fraction of the maximum sentence imposed by the court.

89. In *Greenholts v. Inmates, etc.*, 442 U.S. 1 (1978) the United States Supreme Court held that, except in exceptional circumstances, states are not required to provide a formal hearing and other due process when discretionary parole is being considered by the parole board, nor is it required to give reasons for the denial of parole.

90. (Deterrence and incapacitation) Alfred Blumstein, Jacqueline Cohen, and Daniel Nagin, eds., *Deterrence and Incapacitation: Estimating the Effects of Criminal Sanctions on Crime Rates* (Washington, D.C.: National Academy of Sciences, 1978); Jack P. Gibbs, *Crime, Punishment and Deterrence* (New York: Elsevier, 1975); David F. Greenberg, "The Incapacitative Effect of Imprisonment: Some Estimates," *Law and Society Review* 9 (Summer, 1975): 541–80. (Rehabilitation) Douglas Lipton, R. Martinson, and J. Wilks, *The Effectiveness of Correctional Treatment: A Survey of Treatment Evaluation Studies* (New York: Praeger, 1975); Gene Kassebaum, D. A. Ward, and D. M. Wilner, *Prison Treatment and Parole Survival: An Empirical Assessment* (New York: John Wiley, 1971); David A. Ward, "Evaluative Research for Corrections," in Lloyd E. Ohlin, ed., *Prisoners in America* (Englewood Cliffs, N.J.: Prentice-Hall, 1973); Paul Lerman, *Community Treatment and Social Control* (Chicago: University of Chicago Press, 1975).

## CHAPTER 8

1. See Mueller and LePoole-Griffiths, *Comparative Criminal Procedure*, 210–12. The right of appeal was recognized earlier on the continent of Europe than in Great Britain and North America. See Damaška, *Structures of Authority*, 489, n. 11.

2. Appeals, in the strict sense, did not exist in criminal cases in England until the passage of the Criminal Appeal Act, 1907 (7 Edw. VII, c. 23).

3. See Commentary to Standard 1.1., American Bar Association *ABA Project on Standards for Criminal Justice: Standards Relating to Criminal Appeals,* Supplement (New York: Institute of Judicial Administration, March, 1969), 16.

4. *Estelle v. Dorrough,* 420 U.S. 534, 536 (1975); *Ross v. Moffitt,* 417 U.S. 600, 610–11 (1974); *Griffin v. Illinois,* 351 U.S. 12, 18 (1956); *McKane v. Durston,* 153 U.S. 684, 687 (1894).

5. Sheehan, *Criminal Procedure in Scotland and France,* 64; see also Stefani and Levasseur, *Procédure Pénale,* 525–26.

6. Sheehan, ibid., 90–92; Stefani and Levasseur, ibid., 668–69.

7. Sheehan, ibid., 92–93; Stefani and Levasseur, ibid., 670–71.

8. Berman, *Soviet Criminal Law and Procedure,* 211, 272, 301–09, 316–21.

9. Berman, *Justice in Russia,* 303.

10. See Article 377, CCP, RSFSR; Lapenna, *Soviet Penal Policy,* 131–33.

11. See Article 371, ibid.; Lapenna, ibid., 132.

12. See Articles 384–390, ibid.; Lapenna, ibid., 133.

13. Articles 129–142, CPL, PRC. Article 143 of the Procedure Law stipulates: "The judgments and orders of second instance and the judgments and orders of the Supreme People's Court are all judgments and orders of final instance" (i.e., there is no further appeal, although further review by "adjudication supervision" is still possible). In China local people's courts are divided into three levels: basic people's courts, intermediate people's courts, and higher people's courts. At the national level is the Supreme People's Court. A litigant contesting a judgment of first instance rendered by a local people's court at any level has the right to file an appeal with the people's court at the next higher level. Judgment of this court on this appeal is final. The same holds true for prosecutorial appeals ("protests").

14. Article 131, ibid.

15. Articles 134, 136, 138, ibid.

16. Article 136, ibid. Article 138 indicates that remand for retrial is the appropriate action to be taken if procedural defects are discovered in the trial proceedings of the first instance. However, this action may also be taken if the facts underlying the original judgment are unclear or the evidence insufficient. Article 136 (subpara. 3).

17. Article 137 provides that a people's court retrying a case on appeal from a lower court may not increase the defendant's punishment. Leng remarks that as a result of this new provision and new protection, more people have now sought redress through appellate proceedings, citing statistics of 290,000 appeals accumulating over a two-year period. Leng, "Preliminary Observations," 232; see also *FBIS Daily Report [People's Republic of China]* (Supplement) (September 23, 1980): 42.

18. Articles 148–50, CPL, PRC; see also Leng, "Preliminary Observations," 232; Berman, Cohen and Russell, "Comparison of the Chinese and Soviet Codes," 245.

19. Article 148, CPL, PRC.

20. Articles 149, 150, ibid.

21. Articles 144–147, ibid.

22. "Appeal and Error," *American Jurisprudence 2d*, vol. 5 (1962), 305–6 (sec. 867); *Adkins v. Commonwealth*, 175 Va. 590, 9 S.E. 2d 349, 352 (1940).

23. Kerper and Kerper, *Legal Rights*, 207–44.

24. "Criminal Law," *Corpus Juris Secundum*, vol. 23A (1961), secs. 1143–49; and vol. 24 (1961), secs. 1418–1555.

25. Therefore, judgments of trial courts must usually be "stayed" pending the appeal process, or else the sentences will be executed before the appellate process is completed.

26. "Criminal Law," *Corpus Juris Secundum*, vol. 24 (1961), sec. 1659.

27. Address of Chief Justice Warren Burger to American Bar Association convention held in Houston, Texas, on February 8, 1981; *New York Times*, February 9, 1981, D10; see also Macklin Fleming, *The Price of Perfect Justice* (New York: Basic Books, 1974).

28. Peter Dunne Finley [Mr. Dooley on] "Criminal Trials" in Elmer Ellis, ed., *Mr. Dooley at his Best* (New York: Scribners, 1938), 282.

## CHAPTER 9

1. Esmein, *History*; William S. Holdsworth, *A History of English Law*, 13 vols. (London: Methuen, 1922–1952); Plucknett, *Concise History*; Pollock and Maitland, *History of English Law*; John P. Dawson, *A History of Lay Judges* (Cambridge, Mass.: Harvard University Press, 1960).

2. Berman, *Law and Revolution*.

3. Max Gluckman, *Politics, Law and Ritual in Tribal Society* (Chicago: Aldine, 1965), 183–89; Gluckman, *Judicial Process among the Barotse*, 80–81. As Gluckman points out, however, this aspect of "primitive" criminal procedure may be little more than a function of the customary intimacy of the relationship between litigants and intercessors. Where litigants are strangers to each other, there is no need for the court to reconcile them and proceedings may be more formal and adjudicative.

4. For this reason the analytical model has no application to the punishment of crime in primitive societies, assuming such a concept of "crime" as we understand it exists in such societies.

5. Esmein, *History*, 121; J.H. Baker, "Criminal Courts and Procedure at Common Law," 17.

6. It is no longer the case in all Western non-Communist inquisitorial nations that pretrial investigation is carried out by an independent "judicial" official. In 1975, West Germany amended its law to transfer the examining magistrate's task to the prosecutor.

7. First of all, I have made it my concern to refer the proofs of things touching the law of nature to certain fundamental conceptions which are beyond question, so that no one can deny them without doing violence to himself. For the principles of that law, if only you pay strict heed to them, are in themselves manifest and clear, almost as evident as are those things we perceive by external senses; and the senses do not err if the organs of perception are properly

formed and if the other conditions requisite to perception are present. Thus in his *Phoenician Maidens* Euripides represents Polynices, whose cause he makes out to have been manifestly just, as speaking thus:

Mother, these words, that I have uttered, are not inwrapped with in direction, but, firmly based on rules of justice and of good, are plain alike to simple and to wise.

Translation from Hugo Grotius, *The Laws of War and Peace*, trans. Francis W. Kelsey (Indianapolis: Bobbs–Merrill, 1962), 23.

# BIBLIOGRAPHY

Abraham, Henry, J. *The Judicial Process*. 2d ed., rev. and enl. New York: Oxford University Press, 1968.

American Bar Association. *ABA Project on Standards for Criminal Justice*. 18 vols. New York: Institute of Judicial Administration, 1967–1974.

———. *ABA Project on Standards for Criminal Justice: Standards Relating to Criminal Appeals*. New York: Institute of Judicial Administration, March, 1969.

———. *ABA Project on Standards for Criminal Justice: Standards Relating to Discovery and Procedure Before Trial*. New York: Institute of Judicial Administration, 1969.

———. *ABA Project on Standards for Criminal Justice: Standards Relating to The Prosecution Function and the Defense Function*. New York: Institute of Judicial Administration, 1970.

*American Jurisprudence, Second Series*. 91 vols. Rochester, N. Y. The Lawyers Co-operative Publishing Co., 1962.

Anderson, Gary L. "The Preliminary Hearing—Better Alternatives or More of the Same?" *Missouri Law Review* 35 (1970): 281–325.

Arnold, Thurman. *The Symbols of Government*. New Haven: Yale University Press, 1935.

Babaev, M.M. *Individualizatsiia nakazaniia nesovershennoletnikh*. [Individualization of punishment in the case of minors]. Moscow: Iuridicheskaia literatura, 1968.

Baker, J.H. "Criminal Courts and Procedure at Common Law 1550–1800." Pp.

15–48 in J.S. Cockburn, ed. *Crime in England, 1550–1800*. London: Methuen, 1977.

Barton, R.F. *Ifugao Law*. Berkeley and Los Angeles: University of California Press, 1969.

Bassiouni, M. Cherif. "A Survey of the Major Criminal Justice Systems in the World." Pp. 527–92 in Daniel Glaser, ed. *Handbook of Criminology*. Chicago: Rand McNally College Publishing Co., 1969.

Berger, Raoul. *Government by Judiciary: The Transformation of the Fourteenth Amendment*. Cambridge, Mass.: Harvard University Press, 1977.

Berman, Harold J. *Justice in Russia*. Cambridge, Mass.: Harvard University Press, 1963.

———. *Justice in the USSR: An Interpretation of Soviet Law*. rev. ed. Cambridge, Mass.: Harvard University Press, 1966.

———. *Law and Revolution: The Formation of the Western Legal Tradition*. Cambridge, Mass.: Harvard University Press, 1983.

———. *Soviet Criminal Law and Procedure*. 2d ed. Translated by Harold J. Berman and James W. Spindler. Cambridge, Mass.: Harvard University Press, 1972.

———. "The Use of Law to Guide People to Virtue: A Comparison of Soviet and U.S. Perspectives." Pp. 75–84 in J.L. Tapp and F.J. Levine, eds. *Law, Justice, and the Individual in Society: Psychological and Legal Issues*. New York: Holt, Rinehart and Winston, 1977.

Berman, Harold J., Susan Cohen, and Malcolm Russell. "A Comparison of the Chinese and Soviet Codes of Criminal Law and Procedure." *Journal of Criminal Law and Criminology* 73 (Spring, 1982): 238–58.

Bernat de Celis, J. "Police et victimisation: Réflexions autour d'une main-courante." *Archives de politique criminelle* (Paris: Pedone, 1983), no. 6, 147–68.

Black, Charles L., Jr. *The People and the Court: Judicial Review in a Democracy*. New York: Macmillan, 1960.

Black, Donald, J. *The Behavior of Law*. New York: Academic Press, 1976.

Blackstone, William. *Commentaries on the Laws of England*. A Facsimile of the First Edition of 1765–1769. 4 vols. Chicago: University of Chicago Press, 1979.

Blumberg, Abraham S. "The Practice of Law as a Confidence Game: Organizational Cooptation of a Profession." *Law and Society Review* 1 (1967): 15–39.

Blumstein, Alfred, Jacqueline Cohen, and Daniel Nagin, eds. *Deterrence and Incapacitation: Estimating the Effects of Criminal Sanctions on Crime Rates*. Washington, D.C.: National Academy of Sciences, 1978.

Bodde, Derk, and Clarence Morris. *Law in Imperial China: Exemplified by 190 Ch'ing Dynasty Cases*. Philadelphia: University of Pennsylvania Press, 1973.

Bonavia, David. "Give them Rice and Circuses." *Far Eastern Economic Review* (December 5–11, 1980): 12.

Bonnichon, André. *Law in Communist China*. The Hague: International Commission of Jurists, 1956.

Brosi, Kathleen B. *A Cross-City Comparison of Felony Case Processing*. Washington, D.C.: Institute of Law and Social Research (INSLAW), April, 1979.

Burger, Warren. Address given to American Bar Association Convention in Houston, Texas, on February 8, 1981. *New York Times*, February 9, 1981.

Carlo, Antonio. "Structural Causes of the Soviet Coexistence Policy." Pp. 57–90 in Egbert Jahn, ed. *Soviet Foreign Policy: Its Social and Economic Conditions*. New York: St. Martin's Press, 1978.

Chazal, Jean. *Les magistrats*. Paris: Grasset, 1978.

Chemithe, Philippe, and Paul Strasburg. "France's 'Sentence Judge.'" *Corrections Magazine* 4 (March, 1978): 39–45, 65.

"China's Lawyers." *Beijing Review* 23 (June 9, 1980): 26.

"Closing Arguments in the Debate over the Exclusionary Rule." *Judicature* 62 (February, 1979): 336–56.

Cohen, Jerome A. *The Criminal Process in the People's Republic of China, 1949–1963*. Cambridge, Mass.: Harvard University Press, 1968.

———. "Will China Have a Formal Legal System?" *American Bar Association Journal* 64 (October, 1978): 1510–15.

Coke, Sir Edward. *The Third Part of the Institutes of the Law of England*. London, 1797 edition.

Cole, George F. "The Decision to Prosecute." *Law and Society Review* 4 (February, 1970): 313–43.

Cole, George F., Stanislaw J. Frankowski and Marc Gertz, eds. *Major Criminal Justice Systems*. Beverly Hills, Calif.: Sage, 1981.

Connor, Walter D. *Deviance in Soviet Society: Crime, Delinquency, and Alcoholism*. New York: Columbia University Press, 1972.

*Constitution of the People's Republic of China*. Adopted on March 5, 1978 by the Fifth National Congress of the People's Republic of China at its First Session. English translation in *Beijing Review* 21, no. 11 (March 17, 1978): 5–14.

*Constitution of the People's Republic of China—1982*. English translation in *Beijing Review* 25 (December 27, 1982): 10–29.

*Corpus Juris Secundum*. 153 vols. Brooklyn: The American Book Co., 1961.

Criminal Procedure Teaching Group, Law Faculty of China People's University. *Basic Knowledge about the Criminal Procedure Law of the People's Republic of China*. Beijing: 1980.

Criminal Procedure Teaching Section, Beijing Political-Legal Institute. *Lectures on the Criminal Procedure Law of the People's Republic of China*. Beijing: 1979.

*Criminal Victimization in the United States, 1973*. A National Crime Panel Survey Report. U.S. Department of Justice, Law Enforcement Assistance Administration. Washington, D.C.: U.S. Government Printing Office, 1976.

*Criminal Victimization in the United States: A Comparison of 1973 and 1974 Findings*. A National Crime Panel Survey Report. Washington, D.C.: U.S. Government Printing Office, 1976.

*Criminal Victimization in the United States: A Comparison of the 1974 and*

*1975 Findings*. A National Crime Panel Survey Report. Washington, D.C.: U.S. Government Printing Office, 1977.

Crockett, George W., Jr., and Morris Gleicher. "Teaching Criminals a Lesson." *Judicature* 61 (January, 1978): 278–88.

Damaška, Mirjan. "Evidentiary Barriers to Conviction and Two Models of Criminal Procedure: A Comparative Study." *University of Pennsylvania Law Review* 121 (1973): 506–89.

————. "Structures of Authority and Comparative Criminal Procedure." *Yale Law Journal* 84 (January, 1975): 480–544.

Darwin, Charles. *The Origin of Species* and *The Descent of Man*. New York: Random House, Modern Library Edition, n.d. [original editions 1859 and 1871].

David, René. *French Law: Its Structure, Sources, and Methodology*. Translated by Michael Kindred. Baton Rouge: Louisiana State University Press, 1972.

Davis, Kenneth Culp. *Discretionary Justice: A Preliminary Inquiry*. Urbana, Ill.: University of Illinois Press, 1973.

Dawson, John P. *A History of Lay Judges*. Cambridge, Mass.: Harvard University Press, 1960.

"Decision of the Standing Committee of the National People's Congress Regarding The Question of Time Limits for Handling Cases." *Renmin Ribao* (September 11, 1981): 1.

Dell'Apa, F., W.T. Adams, J.D. Jorgensen, and H.R. Sigurdson. "Advocacy, Brokerage, Community: The ABC's of Probation and Parole." *Federal Probation* 40 (December, 1976): 37–44.

Del Russo, A.L. "Prisoners' Right of Access to the Courts: A Comparative Analysis of Human Rights Jurisprudence in Europe and the United States." *Journal of International Law and Economics* 13 (1978): 1–39.

"Developments in the Law: Confessions." *Harvard Law Review* 79 (March, 1966): 935–1119.

Diamond, A.S. *Primitive Law, Past and Present*. London: Methuen, 1971.

Dodge, D.C. "Plea Bargaining Revisited." *State Court Journal* 2 (Fall, 1978): 13–18, 38–40.

Doig, J.W., D.E. Phillips, and T. Manson. "Deterring Illegal Behavior by Officials of Complex Organizations." *Criminal Justice Ethics* 3 (Winter/Spring, 1984): 27–56.

Easterbrook, Frank H. "Criminal Procedure as a Market System." *Journal of Legal Studies* 12 (June, 1983): 289–332.

Ehrman, Henry W. *Comparative Legal Cultures*. Englewood Cliffs, N.J.: Prentice Hall, 1976.

Epstein, D., Stephanie Rolfe, et. al. "Volunteers in Corrections: An Effective Resource." *International Journal of Offender Therapy* 18, no. 2 (1974): 171–77.

Erman, Adolf. *Life in Ancient Egypt*. Translated by H.M. Tirard. London: Macmillan, 1894.

Esmein, A[démar]. *A History of Continental Criminal Procedure with Special Reference to France*. The Continental Legal History Series, vol. 5. Translated by John Simpson. South Hackensack, N.J.: Rothman Reprints, and New York: Augustus Kelly, 1968.

"An Examination of the Grand Jury System in New York." *Columbia Journal of Law and Social Problems* 2 (1966): 88–108.

Fallers, Lloyd A. *Law Without Precedent: Legal Ideas in Action in the Courts of Colonial Busoga.* Chicago: University of Chicago Press, 1969.

Farrar, R. T. "Aspects of Police Search and Seizure without Warrant in England and the United States." *University of Miami Law Review* 29 (Spring, 1975): 491–558.

*FBIS Daily Report* [*People's Republic of China*] (June 11, 1981).

———. (Supplement) (September 12, 1980).

*Federal Rules of Civil—Appellate—Criminal Procedure, as Amended to April 30, 1984.* St. Paul: West, 1984.

Feeley, Malcolm M. *The Process is the Punishment: Handling Cases in the Lower Criminal Court.* New York: Russell Sage Foundation, 1979.

Feifer, George. *Justice in Moscow.* New York: Simon and Schuster, 1964.

"Fifth Amendment—Double Jeopardy and the Single Tribunal Rule." *Journal of Criminal Law and Criminology* 60 (Winter, 1978): 563–73.

Finley, Peter Dunne. [Mr. Dooley on] "Criminal Trials." In Elmer Ellis, ed. *Mr. Dooley at his Best.* New York: Scribners, 1938.

Fleming, Macklin. *The Price of Perfect Justice.* New York: Basic Books, 1974.

Fletcher, George P. "The Presumption of Innocence in Soviet Law." *Criminal Justice Ethics* 3 (Winter/Spring, 1984): 69–75.

Fogel, David. "China: Trial by the Masses." *Corrections Magazine* 3 (December, 1977): 42–44.

Frankel, Marvin E., and Gary P. Naftalis. *The Grand Jury: An Institution on Trial.* New York: Hill and Wang, 1977.

Freedman, Monroe H. *Lawyers' Ethics in an Adversary System.* Indianapolis: Bobbs-Merrill, 1975.

Friendly, Alfred, and Ronald F. Goldfarb. *Crime and Publicity: The Impact of News on the Administration of Justice.* New York: Vantage Books, 1968.

Fuller, Lon L. "The Adversary System." Pp. 30–43 in Harold J. Berman, ed. *Talks on American Law.* New York: Random House, 1961.

Galanter, Marc. "The Radiating Effects of Courts." Pp. 117–42 in K.O. Boyum and L. Mather, eds. *Empirical Theories about Courts.* New York: Longman, 1983.

Garbus, Martin. "Justice without Courts: A Report on China Today." *Judicature* 60 (March, 1977): 395–402.

Gard, Spencer A. *Jones on Evidence: Civil and Criminal.* 6th ed. 4 vols. Rochester, N.Y.: Lawyers Co-operative Publishing Co., 1972.

Gelatt, Timothy A. "The People's Republic of China and the Presumption of Innocence." *Journal of Criminal Law and Criminology* 73 (Spring, 1982): 259–316.

Gibbs, Jack P. *Crime, Punishment and Deterrence.* New York: Elsevier, 1975.

Ginsburg, Ruth Bader. "American Bar Association Delegation Visits People's Republic of China." *American Bar Association Journal* 64 (October, 1978): 1516–25.

Glaser, Barney G., and Anselm L. Strauss. *The Discovery of Grounded Theory: Strategies of Qualitative Research.* Chicago: Aldine, 1967.

Gleizal, Jean-Jacques. "Police, Law, and Security in France: Questions of Method and Political Strategy." *International Journal of the Sociology of Law* 9 (November, 1981): 361–82.

Gluckman, Max. *The Judicial Process among the Barotse of Northern Rhodesia.* Manchester: University of Manchester Press for the Rhodes-Livingston Institute, 1955.

———. *Politics, Law and Ritual in Tribal Society.* Chicago: Aldine, 1965.

Goldstein, Abraham S. "Reflections on Two Models: Inquisitorial Themes in American Criminal Procedure." *Stanford Law Review* 26 (1974): 1009–25.

Goldstein, Abraham S., and Martin Marcus. "The Myth of Judicial Supervision in Three 'Inquisitorial' Systems: France, Italy, and Germany." *Yale Law Journal* 87 (December, 1977): 240–83.

Goldstein, Joseph. "Police Discretion Not to Invoke the Criminal Process: Low-Visibility Decisions in the Administration of Justice." *Yale Law Journal* 69 (March, 1960): 543–94.

Greenberg, David F. "The Incapacitative Effect of Imprisonment: Some Estimates." *Law and Society Review* 9 (Summer, 1975): 541–80.

Griffiths, John. "Ideology in Criminal Procedure or a Third Model of the Criminal Process." *Yale Law Journal* 79 (1970): 359–417.

Grotius, Hugo. *The Laws of War and Peace.* Translated by Francis W. Kelsey. Indianapolis: Bobbs-Merrill, 1962.

Hall, L., Y. Kamisar, W.R. La Fave, and J.H. Israel. *Modern Criminal Procedure.* 3d ed. American Casebook Series. St. Paul: West, 1969.

Heumann, Milton. *Plea Bargaining: The Experiences of Prosecutors, Judges, and Defense Attorneys.* Chicago: University of Chicago Press, 1978.

Hexter, Ralph J. *Equivocal Oaths and Ordeals in Medieval Literature.* Cambridge, Mass.: Harvard University Press, 1975.

Higher School of the RSFSR Ministry for the Maintenance of Public Order. *Ispravitel'no-trudovoe pravo* [Labor-educational correctional law]. Moscow: Iuridicheskaia literatura, 1966.

Hirschel, J. David. "What We Can Learn from the English Approach to the Problem of Illegally Seized Evidence." *Judicature* 67 (April, 1984): 427–29.

Hoebel, E. Adamson. *The Law of Primitive Man.* New York: Atheneum, 1970.

Holdsworth, William S. *A History of English Law.* 13 vols. London: Methuen, 1922–1952.

Holloway, D. "Foreign and Defence Policy." Pp. 35–64 in A. Brown and M. Kaser, eds. *Soviet Policy for the 1980's.* Bloomington: Indiana University Press, 1982.

Hrones, S. "Interrogation Abuses by the Police in France—A Comparative Solution." *Criminal Law Quarterly* 12 (1969): 68–90.

Hughes, Charles Evans. *The Supreme Court of the United States.* New York: Columbia University Press, 1936.

Hulsewé, A.F.P. *Remnants of Han Law.* 2 vols. Leiden: E.J. Brill, 1955.

Ingraham, Barton L. *Political Crime in Europe, 1770–1970*. Berkeley and Los Angeles: University of California Press, 1979.

Israel, J.H., and Wayne R. La Fave. *Criminal Procedure in a Nutshell*. St. Paul: West, 1975.

Jackson, Robert H. *The Nuremberg Case*. New York: Knopf, 1947.

Jones, A.H.M. *The Criminal Courts of the Roman Republic and Principate*. Totowa, N.J.: Rowman and Littlefield, 1972.

Jones, W.C. "Possible Model for the Criminal Trial in the People's Republic of China." *American Journal of Comparative Law* 24 (Spring, 1976): 229–45.

Kaiser, Daniel H. *The Growth of the Law in Medieval Russia*. Princeton: Princeton University Press, 1980.

Kaminskaya, Dina. *Final Judgment: My Life as a Soviet Defense Attorney*. Translated by Michael Glenny. New York: Simon and Schuster, 1982.

Kanet, Roger E. "East-West Political Relations: The Challenge of Détente." Pp. 39–55 in Roger E. Kanet, ed. *Soviet Foreign Policy and East-West Relations*. New York: Pergamon Press, 1982.

Kassebaum, Gene, D.A. Ward, and D.M. Wilner. *Prison Treatment and Parole Survival: An Empirical Assessment*. New York: Wiley, 1971.

Kerper, Hazel, and June Kerper. *Legal Rights of the Convicted*. St. Paul: West, 1974.

Kondrashkov, N. "Mery nakazaniia v zakone i na praktike." [Measures of punishment in law and practice]. *Sotsialisticheskaia zakonnost'* No. 2 (1968): 20–26.

Kroeber, A.L. "Law of the Yurok Indians." Pp. 511–16 in *Proceedings of the 22nd International Congress of Americanists (1926)*.

La Fave, Wayne R. "Fourth Amendment Vagaries (of Improbable Cause, Imperceptible Plain View, Notorious Privacy, and Balancing Askew)." *Journal of Criminal Law and Criminology* 74 (Winter, 1973): 1171–1224.

Landsman, Steven. *The Adversary System: A Description and Defense*. American Enterprise Institute Studies in Legal Policy. Washington, D.C.: American Enterprise Institute for Public Research, 1984.

Langbein, John H. "The Criminal Trial Before the Lawyers." *University of Chicago Law Review* 45 (Winter, 1978): 263–316.

———. *Prosecuting Crime in the Renaissance: England, Germany, France*. Cambridge, Mass.: Harvard University Press, 1974.

———. *Torture and the Law of Proof: Europe and England in the Ancien Régime*. Chicago: University of Chicago Press, 1977.

Lapenna, Ivo. *Soviet Penal Policy: A Background Book*. Westport, Conn.: Greenwood Press, 1968.

Leng, Shao-chuan. "Criminal Justice in Post-Mao China: Some Preliminary Observations." *Journal of Criminal Law and Criminology* 73 (Spring, 1982): 204–37.

———. *Justice in Communist China*. Dobbs Ferry, N. Y.: Oceana, 1967.

Leng, Shao-chuan, and Hongdah Chiu. *Criminal Justice in Post-Mao China: Analysis and Documents*. Albany: State University of New York Press, 1985.

Lerman, Paul. *Community Treatment and Social Control*. Chicago: University of Chicago Press, 1975.

Levy, Leonard W. *Against the Law*. New York: Harper Torchbooks, 1974.

Li, Victor H. *Law Without Lawyers*. Stanford, Calif.: Portable Stanford, 1977.

Li Yuchang. "The Role of Chinese Lawyers." *Beijing Review* 23 (November 17, 1980): 24.

Lipton, D., R. Martinson, and J. Wilks. *The Effectiveness of Correctional Treatment: A Survey of Treatment Evaluation Studies*. New York: Praeger, 1975.

Lubman, Stanley. "Form and Function in the Chinese Criminal Process." *Columbia Law Review* 69 (1969): 535–75.

Maine, Sir Henry. *Dissertations on Early Law and Custom*. London: Murray, 1883.

Mao Zedong. "Problems Relating to the Correct Handling of Contradictions among the People." Address at the Eleventh Enlarged Meeting of the Supreme State Conference, February 27, 1957. *FKHP [Fa-kuei hui-pien]* 5 (1957): 13.

Marchenko, Anatoly. *My Testimony*. London: Pall Mall, 1969.

Markovits, Inga. "Law and Order—Constitutionalism and Legality in Eastern Europe." *Stanford Law Review* 34 (February, 1982): 513–613.

Martin, Barry S. "The Razor's Edge of Conflicting Duties." *California Lawyer* 4 (January, 1984): 15–16.

Marx, Gary T. "Undercover Police Tactics." Pp. 1154–60 in vol. 3 of *Encyclopedia of Crime and Justice*, ed. Sanford Kadish. 4 vols. New York: The Free Press, 1983.

Maspero, Henri. "Le serment dans la procédure judiciaire de la Chine antique." Pp. 257–317 in vol. 3 of *Mélanges chinois et bouddhiques*. 3 vols. Brussels: 1934–1935.

Mather, Lynn M. "Some Determinants of the Method of Case Disposition: Decision-Making by Public Defenders in Los Angeles." *Law and Society Review* 8 (Winter, 1974): 187–216.

McConville, Michael, and John Baldwin. *Courts, Prosecution, and Conviction*. Oxford: Clarendon Press, 1981.

Merle, Roger, and André Vitu. *Traité de droit criminel: Procédure pénale*. Troisième édition. Paris: Éditions Cujas, 1977.

Miller, Frank. *Prosecution: The Decision to Charge a Suspect with a Crime*. Boston: Little, Brown, 1969.

Miller, Gerald R. "Banishment—A Medieval Tactic in Modern Criminal Law." *Utah Law Review* 5 (Spring, 1957): 365–80.

Miller, Herbert S., William F. McDonald, and James A. Cramer. *Plea Bargaining in the United States*. National Institute of Law Enforcement and Criminal Justice, Department of Justice. Washington, D.C.: U.S. Government Printing Office, September, 1978.

Ministère de la Justice (France). *Compte Générale, 1974*. 2 vols. Paris: La Documentation Française, 1977.

Mnookin, Robert H. and Lewis Kornhauser. "Bargaining in the Shadow of the Law: The Case of Divorce." *Yale Law Journal* 88 (1979): 950–97.

Montet, Pierre. *Everyday Life in Egypt in the Days of Ramses the Great*. Trans-

lated by A.R. Maxwell-Hyslop and M.S. Drower. Westport, Conn.: Green-
   wood Press, 1974.
Morse, Wayne. "A Survey of the Grand Jury System." *Oregon Law Review* 10
   (February and April, 1931): 101–60, 217–57.
Mueller, Gerhard O.W. and Fré Le Poole-Griffiths. *Comparative Criminal Procedure*. New York: New York University Press, 1969.
Naroll, Raoul. "Some Thoughts on the Comparative Method in Cultural An-
   thropology." Pp. 236–77 in H.M. Blalock and A.B. Blalock, eds. *Meth-
   odology in Social Research*. New York: McGraw-Hill, 1968.
National Advisory Commission on Criminal Justice Standards and Goals. *Re-
   ports*. U.S. Department of Justice, Law Enforcement Assistance Admin-
   istration. 6 vols. Washington, D.C.: U.S. Government Printing Office,
   1973.
Neely, Richard. *How Courts Govern America*. New Haven: Yale University
   Press, 1981.
Newman, Donald. *Conviction: The Determination of Guilt or Innocence without
   Trial*. Boston: Little, Brown, 1966.
Newman, Graeme. *The Punishment Response*. Philadelphia: J.B. Lippincott,
   1978.
"NPC Promulgates New Regulations on Arrests, Detentions." *FBIS Daily Re-
   port (People's Republic of China National Affairs)* (February 26, 1979):
   E2–E5.
Oaks, Dallin, and Warren Lehman. *A Criminal Justice System and the Indi-
   gent: A Study of Chicago and Cook County*. Chicago: University of Chi-
   cago Press, 1968.
Packer, Herbert L. *The Limits of the Criminal Sanction*. Stanford: Stanford
   University Press, 1968.
Pekelis, Alexander H. "Legal Techniques and Political Ideologies: A Compar-
   ative Study." *Michigan Law Review* 41 (February, 1943): 665–92.
Pelletier, G.A. "Legal Aid in France." *Notre Dame Lawyer* 42 (June, 1967):
   627–46.
Pieck, Manfred. "The Accused's Privilege Against Self-Incrimination in the
   Civil Law." *American Journal of Comparative Law* 11 (1962): 585–601.
Pittman, R. Carter. "The Colonial and Constitutional History of the Privilege
   against Self-Incrimination in America." *Virginia Law Review* 21 (1935):
   763–82.
Plucknett, Theodore. *A Concise History of the Common Law*. 5th ed. Boston:
   Little, Brown, 1956.
"Policy Toward Descendants of Landlords and Rich Peasants." *Beijing Review*
   22, no. 4 (1979): 8.
Pollock, Sir Frederick, and Frederic W. Maitland. *The History of English Law
   Before the Time of Edward I*. 2d ed. 2 vols. Cambridge: University Press,
   1968.
Pound, Roscoe. *The Causes of Popular Dissatisfaction with the Administration
   of Justice*. First published in 1906; republished Chicago: American Ju-
   dicature Society, 1963.
———. "Law in the Books and Law in Action." *American Law Review* 44 (1910):
   12–36.

President's Commission on Law Enforcement and Administration of Justice. *Final Report: The Challenge of Crime in a Free Society.* Washington, D.C.: U.S. Government Printing Office, 1967.

"Procuratorates in Beijing." *Beijing Review* 22 (December 28, 1979): 18.

Radin, Max. *Handbook of Roman Law.* St. Paul: West, 1927.

Robin, Gerald D. *Introduction to the Criminal Justice System.* 2d ed. New York: Harper and Row, 1984.

Rubin, Sol. *The Law of Criminal Correction.* 2d ed. St. Paul: West, 1973.

Schlesinger, R.B. "Comparative Criminal Procedure: A Plea for Utilizing Foreign Experience." *Buffalo Law Review* 26 (Spring, 1977): 361–85.

Schmidt, Eberhard. *Inquisitionsprozess und Rezeption.* Leipzig: Weicher Verlag, 1940.

"Seven PRC Laws Adopted at the Fifth NPC Second Session." *FBIS Daily Report [People's Republic of China].* Part I, vol. 1, no. 146, supp. 019 (July 27, 1979): 27–33 (Organic Law of the People's Procuratorates); 33–62 (Criminal Law). Part II, vol. 1, no. 147, supp. 020 (July 30, 1979):1–30 (Code of Criminal Procedure).

Sheehan, A.V. *Criminal Procedure in Scotland and France.* Edinburgh: Her Majesty's Stationery Office, 1975.

Shifrin, Avraham. *The First Guidebook to Prisons and Concentration Camps of the Soviet Union.* New York: Bantam Books, 1982.

Shunhua, Wang, Xu Yichu, Zhang Zhonglin, Xiao Xianfu, and Chuan Kuanzhi. *Annotation of the Criminal Procedure Law of the People's Republic of China.* Beijing: 1980.

Silberman, Charles E. *Criminal Violence, Criminal Justice.* New York: Random House, 1978.

Simis, Konstantin. *USSR: The Corrupt Society.* Translated by Jacqueline Edwards and Mitchell Schneider. New York: Simon and Schuster, 1982.

Simson, Gary J. "Jury Nullification in the American System: A Skeptical View." *Texas Law Review* 54 (1976): 488–525.

Smith, Sir Thomas. *De Republica Anglorum.* L. Alston edition (1906). Reprinted edition. New York: Barnes and Noble, 1972.

Snee, J.M., and A.K. Pye. "Due Process in Criminal Procedure: A Comparison of Two Systems." *Ohio State Law Journal* 21 (1960): 467–502.

Solzhenitsyn, Aleksandr I. *The Gulag Archipelago: 1918–1956.* 4 vols. New York: Harper and Row, 1973, 1974.

Sowle, Claude R., ed. *Police Power and Individual Freedom.* Chicago: Aldine, 1962.

Stefani, G., and G. Levasseur. *Procédure Pénale,* Dixième édition. Paris: Dalloz, 1977.

Stein, Melvin P. "Preliminary Hearings in Pennsylvania: A Closer Look." *University of Pittsburgh Law Review* 30 (Spring, 1969): 481–99.

Strick, Anne. *Injustice for All.* New York: Penguin Books, 1978.

"Supplemental Regulations of the State Council on Rehabilitation Through Labor, Approved at the Twelfth Meeting of the Standing Committee of the Fifth Session of the National People's Congress, November 29, 1979, promulgated by the State Council, November 29, 1979." *FBIS Daily Report [People's Republic of China].* (February, 26, 1980): L5.

Sutherland, Edwin H., and Donald R. Cressey. *Criminology*, 9th ed. Philadelphia: J.B. Lippincott, 1974.

Terrill, Richard J. *World Criminal Justice Systems: A Survey*. Cincinnati: Anderson Publishing Co., 1984.

Thibault, John, and Laurens Walker. *Procedural Justice: A Psychological Analysis*. Hillsdale, N.J.: Lawrence Erlbaum Associates, 1975.

————. "A Theory of Procedure." *California Law Review* 66 (1978): 541–66.

Tracy, John Evart. *Handbook of the Law of Evidence*. New York: Prentice-Hall, 1952.

*USSR Constitution of 1977*. English translation in *Great Soviet Encyclopedia* vol. 31, 9–19. London: Macmillan Education Co., 1982.

Utz, Pamela J. *Settling the Facts: Discretion and Negotiation in Criminal Court*. Lexington, Mass.: Lexington Books, 1978.

Van der Sprenkel, Sybille. *Legal Institutions in Manchu China: A Sociological Analysis*. London: Athlone Press, University of London, 1966.

Vouin, R. "France." In Claude R. Sowle, ed. *Police Power and Individual Freedom: The Quest for Balance*. Chicago: Aldine, 1962.

————. "The Protection of the Accused in French Criminal Procedure." *International and Comparative Law Quarterly* 5 (1956): 1–25.

Ward, David A. "Evaluative Research for Corrections." In Lloyd E. Ohlin, ed. *Prisoners in America*. Englewood Cliffs, N.J.: Prentice-Hall, 1973.

Weber, Max. *Max Weber on Law in Economy and Society*. Edited by Max Rheinstein and translated by Edward Shils and Max Rheinstein. Cambridge, Mass.: Harvard University Press, 1954.

Wechsler, Herbert. "Toward Neutral Principles of Constitutional Law" [1959]. Reprinted (pp. 3–48) in Herbert Wechsler, ed. *Principles, Politics, and Fundamental Law: Selected Essays*. Cambridge, Mass.: Harvard University Press, 1961.

Weigend, Thomas. "Continental Cures for American Ailments: European Criminal Procedure as a Model for Law Reform." Pp. 381–428 in Norval Morris and Michael Tonry, eds., *Criminal Justice: An Annual Review of Research*. Vol. 2. Chicago: University of Chicago Press, 1980.

Weinreb, Lloyd L. *Denial of Justice: Criminal Process in the United States*. New York: The Free Press, 1977.

Wilkey, Malcolm R. "The Exclusionary Rule: Why Suppress Valid Evidence?" *Judicature* 62 (November, 1978): 215–32.

Yin, Robert K., et al. *Patrolling the Neighborhood Beat: Residents and Residential Security*. Santa Monica: Rand, March, 1976.

Yngvesson, Barbara, and Lynn Mather. "Courts, Moots, and the Disputing Process." Pp. 51–83 in K.O. Boyum and L. Mather, eds. *Empirical Theories About Courts*. New York: Longman, 1983.

Zipei, Zhang. "Basic Principles of the Law of Criminal Procedure." *Beijing Review* 23 (June 9, 1980): 23–26.

# INDEX TO CASES CITED

# SUBJECT INDEX

Accusatorial procedure. *See* Adversarial procedure

Adjudication, 24, 61, 82, 85–96; during early Middle Ages in Europe, 131–32n.8; in primitive societies, 26–27, 119. *See also* Trials

Adversarial procedure, 20, 21, 25; in the common law tradition, 7; and crime, how regarded in, 4, 117; diffusion of, 30; inquisitorial procedure distinguished and compared, 121–22, 125n.4; lawyers' control over process in USA, 95–96; major flaws in, 11; primitive criminal procedure accusatorial, 26; procedural justice, greater emphasis on, 117, 121; its objective, 85, 132–33n.12; in the 20th Century, 32, 138n.47; in USA, 3, 4, 7–9, 21

Analytical model. *See* Structural Model

Appeal: absence of, in primitive societies, 27, 137n.37; in Anglo-American law, 109; in China, 113–14, 169nn.13, 16; collateral review (USA), 115; essentiality of, 110; finality of judgement, 115, 170n.25; in France, 50, 111–12; in general, 109–11, 118–19, 168–69nn.1, 2; hypertrophy of, in USA, 32, 138–39n.53; in inquisitorial procedure, 29, 30, 110–11, 136n.31; interlocutory appeals, 114; motion for new trial, 115; number of, 115; review, right of, 23; in Soviet Union, 54, 112–13, 146n.35; summary and comparison, 115; as task of criminal procedure, 24; in USA, 114–15

Arrest: in China, 40–44, 67–68, 143nn.40–42, 151n.35; in France, 38, 66; intake, as part of, 22; probable cause, definition (USA), 143–44n.47; in Soviet Union, 66; in USA, 45–46, 69–70. *See also* Pretrial detention; Search and seizure

## About the Author

BARTON L. INGRAHAM is Associate Professor at the Institute of Criminal Justice and Criminology of the University of Maryland, College Park. He is the author of *Political Crime in Europe, 1770–1970*.